Gender Justice and Legal Pluralities

Gender Justice and Legal Pluralities: Latin American and African Perspectives examines the relationship between legal pluralities and the prospects for greater gender justice in developing countries. Rather than asking whether legal pluralities are "good" or "bad" for women, the starting point of this volume is that legal pluralities are a social fact. Adopting a more anthropological approach to the issues of gender justice and women's rights, this book analyzes how gendered rights claims are made and responded to within a range of different cultural, social, economic and political contexts. By examining the different ways in which legal norms, instruments and discourses are being used to challenge or reinforce gendered forms of exclusion, contributing authors generate new knowledge about the dynamics at play between the contemporary contexts of legal pluralities and the struggles for gender justice. Any consideration of this relationship must, it is concluded, be located within a broader, historically informed analysis of regimes of governance.

Rachel Sieder is Senior Research Professor at the Centro de Investigaciones y Educación Superior en Antropología Social (CIESAS) in Mexico City, visiting professor at the Chr. Michelsen Institute, Bergen and research fellow at the Institute for the Study of the Americas at the University of London.

John-Andrew McNeish is Associate Professor at the Norwegian University of Life Sciences and senior researcher at the Chr. Michelsen Institute.

Law, Development and Globalization
Series Editor—Julio Faundez, University of Warwick

During the past decades, a substantial transformation of law and legal institutions in developing countries has taken place. Whether prompted by market-based policies or the international human rights movement, by the relentless advance of the process of globalization or the successive waves of democratization, no area of law has been left untouched. The aim of this series is to promote cross-disciplinary dialogue and cooperation among scholars and development practitioners interested in understanding the theoretical and practical implications of the momentous legal changes taking place in developing countries.

Titles in the series:

State Violence and Human Rights: State Officials in the South
Andrew M. Jefferson and Steffen Jensen (eds)

The Political Economy of Government Auditing: Financial Governance and the Rule of Law in Latin America and Beyond
Carlos Santiso

Global Perspectives on the Rule of Law
James J. Heckman, Robert L. Nelson and Lee Cabatingan (eds)

Marginalized Communities and Access to Justice
Yash Ghai and Jill Cottrell (eds)

Law in the Pursuit of Development: Principles into Practice?
Amanda Perry-Kessaris (ed.)

Governance through Development: Poverty Reduction Strategies and the Disciplining of Third World States
Celine Tan

Lawyers and the Rule of Law in an Era of Globalization
Yves Dezalay and Bryant Garth (eds)

Policing and Human Rights: The Meaning of Violence and Justice in the Everyday Policing of Johannesburg
Julia Hornberger

Lawyers and the Construction of Transnational Justice
Yves Dezalay and Bryant Garth (eds)

Forthcoming titles in the series:

Social Movements, Law and the Politics of Land Reform
George Meszaros

From the Global to the Local, How International Rights Reach Bangladesh's Children
Andrea Schapper

Gender Justice and Legal Pluralities: Latin American and African Perspectives
Rachel Sieder and John-Andrew McNeish

Justice and Security Reform: Development Agencies and Informal Institutions in Sierra Leone
Lisa Denney

Multinational Integration, Cultural Identity and Regional Self-Government: Comparative Experiences for Tibet
Roberto Toniatti and Jens Woelk

Gender Justice and Legal Pluralities

Latin American and African Perspectives

Edited by
Rachel Sieder and
John-Andrew McNeish

LONDON AND NEW YORK

First published in 2013
by Routledge
2 Park Square, Milton Park, Abingdon, Oxfordshire OX14 4RN

Simultaneously published in the USA and Canada
by Routledge
711 Third Avenue, New York, NY 10017

First issued in paperback 2015

Routledge is an imprint of the Taylor & Francis Group, an informa business

A GlassHouse Book

© 2013 Rachel Sieder and John-Andrew McNeish

The right of Rachel Sieder and John-Andrew McNeish to be identified as authors of the editorial material, and the chapter authors of their individual material, has been asserted by them in accordance with sections 77 and 78 of the Copyright, Designs and Patents Act 1988.

All rights reserved. No part of this book may be reprinted or reproduced or utilised in any form or by any electronic, mechanical, or other means, now known or hereafter invented, including photocopying and recording, or in any information storage or retrieval system, without permission in writing from the publishers.

Trademark notice: Product or corporate names may be trademarks or registered trademarks, and are used only for identification and explanation without intent to infringe.

British Library Cataloguing in Publication Data
A catalogue record for this book is available from the British Library

Library of Congress Cataloging in Publication Data
A catalog record for this book has been requested

ISBN13: 978-1-138-93485-6 (pbk)
ISBN13: 978-0-415-52606-7 (hbk)

Typeset in Times New Roman
by Taylor & Francis Books

Contents

Acknowledgements	ix
Notes on contributors	x

Introduction RACHEL SIEDER AND JOHN-ANDREW MCNEISH	1
1 Gender, human rights and legal pluralities: experiences from Southern and Eastern Africa ANNE HELLUM	31
2 Indigenous women fight for justice: gender rights and legal pluralism in Mexico MARÍA TERESA SIERRA	56
3 The gender of law: politics, memory and agency in Mozambican community courts BJØRN ENGE BERTELSEN	82
4 Sexual violence and gendered subjectivities: indigenous women's search for justice in Guatemala RACHEL SIEDER	109
5 Between Sharia and CEDAW in Sudan: Islamist women negotiating gender equity LIV TØNNESSEN	133
6 Indigenous rights and violent state construction: the struggle of Triqui women in Oaxaca NATALIA DE MARINIS	156

viii Contents

7 Opening Pandora's Box: human rights, customary law and the
"communal liberal self" in Tanzania 180
NATALIE J. BOURDON

8 An Accumulated Rage: legal pluralism and gender
justice in Bolivia 200
JOHN-ANDREW MCNEISH AND ANA CECILIA ARTEAGA BÖHRT

Index 224

Acknowledgements

This volume owes a great deal to a number of individuals and institutions. It started life as the collective research project *Poverty Reduction and Gender Justice in Contexts of Legal Pluralism* coordinated by John-Andrew McNeish and Rachel Sieder in collaboration with the Chr. Michelsen Institute, Bergen and the Centro de Investigaciones y Estudios Superiores en Antropología Social (CIESAS) in Mexico City.

We are extremely grateful to the Poverty and Peace Programme (POV-PEACE/NORGLOBAL) at the Norwegian Research Council (NFR) for its financial support for this project.

At the Chr. Michelsen Institute we were particularly fortunate to count on the organizational skills and intellectual input of Eyolf Jul-Larsen, Steinar Hegre, Siri Gloppen, and Elin Skaar. At CIESAS, we wish to thank director Virginia García-Acosta for her enthusiasm for the project, and Aida Hernández Castillo, Morna Macleod and Adriana Terven for their contributions to a workshop held in Tepoztlán in 2010. Yacotzin Bravo worked as research assistant to the project in Mexico City and has tirelessly organized everyone and everything.

The intellectual contribution of Bjørn Enge Bertelsen, who has a chapter here, has been essential to shaping this volume. Bjørn also organized a highly productive workshop in Maputo in 2011 where drafts of some of the chapters that appear in this volume were first discussed. We were fortunate to have the input of Anne Hellum, particularly in the latter stages of the project, and her contribution to this volume has been invaluable.

We want to thank all the authors, who produced a set of original research papers and who have been enormously responsive to the suggestions of the editors. We hope that the relationships we have forged in this collaboration will lay the basis for future endeavours to advance our understanding of legal pluralities and gender justice.

Rachel Sieder
John-Andrew McNeish
Mexico City and Oslo
March 2012

Notes on contributors

Ana Cecilia Arteaga Böhrt is currently candidate for an MA in social anthropology at the Centro de Investigaciones y Estudios Superiores en Antropología Social (CIESAS) in Mexico City. She has researched extensively on indigenous law, political reform, women and domestic violence in her native Bolivia.

Bjørn Enge Bertelsen is a postdoctoral fellow at the Department of Social Anthropology, University of Bergen and affiliated senior researcher at the Chr. Michelsen Institute, Bergen. He has researched issues such as state formation, violence, poverty and rural–urban connections in Mozambique since 1998.

Natalie J. Bourdon is assistant professor of anthropology and gender studies at Mercer University. Her research interests include legal pluralism, gender justice, land and inheritance reform and non-governmental organization human rights advocacy in Tanzania.

Natalia De Marinis holds an MA in social anthropology from the CIESAS in Mexico City. She is currently a PhD candidate at CIESAS. Her research interests include the state, violence, security and indigenous rights.

Anne Hellum is professor in the Department of Public and International Law and director of the Institute of Women's Law at the University of Oslo. She is a lawyer and anthropologist. She has written extensively on women's human rights and legal pluralism in Southern Africa with a focus on family, reproduction, land and water.

John-Andrew McNeish is associate professor at the Norwegian University of Life Sciences and senior researcher at the Chr. Michelsen Institute. His research interests include indigenous rights and politics, the politics of participation, the political and legal anthropology of Bolivia and Latin America, environmental politics and governance and critical development studies.

Rachel Sieder is senior research professor at the Centro de Investigaciones y Estudios Superiores en Antropología Social (CIESAS) in Mexico City and Visiting Professor at the Chr. Michelsen Institute, Bergen, and research fellow at the Institute for the Study of the Americas at the University of London. Her research interests include indigenous rights, human rights, gender, access to justice, and indigenous law, particularly in Guatemala where she has worked since 1995.

María Teresa Sierra is senior research professor at the CIESAS in Mexico City. Her research interests include political and legal anthropology in Mexico and Latin America, particularly legal pluralism, indigenous law and community justice, gender and multiculturalism, particularly in Mexico.

Liv Tønnessen is a senior researcher at the Chr. Michelsen Institute, Bergen. Her research focuses on the intersection between Islam(ism), politics and gender in the Middle East and Northern Africa generally and Sudan in particular. She has published on Islamism, Islamic feminism, legal pluralism and gender justice, women's political representation, and women's rights activism.

Introduction

Rachel Sieder and John-Andrew McNeish

Since the adoption in 1979 of the United Nations Convention on the Elimination of all forms of Discrimination against Women (CEDAW), principles of gender equity and non-discrimination have been incorporated into constitutional and statutory law in many countries across the world. International law on the human rights of women has also become entrenched in global development practice. Rights-based approaches to development generally assume that the strengthening of respect for human rights, involving a range of legislative and institutional reforms, education and training will combat gendered forms of discrimination and contribute to greater gender justice and equity.[1] However, the connections between law, rights and gender relations are often over-simplified and the legal, political and social contexts where human rights and development initiatives are promoted insufficiently understood.

One issue which deserves more systematic consideration in the development literature concerned with gender justice and women's rights is that of legal pluralism. In this volume we prefer the term "legal pluralities" to legal pluralism, believing that the former best evokes the fluid, multilayered, contradictory and transnational forms of legal ordering that shape women's life prospects today. Most developing countries are characterized by multiple overlapping and sometimes competing legal and normative orders, including codified statutory law, "custom," transnational norms and procedures, and various informal norms and rules, many of which are often highly ambiguous and difficult to discern. Yet development theory and practise has only recently begun to consider the impact of legal pluralities on the life prospects of marginalized sectors and populations, such as women. As Anne Hellum has argued, in order to effectively contribute to greater gender equity and an improvement in women's development prospects, the human rights based approach to development must be expanded to take account of a plurality of legal orders (Hellum *et al.* 2007). However, despite general agreement today on the importance of legal pluralities in determining women's livelihood options in many developing countries, there is surprisingly little consolidated research examining the relationship between legal pluralities and the prospects for greater gender justice.[2]

2   Introduction

This volume seeks to explore the relationship between legal pluralities and gender justice and injustice. Rather than asking whether contexts of legal plurality are "good" or "bad" for women – a normative stance that we find singularly unhelpful – we understand plural legal orderings as a social fact and seek to analyze how gendered rights claims are made and responded to within a range of different cultural, social, economic and political contexts. Examining cases from a range of different contexts marked by gendered marginalization, the contributors ask how human rights discourses and instruments, and processes of state reform to promote greater gender equality, are affecting different constellations of normative orders over time and, critically, with what concrete effects? Different rights may be invoked, but the extent to which they are realizable depends on multiple factors, including complex historical legacies and power relations. It is therefore important to analyze how individuals and communities are able to negotiate to protect and promote their interests within legally plural settings.

A number of key questions are identified here and are taken up within the following chapters: how do different constellations of governance and legal pluralities constrain and enable greater gender justice? How do they affect women's political participation, their access to economic resources, and their ability to live a life free from violence? What strategies do women and men use to claim and obtain resources, protection, security and voice? How are rights and obligations understood and negotiated? Under what conditions are complex legal pluralities a factor in producing gendered forms of exclusion? And under what conditions do they constitute a resource for women – and men – to challenge their marginalization? Does the existence of a plurality of legal orders offer ordinary people multiple options ("forum shopping"), or does it rather produce situations of ambiguity, lack of legal enforceability and the absence of clear mechanisms for rights protection?[3] Our case studies, drawn from Africa and Latin America, explore the ways in which individuals and groups make resort to legal and quasi-legal norms, instruments, processes and discourses. We hope that by examining the different ways in which legal norms, instruments and discourses are being used to challenge or reinforce gendered forms of exclusion, we will generate new knowledge about dynamics at play between contemporary contexts of legal pluralities and the struggles for gender justice. We argue here that any consideration of these dynamics – and of related development interventions – must, however, be located within a broader analysis of regimes of governance. We hope that through such analysis we will contribute to greater gender justice by influencing ongoing debates within development policy about legal pluralities and gender inequalities. Our approach privileges women's and men's agency and perceptions, underlining the importance of local, grounded understandings. But we also emphasize the role that structure and long-run historical processes play in shaping constellations of legal pluralities and governance, and current prospects for positive change. Lastly, while broadly endorsing a

Introduction 3

rights-based approach to securing greater gender justice, we do not necessarily perceive a unidirectional advance towards shared, rights-based understandings in the different contexts we examine. While they are an important part of globalized legal pluralities, rights are just one amongst many ways of understanding personhood or of challenging injustice. In the end it is only by understanding the complex processes whereby human rights are or are not "vernacularized" (Merry 2006) in specific contexts that we can truly evaluate their emancipatory potential.

This introduction is structured as follows: the first section considers, albeit briefly, the different regional contexts of legal pluralities in Africa and Latin America. The second section summarizes different analytical approaches to legal pluralities and proposes a focus on their role in emerging constellations of governance. The third section considers the ways in which contemporary development practice has increasingly engaged with the issue of legal pluralities. The fourth section discusses the intersection of debates on gender justice and legal pluralities. A final section suggests some overall conclusions.

Cross-regional considerations

While this volume focuses on cases from countries in the global south, legal pluralities are not confined to so-called "developing" countries but are rather a global phenomenon. Indeed, important recent work examines issues of migration, multiculturalism and legal pluralism in Northern Europe (Hellum *et al.* 2011). When discussing legal pluralities, however, it should be emphasized that the use of a standard terminology to describe different forms of sub-national law is highly problematic. An enormous range of practices, institutions and traditions have been defined as informal, traditional or customary law in widely differing historical, socio-economic and political contexts. "Customary law," for example, often means quite different things depending on the colonial and postcolonial history of the country or region in question. Similarly, understandings and histories of "community justice systems" differ enormously from place to place, and depend also on the specific policy and practitioner debates within which they are invoked. Neither is the distinction between "formal" and "informal" kinds of law always clear in practice. This all greatly complicates cross-regional discussions about legal pluralities and alerts us to the dangers of deriving general conclusions from specific regional and historical contexts, something we aim to emphasize in this volume. In some contexts non-state forms of law are generally understood to be subaltern expressions of historically marginalized groups, such as indigenous peoples or marginal urban dwellers in Latin America (Sierra 2004; de Sousa Santos 1977) or instances of lynchings in Africa (Serra 2008). However, in others, non-state forms of law constitute an important resource for dominant groups in society to structure patterns of governance, for example the "traditional" or "customary" legal orders of

4 Introduction

particular tribal or ethnic groups, or religious laws such as Sharia (Bellagamba and Klute 2008; Hinz 2006; Perrot and Fauvelle-Aymar 2003; Vaughan 2005). Academic analysts and development practitioners alike need to understand how different terms have been deployed and re-signified over time in different historical and geographical contexts. In addition, whether invoked or defended by subaltern or dominant groups, non-state forms of law always tend to reflect local politics, which are never homogenous. Legal discourses and mechanisms therefore constitute resources for different groups within society.

Constellations of governance and the role that complex legal pluralities play in these have differed greatly across Africa and Latin America. While we cannot provide an exhaustive account of developments in the two regions, we draw here some general contrasts in order to situate the individual chapters that follow. The regulatory norms and practices of colonized peoples were reshaped and utilized in very different ways under colonial rule, which ended over 150 years earlier in Latin America than in Africa. In the colonial Spanish Americas a dual system established separate courts for settlers and indigenous subjects of the Spanish Crown: the *"república de Españoles"* and the *"república de Indios."* In effect, a system of indirect rule prevailed in the more densely settled highland areas, whereby settlers relied on local indigenous authorities to ensure the supply of labor and produce. These indigenous authority structures developed in a dynamic relation with colonial mechanisms of domination, but were never transformed in as wholesale a fashion as occurred in much of Africa under colonialism. After independence in the early nineteenth century, this dual system was gradually broken down and replaced with a unitary legal system. Following the triumph of liberal ideologies in the mid-nineteenth century, elites generally opposed different forms of law for particular religious or ethnic groups. This was directly tied to the appropriation and concentration of land resources in the hands of governing elites that required the breakdown of special regimes of protection for indigenous groups. Semi-autonomous, community-based indigenous authority structures continued to exist in practice, but they were not formally recognized as an explicit part of the structure of governance. Indeed indigenous people were systematically marginalized and dispossessed of their lands, and their authority systems were circumscribed and often criminalized. Nineteenth-century liberalism also involved racialized forms of inequality and exploitation, along with de facto segregation, denying indigenous people citizenship rights until well into the twentieth century. Today indigenous peoples remain amongst the most marginalized sectors of the population in Latin America and it for this reason that our focus on legal pluralities in this region is on indigenous peoples (see the chapters by Sierra and De Marinis on Mexico, Sieder on Guatemala, and McNeish and Arteaga Böhrt on Bolivia). In Latin America the term "customary law" (*derecho consuetudinario*) tends to be rejected by indigenous peoples' organizations because of its colonial associations. The terms "indigenous law" (*derecho indígena*), our "own law" (*derecho propio*) or "justice systems of indigenous peoples" (*sistemas jurídicos de los pueblos indígenas*) are now more commonly used. Only in the last two decades have indigenous peoples' forms of law and governance been formally incorporated into national systems of governance through ratification of international instruments on the collective rights of indigenous peoples and constitutional reforms providing for greater autonomy. Unsurprisingly perhaps, as indigenous claims for parity or sovereignty have gained ground, "indigenous law" has become increasingly problematized. At the same time, however, indigenous law has become rapidly accepted as part of an increasingly plural legal landscape in many countries, including Bolivia, Ecuador, Colombia and Guatemala.

In Africa "customary law" was radically reshaped – some would say invented – by the colonial powers, who multiplied chieftainships and their associated institutional structures of dispute adjudication, using legal pluralism to secure domination.[4] British colonial authorities appointed new elders and chiefs, and made them responsible for dealing with local disputes and for allocating communal lands for use through "customary courts."[5] They also installed a series of colonial officials to oversee them. In this way customary law was formalized and sanctioned as part of the legal landscape of colonial governance. As Mamdami has observed, such measures imposed hierarchies in "traditional" systems of governance where in many cases no such hierarchies had previously existed, leading to a system of "decentralized despotism." In effect, colonial power in Africa was dependent on indirect rule exercised through the creation of formalized customary law that fundamentally transformed pre-existing balances of power (Bayart 1993; Herbst 2000; Mamdami 1996; Moore 1986; Young 1994).

The customary system of authorities was retained in many African countries after independence, with national officials appointed in place of colonial officers to oversee ethnic "self-governance" or to ensure "modernization." Yet evidently:

> expressions such as "customary" or "traditional" law are only convenient labels for what is in fact a very complex set of rules that, in particular localities, have with time acquired the force of habit, backed by mechanisms of social coercion and ... state power.
>
> (Anselm Odinkalu 2006: 144)

In effect, formal and customary systems of law are often so intertwined in postcolonial African countries that it is very difficult to distinguish between the two. In some places the customary court system is a secondary source of law for formal courts. There have been periods when custom was demonized in almost all countries – Tanzania's socialist experiment is perhaps the best

6 Introduction

and most long-lasting example. Yet customary law also gained legitimacy as part of the movement away from colonial rule and institutions, and the search for specifically "African" forms of governance. Thus the postcolonial period has been characterized by a back and forth between lionizing and demonizing custom. Contemporary reforms tend to recognize the reality of complex legal pluralities and try to ensure greater gender equity and non-discrimination throughout different legal orders and spheres (see the contributions by Hellum on Southern and Eastern Africa, Chapter 1 in this volume, and Bourdon on Tanzania, Chapter 7 in this volume). For example, the new South African constitution of 1996 specifically recognizes customary law yet also enshrines rights guarantees, gender equity and so forth. The specter of "tribalism" and the politics of ethnic chauvinism, autochthony and belonging continue to dominate political debate in many parts of contemporary Africa. However, it is also the case that in countries such as Mozambique, South Africa, Malawi and Tanzania political debate is oriented towards continued national unity (Englund and Nyamnjoh 2004; Geschiere and Nyamnjoh 2000).

In this respect it is important to understand the differences in historical processes of colonial and postcolonial state construction and the ways in which debates on liberalism, universal rights and the recognition of difference have featured – or not featured – in these at different moments in time. In Latin America liberalism has been the dominant ideology of elites since the mid-nineteenth century and was used to exploit and subjugate native populations. Yet liberalism and universalism are not simply ideologies of domination. Demands for citizenship and latterly human rights have played a central role in subaltern politics of resisting oppression and struggling for greater inclusion and equality (Mallon 1995). In contrast to much of Africa, the legal recognition of ethnic or racial difference was not part of the structures of postcolonial governance and domination. During the twentieth century calls for the recognition of ethnic difference and specificity originated amongst historically marginalized indigenous peoples. However, constitutional and policy reforms during the 1990s that recognized ethnic difference were criticized by some scholars and indigenous rights activists as a form of "neoliberal governance" – a global regime that accepts cultural specificity but denies social and economic rights to the majority (Hale 2002). In Africa, by contrast, the creation of a bifurcated legal system in many African contexts was key to creating forms of difference undergirding colonial (and in some cases postcolonial) regimes for decades. Universal doctrines of equality of rights therefore held out the promise of overcoming the segregated, racialized systems of rule associated with colonialism and apartheid. Yet it is also true that liberalism has much shallower historical roots across much of the continent than in Latin America. In addition, in many African countries the introduction of human rights doctrines has coincided with the regional and global shift to neoliberal models of economic

Introduction 7

organization. Both phenomena are strongly associated with international agencies such as the World Bank and have been criticized by some sectors as new forms of colonial imposition (Ferguson 2006; Englund 2006). The historical timing and broader political and economic context surrounding debates on the recognition of rights or ethnic difference is therefore a key factor in any analysis.

Analyzing legal pluralities

Legal pluralities entail multiple forms of law or legal ordering within the same social field. These can include a multitude of legal phenomena: the "customary," "traditional" or "neo-traditional" law practiced by and/or ascribed to different ethnic groups; distinct forms of religious law applying to specific denominational communities; the official statutory law of nation states; international human rights law; the transnational "soft law" of international organizations or multinational corporations; the "project law" of non-governmental organizations (NGOs); and international commercial law or *lex mercatoria*.[6] For most people across the world, social, economic and political life is structured by the coexistence of these multiple formal and informal norms and institutions, and by the interaction of a variety of beliefs and practices. Different normative orders define categories of inclusion. They set out the entitlements and obligations of collective and individual subjects. They also establish rules for the exercise of power. Distinct normative orders may compete or conflict with one another in what is often a context of highly decentralized governance, involving a wider range of non-state actors and institutions (Benda-Beckmann *et al.* 2009a). Clearly statutory law alone does not define social, political and economic life. As Roger Cotterrell has noted, as an analytical approach legal pluralism rejects typical legal positivist assumptions that privilege the authority of state law. "Instead it signals that [...] authority is unsettled in many social fields, a matter of conflict to be resolved ... by negotiation, power or influence" (Cotterrell 2009: 485).

Much debate on legal pluralism has aimed to determine what is new about its contemporary forms and how we should best approach their analysis. Most accounts draw distinctions between "old" and "new" legal pluralism: the "old," mostly associated with mid-twentieth century legal anthropology, conceived of multiple legal orders within the boundaries of the nation state and focused primarily on the relationship between state law and non-state "ethnic" or "religious" law in colonial and postcolonial settings (Chanock 1985; Griffiths 1986; Guedes and Lopes 2006; Merry 1988; Moore 2005). The more recent wave of legal pluralism studies is concerned with the transnational and international dimensions of legal ordering. Contemporary research also tends to be much more interdisciplinary: legal anthropologists have consistently pointed to the multiple sources of law and authority in society, but contemporary patterns of globalization have now led legal

8 Introduction

sociologists and social theorists to analyze the nature and significance of non-state forms of law (Michaels 2009; Schiff Berman 2009).[7]

Recent analytical approaches towards legal pluralism have tended to move away from a conception of multiple "systems" or semi-autonomous spheres ("state law," "customary law") existing in relation to one another. Instead perspectives that understand different legal orders as hybrid, fluid and mutually constituted have come to define the field.[8] Boaventura de Sousa Santos' concept of "interlegality," with its emphasis on the role of human agency in the constitution of constantly evolving legal hybrids, has been particularly influential. All rules and laws are subject to negotiation, reinterpretation and change, much of this driven by people invoking different normative and cognitive orders. De Sousa Santos's formulation encourages us to analyze the ways in which social actors perceive of, deploy, resist, appropriate and construct different legal repertoires, and to explore the manner in which "legal life is constituted by an intersection of different legal orders" (de Sousa Santos 1987: 298). It also encourages us to explore the ways in which contemporary legal constellations are constituted diachronically through complex historical trajectories and sedimentations, something emphasized in the different contributions to this volume. Following de Sousa Santos's reformulation of legal pluralism, other authors have emphasized the ways in which contemporary globalization has de-centered key transnational legal concepts, such as human rights, which can be understood as "a set of complicated social and ethical knowledge practices that appear in discrete places at discrete time with enough autonomy that they can be isolated analytically and studied in what is often described as their 'local context'" (Goodale 2007: 11–12).[9]

At the same time, previous tendencies within the literature towards either celebrating or demonizing legal pluralities have largely given way to more nuanced analyses that strive to understand them as dynamic social formations with varying effects and consequences. "The idea of legal pluralism drawing attention to the possibility that there may be sources of law other than the nation state has become far more widely accepted than it was only a few decades ago" (Benda-Beckmann *et al.* 2009b: 1). This is partly due to the global shift towards greater acceptance of sub-national ethnic and cultural difference: degrees of autonomy for different peoples or communities are increasingly endorsed within the architecture of neoliberal governance. It is also due to the ways in which contemporary patterns of globalization – and particularly legal globalization – have transformed all nation states. As regional and international sources of law have become increasingly important, traditional state-centered positivist understandings have become harder to sustain. As Michaels recently observed, "several themes of legal pluralism have [now] become common sense: the plurality of legal orders, the decentralized position of the state, the strengthening of non-state norms" (Michaels 2009: 255).

Introduction 9

So what then, if anything, is new about the "new" legal pluralities? A number of empirical phenomena can be identified, all of which pose new challenges for understanding the dynamics between legal pluralities and the prospects for greater gender justice:

First, recent decades have seen the rapid multiplication of new forms of transnationalized law and international norm development, including human rights and regional interstate legal systems. As many have noted, legal globalization itself is far from new. Yet, as Franz von Benda-Beckmann has observed, "transnational and international law presently play a far greater role in the international order and within legal orders in states than in earlier post-colonial periods" (Benda-Beckmann 2006: 55). Human rights have been a particularly important innovation, particularly since the end of the cold war, effectively "transform[ing] individuals into international law stakeholders possessing their own entitlements against the state" (Schiff Berman 2009: 230). Human rights have also given rise to specifically rights-based approaches to international development (Jefferson and Jensen 2009).

Second, together with the "rights revolution," the global paradigm shift to neoliberalism has increasingly shaped constitutional and legal arrangements in a range of countries across the world. Recurring features of the neoliberal paradigm include the outsourcing or delegation of previously public, governmental functions to private enterprises, NGOs, communities or individuals. This increasingly blurs the lines between the exercise of state and non-state power. Other specifically legal features of neoliberalism include an emphasis on the primacy of the individual citizen, and the institutionalization of inequalities through differentiated forms of law and security. For example, Aiwha Ong's work on Southeast Asia has pointed to the phenomenon of "graduated sovereignty," "whereby citizens in zones that are differently articulated to global production and financial circuits are subjected to different kinds of surveillance and in practice enjoy different sets of civil, political and economic rights" (Ong 2003: 41; see also Ong 2006).

Third, the recognition of cultural difference has become a significant feature of contemporary constitutional design. Modernizing visions involving the abolition or outlawing of non-state forms of law and the subordination of all ethnic, racial, religious and tribal groups to a single legal order have increasingly fallen out of political favor, recognized as unviable. Instead different kinds of "multicultural constitutionalism" have been adopted, which explicitly define governance roles – or semi-autonomous spheres – for different ethno-cultural and religious forms of law and authority. In Western Europe, for example, large-scale migration, religious diversity and the growing importance of Islam have led to the adoption of various kinds of multiculturalism. As Benda-Beckmann and his co-authors observe, "states, rather than governing directly, now attempt to determine the shape of the constellations of governance" (Benda-Beckmann *et al.* 2009a: 5). Indeed, this often results in the forced recognition of competing and overlapping sovereignties within one national territory (Blom Hansen and Stepputat 2001). However, written constitutions and central government edicts rarely determine how constellations of governance will operate on the ground; this requires the more ethnographic forms of analysis privileged in the contributions to this volume.

Fourth, the last two decades have seen the growth of a worldwide trend towards the judicialization of politics and political claims, and the increasing appeal to laws, constitutions and specifically legal forms of legitimacy by dominant and opposition groups alike – a phenomena Jean and John Comaroff have referred to as the "fetishization of law." This appeal to legal forms leads, in turn, to the expansion of "forum shopping" into the regional and global spheres as individuals and social movements seek to reach beyond the boundaries of the nation-state in their struggles for justice (Comaroff and Comaroff 2006, 2009; de Sousa Santos 2002; Sieder et al. 2005; Couso et al. 2010). As political battles are increasingly fought on the legal terrain, all actors seek to expand the repertoire of rules to their own advantage.

Fifth, since 9/11 new global security paradigms have emerged that favor the ever more frequent suspension of constitutional guarantees by governments. Such paradigms effectively blur the line between the legal and the illegal, creating "grey zones" of heightened legal ambiguity. The construction of state legality or the so-called "rule of law" has always been embedded within illegal practices, yet the transnational dynamics within new security paradigms suggest something qualitatively different at work. Understandings of citizenship have been transformed post 9/11: sovereignty is questioned under agreements on the Right to Protect Principle (R2P), human rights violations have become "legalized" (debates on torture) and are increasingly transnational in nature (forced rendition). At the same time, the provision of security has increasingly been privatized or "outsourced" to different non-state actors. Private security companies and the "cultural experts" of human terrain systems now commonly operate side by side with soldiers on the ground to map and win the hearts and minds of internationally determined dangerous populations. In the light of this growing "security-development nexus" (Buur et al. 2007; Duffield 2001; McNeish and Sande Lie 2010), the transnational and localized processes through which these "grey zones" are constituted are a key element in analyses of contemporary legal pluralities.

Some authors have pointed out that although the empirical field of legal pluralism has certainly expanded as a consequence of contemporary globalization, analytically the concept itself has not moved forward very much (Michaels 2009). Indeed many anthropologists have abandoned the idea of legal pluralism altogether, judging it to be of limited purchase. Jean and John Comaroff have emphasized the need for an analytical shift within legal anthropology from concern with legal pluralism per se, to a consideration of the combined problematic of law and governance in the contemporary world, and specifically the new relationships between law and governance in the age of neoliberalism (Comaroff and Comaroff 2009: 32, 39). Such a holistic approach to analyzing legal pluralities holds out much promise. Potentially it can enable a broader consideration of the relationship between plural legal forms and different, shifting configurations of power and rule. We contend that any consideration of the relationship between legal pluralities and gender justice needs to be located within such a broader, historically informed analysis of regimes of governance. A dual focus on legal pluralities and governance will also help to critically consider the nature and effect of different development interventions and to consider the ways in which patterns of governance could or should be transformed.

Legal pluralities and development practice

In recent years, the international development community has become increasingly interested in legal pluralities and specifically non-state justice systems as part of the general shift towards conceiving governance as being more decentered and more "society"- and "market"-oriented than in the past (Benda-Beckmann *et al.* 2009a; Faundez 2005, 2006). Many development practitioners remain cautious about endorsing customary, traditional or religious forms of legal ordering, which often function to protect and promote the interests of powerful or dominant groups to the detriment of the interests of marginalized sectors within those communities. There remains concern about how to make legally plural systems more permeable to international human rights discourses and, within this, how to encourage more equitable gender practices (ICHRP 2009; UN Women 2011).

Nonetheless, in recent years many development specialists have also increasingly come to view non-state justice systems as a development resource for "strengthening the rule of law" and for dealing with conflict. This is particularly the case in post-conflict contexts where non-state forms of justice are often seen as a valuable resource for constructing the rule of law (Isser 2011). For example, the international development community has endorsed traditional courts as a means of addressing "reconciliation" in post-genocide Rwanda and post-war Mozambique (Igreja 2010; Kyed 2009; Waldorf *et al.* 2010). In other contexts, where people cannot access state justice institutions, non-state justice systems are also increasingly viewed as a relevant form of alternative dispute resolution (ADR) (Chirayath *et al.* 2005; Faundez 2005, 2006; Kane *et al.* 2005).[10] Proponents of such approaches argue that non-state justice systems tend to be cheaper and more accessible than the formal courts; that they are invariably socially embedded; and that they are characterized by dynamic and flexible norms and procedures and therefore, at least in the view of some, may be better suited to adapting to environmental, ecological economic and political change than the formal legal system of the state (Meinzen-Dick and Pradhan 2002).

12 Introduction

Developments in policy discussions and soft law amongst multinational organizations also appear to be giving increasing saliency to non-state justice systems and the development of mechanisms to deal with plurality. For example, in its disaggregation of types of violence the World Development Report for 2011 explicitly recognizes that "[t]raditional and community structures for dispute resolution are also potential partners in delivering early results – and it may be unwise to ignore them" (World Bank 2011: 133). Recognizing the sustainability and necessity of diverse tenure systems, many policy makers and practitioners are also making increasing reference to Ellinor Ostrom's (2007) Nobel laureate winning call for a Polycentric Model of Natural Resource Management. This approach to environmental governance proposes to recognize and link together diverse ideas of tenure organization and institutional arrangements, including customary forms of organization, into a singular but differentiated system of management. As evidenced by recent documents produced by the Commission on the Legal Empowerment of the Poor, Ostrom's work has influenced previous thinking that emphasized private tenure rights and opened the way for more diverse forms of policy prescription.[11] Recognizing the need to respond to and address a plurality of claims from indigenous communities, the World Bank (OP 4.10) and the International Finance Cooperation (Performance Standard 7) have introduced a set of official operating guidelines that draw on ADR experience and that are aimed at the definition of social safeguards and grievance mechanisms that respect local and traditional governance institutions. While criticisms can be made with regards to their lack of legal teeth, these guidelines are becoming the standard on which UNREDD,[12] FCPF[13] and other donors are looking to base social safeguards and complaint mechanisms in relation to the diversity of interests and governance structures encountered in the application of policy and projects geared towards the reduction of deforestation.

In the field of human rights, international agencies and think-tanks are increasingly engaging with the complexities of legal plural contexts and addressing questions of how policy makers and advocates can best promote human rights standards, access to justice and gender justice within such settings. For example, in 2009 the Geneva-based International Council on Human Rights Policy published an extensive report on human rights, state and non-state law that included a series of "guiding principles" for human rights advocates engaging with plural legal orders (ICHRP 2009: 147–56). And in 2011 UN Women (formerly UNIFEM) published the flagship report *Progress of the World's Women*, which focused on access to justice and paid considerable attention to legal pluralities, their effects on gender justice and policy recommendations for addressing gender justice in plural legal contexts (UN Women 2011).

Other development practices highlighting a growing acceptance of the realities of legal pluralities in policy are also visible at the regional level. One

Introduction   13

trend that has recently been promoted by the international development community in some African countries is that of "self-statement" or ascertainment of community law: essentially converting oral law into written form. Such moves have been supported by the United Nations Development Programme (UNDP) in Namibia and Sudan (USIP 2010). "Self-statement" is supposedly distinguished from previous attempts at codifying "customary law," tarred as these are by associations with colonial projects of domination and control. Rather it is meant to be an organic process of identifying and writing down "customary law" driven by the community itself. However, it is also clear that international agencies see self-statement as a convenient way to introduce rights debates into communities' norms and practices. Some national governments see it as a tool for state-building, a means of "harmonizing" – or controlling – different forms of non-state law with statutory law. For example, in Southern Sudan the Ministry of Legal Affairs and Constitutional Development, together with the UNDP's rule of law unit, recently elaborated a strategy for "self-statement" of customary law by "communities" together with a "soft human rights approach" to regulate and reform this law.

The emphasis on ascertainment has guided much work on customary law in recent years, resulting in various forms of documentation of the laws of some ethnic groups or regions in Southern Sudan (USIP 2010: 14). There are many potential pitfalls inherent in ascertainment, even in its most community-friendly guise of "self-statement." International agencies can end up driving the process and in any case outcomes are rarely predictable. In addition, irrespective of who actually writes down and interprets "custom," the act of codification may limit its inherently flexible, dynamic and negotiable character, or the ability of actors to determine outcomes depending on the specific circumstances of each case. It may also encourage the rigid policing of ethnic or tribal boundaries, supporting the notion that each group should have its own form of law, when in fact legal pluralities are characterized by hybridity and the blurring of boundaries between different forms of regulation. Codification can also simplify the richness of community-based forms of law, reducing it to lists of norms and procedures. Yet it may be that for some groups, such as indigenous people, codification is a means of asserting the validity of their justice systems and staking their claim to autonomy before dominant groups in society. In addition, the written documents produced through such processes may not in fact always determine the way in which particular disputes are dealt with in practice.[14] How "self-statement" or ascertainment works depends ultimately on context. But given the ways in which such techniques tend to be adopted, exported and replicated by international development agencies, it is vital to maintain a critical approach.

We suggest that donor attempts to engage with legal pluralities invariably prove more complicated than originally anticipated. Approaches promoting non-state justice systems and "forum shopping" tend to treat complex historical legal constellations as some kind of menu of dispute resolution options, devoid of power relations and politics. International cooperation efforts have often supported the strengthening of informal legal systems, such as indigenous peoples' justice, yet development approaches can be over-simplified, ahistorical and instrumentalist, driven by efforts to find the "right formula" for approaching legal pluralities in order to ensure specific development outcomes. Non-state justice systems may be promoted and strengthened as a means of dealing with conflict and the weaknesses of a deficient state justice system. Yet such policies often fail to address the structural roots of conflict, such as inequalities in access to land and resources. In fact some analysts have argued that such policies are in fact aimed at cultivating certain kinds of behavior amongst target populations, encouraging them to "participate" in their own self-regulation (Li 2007). Drawing on Foucault's ground-breaking analysis of "governmentality" (Burchill *et al.* 1991), post-developmentalist scholars such as Escobar (1995) and Ferguson (1994) have highlighted the power of international donors and NGOs to define a hegemonic discourse of the development subject – that is, the poor. They have also criticized the management and de-politicization of their political claims through the development of contradictory technologies of governance premised on individual responsibility and managed decen-tralization. More recent writing (Ferguson 2006; Ong 2006) from this posi-tion has furthermore demonstrated that the result of these developments is an increasing variation and lack of uniformity of citizenship rights. As some people and populations "succeed" in re-orienting their conduct to fit new global conditions, other "fragile" populations are singled out for special treatment or exclusion.

Recognizing that law is a matter of politics the contributors to this book question analytical and practitioner approaches that focus almost exclusively on institutions ("court-centric" approaches), and approaches that focus exclusively on rights ("norm-driven" approaches). Instead we place greater emphasis on personhood, subjectivities and the socio-economic and political contexts of disputes and negotiations over rights and obligations. Rather than viewing law as a fixed ideal that people conform to or deviate from, we emphasize the importance of privileging people's understandings and nego-tiation of law, justice, rights and obligations. Thus in our consideration of different plural legal constellations, we place the emphasis on social actors and the ways in which they shape and interact with legal institutions, norms and discourses. For many international development agencies, local forms of law are endorsed only to the extent that they support Western conceptions of the rule of law or international human rights norms. Most countries that have recently recognized indigenous peoples' justice systems specify that these must respect fundamental human rights guarantees and gender equity. Yet instead of asking how traditional, customary or religious law can be made to support gender equity or other abstract international human rights norms, the key is surely to develop more holistic understandings of how communities can be adequately supported in processes of change over time that emphasize the human dignity of all their members, including women.

Legal pluralities play a fundamental role in shaping understandings of gender relations, justice, community and personhood. Discourses and practices rooted in culture, custom, tradition and religion exercise considerable power in shaping, regulating and ordering personal, social, political and economic conduct in all societies, as increasingly do notions of rights. By determining opportunities for personal autonomy, political participation and access to economic resources, such as education, health, land, water or employment, legal pluralities play a critical role in gendered livelihood prospects. Gendered norms and practices that discriminate against women mean they enjoy lower levels of health, nutrition, education and security than men and invariably hold fewer assets than male family members.

In countries where different religious or tribal laws apply to specific communities for civil matters, such as marriage, divorce, inheritance or child custody, the development focus has been on how to reduce discrimination and ensure basic guarantees and safeguards for women and children (Joseph 2000). In many parts of sub-Saharan Africa debates about development, gender and legal pluralities have centered largely on the role that "traditional" or "customary" law of different ethnic and tribal groups plays in the social regulation of rights to allocate and use land, water and natural resources. Here access to such resources is generally mediated through kinship groups: women usually have secondary or use rights to the land of their husbands or male kin. This means that if they are widowed or divorced they can face eviction by their husband's relatives. In many countries new constitutions and statutory land reforms were passed in the 1990s and early 2000s stipulating gender equity in land tenure. These reforms aimed to clarify and formalize title to land in order to promote agricultural production, improve livelihoods and increase women's economic security (Ikdahl *et al.* 2005).[15] Many of the new laws endorsed hybrid or plural legal models, recognizing both official and customary law and mandating gender equality in both, often through non-discrimination clauses and positive discrimination to ensure women's representation in customary institutions. Yet implementation of these changes has been slow and norms and practices that discriminate against women often prevail. Some analysts have seen customary law and legal pluralities as an impediment to achieving greater gender equity and livelihood security for women. Others take a less normative stance and instead stress the need for research examining how statutory and customary law interact and change over time, and how this interaction affects gender relations (Henrysson and Joireman 2009; Chimhowu and Woodhouse 2006; Ikdahl *et al.* 2005; Whitehead and Tsikata 2003; Bourdon,

16 Introduction

Chapter 7 in this volume; Hellum, Chapter 1 in this volume; Tønnessen, Chapter 5 in this volume).

In Latin America, where indigenous peoples' normative and legal systems have increasingly been recognized within new constitutions, policy debates around legal pluralities have centered on issues concerning law and order and intra-familial violence, as well as territorial autonomy and control of natural resources. Concerns have been voiced that officially recognizing indigenous law may result in violent, vigilante-style justice (Arias and Goldstein 2010) that can unfairly discriminate against women (Cumes 2009). Other concerns have been voiced that formal recognition of non-state justice systems may prejudice indigenous women's access to justice by legitimizing and entrenching discriminatory patriarchal norms and practices. These debates raise substantive questions about how to harmonize and strengthen different legal orders in order to ensure respect for human dignity, and how to protect disadvantaged groups against discrimination or victimization at the same time as ensuring that the collective rights to autonomy of indigenous peoples are respected.

Gender justice

While at first glance suggestive of emancipatory potential, the phrase "gender justice" is rarely given precise definition and is often used interchangeably with notions of "gender equality", "gender equity", "women's empowerment", and "women's rights" (Goetz 2007: 17). Wanting to establish the applicability of gender justice as both goal and process in relation to the legal complexities explored in our research and writing, we therefore see it as important to define more clearly the significance of the term. As such, we specifically emphasize here the importance of a three-dimensional approach to gender justice. We argue that this approach can, through critical engagement, overcome previous splits in feminist theory, in particular those between universalist analysis associated with both socialist and liberal ideas of rights-based development, and culture-centric analysis associated with putatively "post-Marxist" strands of feminist thought. Importantly, our approach also re-emphasizes the inter-sexual relational basis of gender and development (Chant and Gutmann 2002).

The phrase "gender justice" has been increasingly referred to by activists and academics in recent years because of a growing concern and realization that phrases like "gender equality" and "gender mainstreaming" have failed to communicate, or provide redress for, the ongoing gender-based injustices from which women suffer. However, despite its rising currency there remains little agreement on its meaning or intended goals and outcomes (Mukhopadyay and Singh 2007; Molyneux and Razavi 2003; Hellum *et al.* 2007). Contemporary discussions of gender justice include political philosophy discussions of human agency, autonomy, rights and capabilities; debates within political science about democratization, citizenship and constitutionalism; and discussions in the field of law about judicial reform and practical matters of access to justice (Goetz 2007). Similar unresolved dilemmas are also found across these discussions: can absolute and universal standards be set for determining what is right or good in human social relations? How should the rights of the individual be offset against the needs of the family, the community, the ethnic "nation" or the territorial state? What is the appropriate role for the state and the international community in promoting social welfare and human equality? The answers given to each of these questions betray in general political positions in a debate about what is "right" and "good" in human relationships, and how these desirable outcomes may be achieved (Mukhopadyay and Singh 2007). Ideologies and conventions about women's subordination to men and the family are often rooted in assumptions about what is "natural" or "divinely ordained" in human relationships. While there are clear overlaps, these different assumptions and convictions can be seen to have formed the basis of three roughly contrasting camps in recent thought about gender justice.

The first and perhaps most formalized of the positions on gender justice is that which is most firmly founded on an idea of setting minimum universal standards for women's freedom. Referring directly to the CEDAW convention which makes the absence of gender-based discrimination the indicator of gender justice, this position emphasizes the need to establish universally applicable principles of justice and to apply them as impartially as possible. Here the phrase "discrimination against women" is strictly held to be any distinction, exclusion, or restriction made on the basis of sex which has the effect of impairing or nullifying the recognition, enjoyment or exercise by women, irrespective of their marital status, on a basis of equality of men and women, of human rights and fundamental freedoms in the political, economic, social, cultural, civil or any other field (Cook 1997: 189). This position of universality is partially a legacy of earlier socialist approaches to feminism that emphasized a singular class analysis and located gender relations in the terrain of political economy and was primarily concerned with the issues of division of labor, reproduction and sexuality. However, as these ideas were increasingly critiqued for their economic determinism and limitations to issues of body and materiality, Marxist positivism was replaced by a liberal positivism that drew largely on European legal traditions and a framework of human rights that took on new salience with the spread of neoliberalism. While emphasizing market freedoms, this position also stressed the importance of political and legal institutions in forming the enabling environment for economic development. Acknowledging that power relations understood as *agency* affect the outcome of policies, this approach to gender justice proposed that a state of law and basic accountability is needed in order to advance human development – to enable people to make the most of their basic endowments in resources and skills. This position stresses the

18   Introduction

relationship between the articulation of individual and collective preferences ("voice") and state responses, and furthermore aims to establish the basic rights that citizens may legitimately claim from the state. Following the impact of the work of the Nobel laureate Amartya Sen emphasizing the importance of basic capabilities or freedoms in the creation of development, a number of feminist scholars have debated the minimum economic, social and even psychological conditions under which women might be able to refuse or renegotiate the social arrangements in which they find themselves (O'Neill 2000: 163; Nussbaum 2000; Young 1990). This "minimum capabilities" approach to gender justice aims to construct the basic universal conditions required for free and rational individual choice.

Taking strong exception with both the universalist assumptions and legal determinism of the liberal position, contrasting approaches to gender justice have taken a "cultural turn" (Frazier 2007). These more culturally oriented perspectives emphasize both the need to recognize that gender struggles in the world have increasingly emphasized issues of identity and representation, and draw attention to the falseness of universalist approaches that characterize the state as the hegemonic legal authority (Goetz 2007). Rights-based approaches are described as impractical and deceptively easy to promulgate while being deeply evasive on the matter of identifying the agents obliged to satisfy rights claims, and the degrees to which they should do so (O'Neill 2000: 97; Jefferson and Jensen 2009). Anne Phillips (2001) has been particularly pointed in her critique of Nussbaum's capabilities' approach and its emphasis on minimum necessary requirements. This approach, she argues, retreats from the profound challenges of the struggle for human equality – not just between women and men, but across social groups both within or across nations. Moreover, she highlights that this retreat "meshes with an almost universal shift in social-democratic politics, where the problem of poverty has supplanted the problem of inequality, and ensuring a humane minimum has taken over from worries about the overall income gap" (Phillips 2001: 16–17). The ideas of agency suggested by liberal approaches to gender justice are also criticized for being overly romanticized due to their lack of consideration of how power relations are historically transformed and produced (Abu-Lughod 1990). Kandiyoti (1998: 147) has asserted, for example, in a moment of self-criticism of her concept of "bargaining with patriarchy" that explaining resistance has often relied on the notion of the autonomous, self-determining individual, thus naively assuming the subordinates' capacities to see through the discourse of the dominant. She indicates here, as other feminist scholars do (Abu-Lughod 1990; Mahmood 2001), the danger of romanticizing resistance and points to the fact that women's agencies are not always tied to clear ideas of emancipation or the challenge to male domination. Through her analysis of women's mosque movements in Cairo, Mahmood (2001), for example, has demonstrated that women may challenge patriarchal norms, but may also reinforce and accommodate these norms (see also Tønnessen on Sudan, Chapter 5 in this volume). Mahmood analyzes piety and underlines the importance of patience (*sabr*) and modesty (*al-hayat*) for women's agencies and their conception of justice. Her work encourages us "to conceptualize agency not simply as a synonym for resistance to relations of domination, but as a capacity for action that specific relations and subordination create and enable" (Mahmood 2001: 212). As such, women's agency may have the effect of reinforcing continuity and stability, rather than somehow implying a break with existing norms (Charrad 2010).

Drawing on the literature on legal pluralism and inter-legality, culturally oriented perspectives highlight that in most states, and particularly in developing postcolonial societies, there are plural and overlapping legal systems, and multiple social authorities – clan or tribe elders, religious leaders, feudal elites. Recognizing that this highlights the limits of formal law in many contexts, and casts doubts on the effectiveness of a feminist focus on the state or institutions as the medium through which to enforce changed rules and norms in gender relations (Manji 1999: 439). There are few states in which norms, prejudices and affections that have been developed in particular communities are excised from the deliberations of public actors in deciding who should benefit from public resources. In some contexts, these non-state normative and authority systems are particularly strong. Therefore, the state's rulings on justice are ignored by powerful groups, and the rights it extends to all citizens are not deemed legitimate or relevant to those who most urgently require them in order to transform oppressive social relations. Moreover, as Molyneux and Razavi (2003) suggest, recognizing the plural character of social formations entails the adoption of a cultural and moral relativism that is at variance with universal legal standards. From this camp it is argued that we are also practically obliged to examine how rule-making and enforcement works in other enduring normative systems such as clan and kinship networks, how these position women and men in relation to one another, and how these positions might either be influenced by changes in formal state law, or by other means.

A third position on gender justice has developed out of an effort to reconsider the meaning of "gender mainstreaming" and acknowledgement of the need to reconsider the position of men as part of the relational equation it covers. Men as a human category have always been present, involved, consulted, obeyed and disobeyed in development work, and expressly so since the coining of the idea of Gender in Development (GAD) in the 1990s. Yet men as a gendered category in a feminist sense, recognizing the unequal power relations between men and women and between men, have rarely been drawn into development in any substantial manner (Chant and Gutmann 2002: 271). Although women-only approaches to gender have been recognized to be insufficient to deal with and overturn embedded patriarchal structures, most gender projects remain focused on only one side of the

20 Introduction

relationship. The argument made in this third approach to gender justice is that mainstreaming requires men to be more involved both at the operational and project levels. Planning for change in women's lives entails changes for men, with structural and normative shifts in male–female power relations being a necessary precondition for any development process with long-term sustainability (Pineda 2000). While not losing sight of the fact that women are in general worse off, it also requires recognition that men's power and privileges are not uniform, fixed and universal (Kajifusa 1998). Changing socio-economic conditions mean that in many parts of the world patriarchal family units dependent primarily or exclusively on male incomes are declining, and ideological challenges to traditional gender relations overall are growing. A reconsideration of patriarchal power also requires a critical approach to a typical "problematic male" discourse, whereby opposition between men and women – which pose the former as useless, irrelevant, parasitic and so on, and the latter as either victims or heroines – are taken as a norm, regardless of context or intra-group heterogeneity (Cornwall 2000: 21).

In this volume critical inspiration is taken from each of these three separate approaches to the question of gender justice and a more integrated three-dimensional approach adopted. This approach accepts the criticism made of universalism, but also recognizes that the dangers inherent in a culturally sensitive human rights approach should not be underestimated (Hellum *et al.* 2007). Although we argue that an understanding and appreciation of local norms and customs can be a tool for engaging in meaningful change, we emphasize in line with Hellum *et al.* (2007: xvii) that there is a need to be constantly alert to the risk of uncritically buying into customary and religious approaches and losing out on human rights entitlements. There is also always a risk that findings on the harsh realities of women's and girl's lives and consequent analysis of their needs will be overridden or compromised in the local, national and international processes in which rights, culture and religious values are negotiated. While there is apparent room for culturally defined concepts such as the Andean "*buen vivir*" in accepted development parlance as ostensible locally grounded expressions of liberty and prosperity, critical analysis is needed to consider whether in transference to other levels of application original meanings are retained, diluted or hollowed out in conformity with dominant preoccupations with a limited form of individual citizenship (Walsh 2010). As such we argue that there is a need to develop an approach that takes human rights from the plane of abstract principles and places them in dialogue with local problems and principles, but also vice versa. Again, we agree with Hellum *et al.* (2007) that what is needed is knowledge that can facilitate the translation of the complex realities and legalities of women's lives into human rights measures that respond to the situation at hand and engage the tension between the complexities of women's lived realities and achieving basic universal rights through exploring locally appropriate implementation approaches. We therefore support the idea of a constructivist approach to law and culture, which as Hernández Castillo (2002) recognizes, helps women in claiming their rights since it frees them from having to choose between endorsing national law or indigenous customs.

In addition we also emphasize the need to come to terms with the relational nature of gender. Gender justice can be defined as the ending of – and of necessary provision for redress for – inequalities between women and men that result in women's subordination to men. As such men, but also recognition of the interplay between structure and agency, are important elements of a refined approach. In order to better understand the power relation structuring men's and women's lives, we must consider both men's and women's real-life gendered experiences and avoid recourse to stereotyped gender roles and power relations (Sooriyakumaran 2010). Moreover, from a strategic perspective, the involvement of men in the quest for gender justice promotes joint responsibility for achieving gender equality (Esplen 2008), and invites a discussion of "intersectionality:" that is, an analysis of the multiplicity and "simultaneity" of oppression where systems of inequality such as class, gender, and ethnicity come together (Crenshaw 1991; Collins 1998; FIMI 2006). While recognizing the common imbalances of existing structures of patriarchal bargaining, our approach proposes that rather than suggesting a simple conclusion of male power and female exploitation, levers for change can only be identified through acceptance, study and engagement with the complex natures of the economies of influence and power between men and women of different classes, ethnic, racial and religious groups. We furthermore recognize that while patriarchal mindsets and social relations are produced in the private sphere they are not contained there, but rather infuse most economic, social and political institutions. Indeed, the phrase "gender justice" provides a direct reminder of the problem of institutionalized bias by reminding us that justice itself, in its conception and administration, is very often gendered, responding to a patriarchal standard derived from the domestic arena (Goetz 2007: 17–18).

Recognizing the interplay between structures and agency in these processes, our approach furthermore proposes that gender justice includes unique and context-specific elements that go beyond related concepts of justice in class or race terms, which complicate both its definition and enactment (Goetz 2007). Inequalities may exist in the distribution of resources and opportunities that enable individuals to build human, social, economic, and political capital. Or they may be located in the conceptions of human dignity, personal autonomy and rights that deny women physical integrity and the capacity to make choices about how to live their lives. Gender justice implies then both access to and control over resources (including bodies), combined with agency. In this sense it does not differ from many definitions of women's empowerment. However, emphasizing the issue of justice

22 Introduction

implies an additional element: that of accountability. Gender justice is therefore understood as a process that requires that women are able to ensure that power-holders – whether in the household, the community, the market, or the state – can be held to account so that actions that limit, on the grounds of gender, women's access to resources or capacity to make choices, are prevented or punished (Goetz 2007: 30–31). It is furthermore understood here as a process that seeks parity of participation. Borrowing and building on Nancy Frazier's (2007) proposals for parity in gender justice, this principle aims to build or identify social arrangements that permit all adult members of society to interact with one another as peers. This requires both the redistribution of resources needed to ensure independence and voice, and institutionalized patterns of cultural values that express respect for all participants and ensure equal opportunity for achieving social esteem.

The complex intertwining of gendered power relations makes clear the need for a three-dimensional vision of gender justice. In summary, this is an approach that critically considers the relationship between rights and legal practice, that actively applies a relational analysis of gender relations where both men and women are present, and which practically engages with the limitations and possibilities of both distribution and recognition as steps towards gender parity and as part of a process aimed at wider human emancipation.

Conclusions

While not claiming to be exhaustive of the relevant literature on legal pluralism and gender, this introductory chapter demonstrates the complexity of the relationship between these two areas of study. Moreover, we contend here that despite the need to highlight complexity and ambiguity, it is nonetheless possible to say something concrete about the relationships between what have until now been largely kept separate fields of study. Our work emphasizes the artificiality of this division and the need for both fields to come into tension with each other. In doing so we have emphasized here that hybrid legal pluralities are a feature of governance and patterns of rule, both past and present, throughout the world. Promoting gender justice requires engagement with legal pluralities and hybrid legal systems. It also entails recognition that constellations of governance – like identities – are mobile, dynamic, historically shaped and often highly contested. Ultimately legal systems need to provide for conciliation and the restoration of social relations; to provide justice and reparations in order to prevent retaliatory violence and conflict; and to have the power to protect victims and ensure that decisions are carried out. Transnational and global dynamics have increased possibilities for people to appropriate rights discourses: across the world different mediating institutions, including NGOs and social movements, are working to increase women's legal consciousness and to amplify their demands for justice. Certain human rights principles, such as non-discrimination and the prohibition on violence against women, are non-negotiable (ICHRP 2009). But human rights advocates face the challenges of how to understand power dynamics within legally plural constellations of governance, and how best to support women – and men – in struggles for more equitable and less violent relations and for human dignity. The approach we have advocated here emphasizes the importance of analyzing context, historical trajectories and local agency and understandings. We hope that the work presented in this volume, bringing together perspectives from Africa and Latin America, contributes to ongoing policy debates about how best to secure greater gender justice.

Acknowledgements

The authors would like to thank the participants in the workshop held in Maputo in February 2011 for their comments on an initial draft of this introduction. They are particularly grateful to Bjørn Enge Bertelsen, Eyolf Jul-Larsen, Anne Hellum and Bill Derman for their close readings and constructive suggestions.

Notes

1 CEDAW places women's rights in a global normative framework of equality and non-discrimination. It defines discrimination against women comprehensively to include any distinction made on the basis of sex that impairs women's equal human rights in any sphere: "political, economic, social, cultural, civil or any other" (Article 1).
2 The volume edited by Anne Hellum, Julie Stewart, Shaheen Ali and Amy Tsanga (Hellum *et al.* 2007) is a notable exception; see also Griffiths (1997). On the history of legal pluralism in development policy, see Benda-Beckmann (2006).
3 In their recent work on legal pluralism and women's access to property rights in Kenya, Henrysson and Joireman provide a clear statement of the position in favor of a unitary regime of law as a means to favor economic development: "Ambiguity in the definition or enforcement of property rights leads to an increase in trans-action costs in the exchange and transfer of land as well as a residual uncertainty after any land contract. ... The disjuncture between public and customary law regulating property rights is a problem for capital formation across Africa" (Henrysson and Joireman 2009: 40).
4 On the invention of tradition see Hobsbawm and Ranger (1983).
5 The means of formalizing custom was not uniform across the British colonies in Africa. In Kenya and Tanzania, for example, no separate customary tribunals were created and the official judiciary adjudicated on matters of customary law. This did not mean of course that the colonial power did not respect the role and to a large extent also the decisions taken by the traditional authority structures.
6 For surveys of debates on legal pluralism, see Griffiths (1986); Griffiths (2002); Merry (1988); Tamanaha (2008); Twining (2000); on project law, see Li (2007); on *lex mercatoria*, see Dezaley and Garth (1996); Teubner (1996).

24 Introduction

7 See, for example, Cotterrell on legal transnationalism and the challenges it poses to legal sociology (Cotterrell 2009); or Rodríguez-Garavito's call for a "post-Westphalian conception of law" (Rodríguez-Garavito 2011).
8 See Merry (1998, 2006); Rajagopal (2003).
9 Goodale and Merry insist that ideas about human rights are not simply "vernacularized" in "local" contexts; rather they unfold "without a clear spatial referent, in part through transnational networks but, also, equally importantly, through the projection of the moral and legal imagination by social actors whose precise locations ... within these networks are (for them) practically irrelevant" (Goodale and Merry 2007: 12).
10 For a critical appraisal of this trend, see Nader 2002.
11 See http://www.undp.org/legalempowerment/report/Making_the_Law_Work_for_Everyone.pdf (accessed March 2012).
12 United Nations Program for Reduced Emissions from Deforestation and Degradation.
13 World Bank Forest Carbon Partnership.
14 Sierra has carried out research on the Coordinadora Regional de Autoridades Comunitarias, better known as the *comunitaria*, a non-governmental alliance of indigenous and non-indigenous communal authorities that provides security and justice services in the state of Guerrero, Mexico. She shows that while the statute of the organization is important for negotiating spheres of autonomy and power with state authorities, it is not necessarily used as a guide for dispute resolution procedures (Sierra 2007).
15 International agencies have promoted different approaches within debates on land reform in Africa; the World Bank emphasized a market-based approach to development, while UN agencies and a variety of NGOs and international non-governmental organizations have promoted rights-based approaches.

References

Abu-Lughod, L. (1990) "The Romance of Resistance: Tracing Transformations of Power through Bedouin Women," *American Ethnologist* 17 (1): 41–55.
Anselm Odinkalu, C. (2006) "Poor Justice or Justice for the Poor? A Policy Framework for Reform of Customary and Informal Justice Systems in Africa," *World Bank Legal Review: Law, Equity and Development*: 141–65.
Arias, E. D. and D. M. Goldstein (eds) (2010) *Violent Democracies in Latin America*, Durham, NC: Duke University Press.
Bayart, J. F. (1993) *The State in Africa: The Politics of the Belly*, London: Longman.
Bellagamba, A. and G. Klute (eds) (2008) *Beside the State: Emergent Powers in Contemporary Africa*, Cologne: Rüdiger Köppe Verlag.
Benda-Beckmann, F. von (2006) "The Multiple Edges of Law: Dealing with Legal Pluralism in Development Practice," in *The World Bank Legal Review: Law, Equity and Development*, Washington, DC: World Bank Publications, pp. 51–86.
——(2009) "Balancing Islam, Adat and the State: Comparing Islamic and Civil Courts in Indonesia," in Benda-Beckmann, F. von, K. von Benda-Beckmann and A. Griffiths (eds) *The Power of Law in a Transnational World: Anthropological Enquiries*, New York, NY and Oxford: Berghan Books, pp. 216–35.
Benda-Beckmann, F. von, K. von Benda-Beckmann and J. Eckert (eds) (2009a) *Rules of Law and Laws of Ruling: On the Governance of Law*, Surrey and Burlington, VT: Ashgate.

Benda-Beckmann, F. von, K. von Benda-Beckmann and A. Griffiths (eds) (2009b) *The Power of Law in a Transnational World: Anthropological Enquiries*, New York, NY and Oxford: Berghan Books.

Blom Hansen, T. and F. Stepputat (eds) (2001) *States of Imagination: Ethnographic Explorations of the Post-colonial State*, Durham, NC: Duke University Press.

Burchill, G., C. Gordon and P. Miller (1991) *The Foucault Effect: Studies in Governmentality*, Chicago, IL: University of Chicago Press.

Buur, L., S. Jensen and F. Stepputat (eds) (2007) *The Security-Development Nexus: Expressions of Sovereignty and Securitization in Southern Africa*, Capetown: HSRC Press.

Chanock, M. (1985) *Law, Custom and Social Order: The Colonial Experience in Malawi and Zambia*, Cambridge: Cambridge University Press.

Chant, S. and M. Gutmann (2002) "Men-Streaming Gender? Questions for Gender and Development Policy in the 21st Century," *Progress in Development Studies* (2): 269–82.

Charrad, M. M. (2010) "Women's Agency Across Cultures: Conceptualizing Strengths and Boundaries," *Women's Studies International Forum* 33: 517–22.

Chimhowu, A. and P. Woodhouse (2006) "Customary vs. Private Property Rights? Dynamics and Trajectories of Vernacular Land Markets in Sub-Saharan Africa," *Journal of Agrarian Change* (6): 346–71.

Chirayath, L., C. Sage and M. Woodcock (2005) "Customary Law and Policy Reform: Engaging with the Plurality of Justice Systems," Background paper for the *World Development Report 2006: Equity and Development.*

Collins, P. H. (1998) "The Tie that Binds: Race, Gender, and US Violence," *Ethnic and Racial Studies*, 21 (5): 917–38.

Comaroff, J. and J. L. Comaroff (eds) (2006) *Law and Disorder in the Postcolony*, Chicago, IL: University of Chicago Press.

Comaroff, J. L. and J. Comaroff (2009) "Reflections on the Anthropology of Law, Governance and Sovereignty," in Benda-Beckmann, F. von, K. von Benda-Beckmann and J. Eckert (eds) *Rules of Law and Laws of Ruling: On the Governance of Law*, Surrey and Burlington, VT: Ashgate, pp. 31–59.

Cook, R. (1997) "Women," in Joyner, C. (ed.) *Towards Equality: Report of the Committee on the Status of Women in India*, New Delhi: Ministry of Education and Social Welfare.

Cornwall, A. (2000) "Missing Men? Reflections on Men, Masculinities and Development: Politics, Policies and Practice," *IDS Bulletin* 31 (2): 1–6.

Cotterrell, R. (2009) "Spectres of Transnationalism: Changing Terrains of the Sociology of Law," *Journal of Law and Society* 36 (4): 481–500.

Couso, J., A. Huneeus and R. Sieder (eds) (2010) *Cultures of Legality: Judicialization and Political Activism in Latin America*, New York, NY: Cambridge University Press.

Crenshaw, K. (1991) "Mapping the Margins: Intersectionality, Identity Politics, and Violence against Women of Color," *Stanford Law Review* 43 (6): 1241–99.

Cumes, A. (2009) "Sufrimos vergüenza: mujeres k'iche' frente a la justicia comunitaria en Guatemala", *Desacatos*, núm. 31, septiembre–diciembre: 99–114.

de Sousa Santos, B. (1977) "The Law of the Oppressed: The Construction and Reproduction of Legality in Pasargada," *Law and Society Review* 12: 5–126.

——(1987) "Law: A Map of Misreading. Toward a Postmodern Conception of Law," *Journal of Law and Society* 14 (3): 279–302.

—— (2002) *Toward a New Legal Commonsense: Law, Globalization and Emancipation*, 2nd edn, Toronto: Butterworths.

—— (2006) "The Heterogenous State and Legal Pluralism in Mozambique," *Law and Society Review* 40: 39–75.

Dezaley, Y. and B. Garth (1996) *Dealing in Virtue: International Commercial Arbitration and the Construction of a Transnational Legal Order*, Chicago, IL: Chicago University Press.

Duffield, M. (2001) *Global Governance and the New Wars: The Merging of Development and Security*, New York, NY and London: Zed Books.

Englund, H. (2006) *Prisoners of Freedom: Human Rights and the African Poor*, Berkeley and Los Angeles, CA: University of California Press.

Englund, H. and F. Nyamnjoh (eds) (2004) *Rights and the Politics of Recognition in Africa*, London: Zed Books.

Escobar, A. (1995) *Encountering Development: The Making and Unmaking of the Third World*, Princeton, NJ: Princeton University Press.

Esplen, E. (2008) "Men and Gender Justice: Old Debate, New Perspective," *Open Democracy*, http://www.opendemocracy.net/print/35918 (accessed March 2012).

Faundez, J. (2005) "Community Justice Institutions and Judicialization: Lessons from Rural Peru," in Sieder, R., L. Schjolden and A. Angell (eds) *The Judicialization of Politics in Latin America*, New York, NY: Palgrave, pp. 187–209.

—— (2006) "Should Justice Reform Projects Take Non-State Justice Systems Seriously? Perspectives from Latin America," in *The World Bank Legal Review: Law Equity and Development*, Washington, DC: World Bank Publications, pp. 113–39.

Ferguson, J. (1994) *The Anti-Politics Machine: Development, Decentralization and Depoliticization in Lesotho*, Minnesota, MN: University of Minnesota Press.

—— (2006) *Global Shadows: Africa in the Neoliberal World Order*, Durham, NC: Duke University Press.

Foro Internacional de Mujeres Indígenas (FIMI) (2006) *Mairin Iwanka Raya: Mujeres Indígenas Confrontan la Violencia*, New York, NY: FIMI.

Frazier, N. (2007) "Feminist Politics in the Age of Recognition: A Two-Dimensional Approach to Gender Justice," *Studies in Social Justice* 1 (1): 23–35.

Geschiere, P. and F. Nyamnjoh (2000) "Capitalism and Autochthony: The Seesaw of Mobility and Belonging," *Public Culture* 12 (2): 423–52.

Goetz, A. M. (2007) "Gender Justice, Citizenship and Entitlements: Core Concepts, Central Debates and New Directions for Research," in Mukhopadyay, M. and N. Singh (eds) *Gender Justice, Citizenship and Development*, Ottawa, Cairo, Dakar, Montevideo, Nairobi, New Delhi and Singapore: Zubaan International Development Research Centre.

Goodale, M. (2007) "Introduction: Locating Rights, Envisioning Law Between the Global and the Local," in Goodale, M. and S. E. Merry (eds) *The Practice of Human Rights: Tracking Law Between the Global and the Local*, Cambridge and New York, NY: Cambridge University Press, pp. 1–38.

Goodale, M. and S. E. Merry (eds) (2007) *The Practice of Human Rights: Tracking Law Between the Global and the Local*, Cambridge and New York, NY: Cambridge University Press.

Griffiths, A. (1997) *In the Shadow of Marriage: Gender and Justice in an African Community*, Chicago, IL: University of Chicago Press.

——(2002) "Legal Pluralism," in Banakar, R. and M. Travers (eds) *An Introduction to Law and Social Theory*, Oxford and Portland, OR: Hart Publishing, pp. 289–310.

Griffiths, J. (1986) "What is Legal Pluralism?" *Journal of Legal Pluralism* 24: 1–50.

Guedes, A. M. and M. J. Lopes (eds) (2006) *State and Traditional Law in Angola and Mozambique*, Coimbra: Edições Almedina.

Hale, C. R. (2002) "Does Multiculturalism Menace? Governance, Cultural Rights and the Politics of Identity in Guatemala," *Journal of Latin American Studies* 34 (3): 485–524.

Hellum, A. and B. Derman (2009) "Government, Business and Chiefs: Ambiguities of Social Justice through Land Restitution in South Africa," in Benda-Beckmann, F. von, K. von Benda-Beckmann and J. Eckert (eds) *Rules of Law and Laws of Ruling: On the Governance of Law*, Surrey and Burlington, VT: Ashgate, pp. 125–50.

Hellum, A., S. Sardar Ali and A. Griffiths (2011) *From Transnational Relations to Transnational Laws (Law, Justice and Power)*, Farnham, Surrey and Burlington, VT: Ashgate.

Hellum, A., J. Stewart, S. Sardar Ali and A. Tsanga (2007) *Human Rights, Plural Legalities and Gendered Realities: Paths are Made by Walking*, Zimbabwe: Weaver Press.

Henrysson, E. and S. F. Joireman (2009) "On the Edge of the Law: Women's Property Rights and Dispute Resolution in Kisii, Kenya," *Law and Society Review* 43 (1): 39–59.

Herbst, J. (2000) *States and Power in Africa: Comparative Lessons in Authority and Control*, Princeton, NJ: Princeton University Press.

Hernández Castillo, A. (2002) "Zapatismo and the Emergence of Indigenous Feminism," *Report on the Americas NACLA* XXXV (6) May/June: 39–59.

Hinz, M. O. (ed.) (2006) *The Shade of New Leaves: Governance in Traditional Authority – A Southern African Perspective*, Berlin and Windhoek: LIT Verlag and Centre for Applied Social Sciences (CASS), University of Namibia.

Hirsch, S. F. (1998) *Pronouncing and Persevering: Gender and the Discourses of Disputing in an African Islamic Court*, Chicago, IL: University of Chicago Press.

Hobsbawm, E. and T. Ranger (eds) (1983) *The Invention of Tradition*, Cambridge: Cambridge University Press.

Igreja, V. (2010) "Traditional Courts and the Struggle against State Impunity for Civil Wartime Offences in Mozambique," *Journal of African Law* 54 (1): 51–73.

Ikdahl, I., A. Hellum, R. Kaarhus, T. A. Benjaminsen, P. Kameri-Mbote (2005) *Human Rights, Formalisation and Women's Land Rights in Southern and Eastern Africa*, Oslo: Institute of Women's Law.

International Council on Human Rights Policy (ICHRP) (2009) *When Legal Worlds Overlap: Human Rights, State and Non-State Law*, Geneva: ICHRP.

Isser, D. (ed.) (2011) *Customary Justice and the Rule of Law in War-Torn Societies*, Washington, DC: US Institute of Peace.

Jefferson, A. M and S. Jensen (eds) (2009) *State Violence and Human Rights: State Officials in the South*, London and New York, NY: Routledge-Cavendish.

Joseph, S. (1999) *Intimate Selving in Arab Families: Gender Self and Identity*, Syracuse, NY: Syracuse University Press.

——(2000) *Gender and Citizenship in the Middle East*, Syracuse, NY: Syracuse University Press.

28 Introduction

Kajifusa, H. (1998) *Towards Mainstreaming Gender Issues in Development Institutions: The Possibilities and Limitations of Men's Involvement in WID/GAD*, Unpublished MSc Dissertation, Brighton: Institute of Development Studies.

Kandiyoti, D. (1998) "Gender, Power and Contestation: Rethinking Bargaining with Patriarchy," in Jackson, C. and R. Pearson (eds) *Feminist Visions of Development: Gender Analysis and Policy*, London and New York, NY: Routledge.

Kane, M., J. Oloka-Onyango and A. Tejan-Cole (2005) "Reassessing Customary Law Systems as a Vehicle for Providing Equitable Access to Justice for the Poor," Working paper for World Bank Conference New Frontiers of Social Policy, Arusha, December 12–15.

Kyed, H. M. (2009) "Traditional Authority and Localization of State Law. The Intricacies of Boundary Marking in Policing Rural Mozambique," in Jefferson, A. M and S. Jensen (eds) *State Violence and Human Rights: State Officials in the South*, London and New York, NY: Routledge-Cavendish, pp. 40–59.

Li, T. M. (2007) *The Will to Improve: Governamentality, Development and the Practice of Politics*, Durham, NC: Duke University Press.

Mahmood, S. (2001) "Feminist Theory, Embodiment, and the Docile Agent: Some Reflections on the Egyptian Islamic Revival," *Cultural Anthropology* 16 (2): 202–36.

——(2005) *Politics of Piety: The Islamic Revival and the Feminist Subject*, Princeton, NJ: Princeton University Press.

Mallon, F. (1995) *Peasant and Nation: The Making of Postcolonial Mexico and Peru*, Berkeley, CA: University of California Press.

Mamdami, M. (1996) *Citizen and Subject: Contemporary Africa and the Legacy of Late Colonialism*, Princeton, NJ: Princeton University Press.

Manji, A. (1999) "Imagining Women's Legal World: Towards a Feminist Theory of Legal Pluralism in Africa," *Social and Legal Studies* 8 (4): 435–55.

McNeish, J. A. and J. H. Sandie Lie (eds) (2010) *Security and Development (Critical Interventions)*, Oxford and New York, NY: Berghahn Books.

Meinzen-Dick, R. S. and R. Pradhan (2002) *Legal Pluralism and Dynamic Property Rights*, Working paper 22, CGIAR Systemwide Program on Collective Action and Property Rights, Washington, DC: International Food Policy Research Institute.

Merry, S. E. (1988) "Legal Pluralism," *Law and Society Review* 22: 869–96.

——(2006) *Human Rights and Gender Violence: Translating International Law into Local Justice*, Chicago, IL: University of Chicago Press.

Michaels, R. (2009) "Global Legal Pluralism," *Annual Review of Law and Social Science* 5: 243–62.

Molyneux, M. and S. Razavi (2003) *Gender Justice, Development and Rights*, New York, NY: Oxford University Press.

Moore, S. F. (1973) "Law and Social Change: The Semi-Autonomous Field as an Appropriate Subject of Study," *Law and Society Review* (7): 719–46.

——(1986) *Social Facts and Fabrications: "Customary" Law on Kilimanjaro, 1880–1980*, New York, NY: Cambridge University Press.

——(2005) "Certainties Undone: Fifty Turbulent Years of Legal Anthropology, 1949–99," in Moore, S. F. (ed.) *Law and Anthropology: A Reader*, Oxford: Blackwells, pp. 346–67.

Mukhopadyay, M. and N. Singh (eds) (2007) *Gender Justice, Citizenship and Development*, Ottawa, Cairo, Dakar, Montevideo, Nairobi, New Delhi and Singapore: Zubaan: International Development Research Centre.

Nader, L. (2002) *The Life of the Law: Anthropological Projects*, Berkeley, CA, Los Angeles, CA and London: University of California Press.

Nussbaum, M. (2000) *Women and Human Development: The Capabilities Approach*, Cambridge: Cambridge University Press.

O'Neill, O. (2000) "Justice, Gender and International Boundaries," in *Bounds of Justice*, Cambridge: Cambridge University Press, pp. 143–67

Ong, A. (2003) "Zones of New Sovereignty in Southeast Asia," in Perry, R.-W. and B. Maurer (eds) *Globalization under Construction: Governamentality, Law, and Identity*, Minneapolis, MN and London: University of Minnesota Press, pp. 39–69.

——(2006) *Neoliberalism as Exception: Mutations in Citizenship and Sovereignty*, Durham, NC: Duke University Press.

Ostrom, E. (2007) "Analyzing Decentralized Resource Regimes from a Polycentric Perspective," *Policy Sciences* 41: 71–93.

Perrot, C.-H. and F.-X. Fauvelle-Aymar (eds) (2003) *Le retour des rois. Les autorités traditionelles et l'État en Afrique contemporaine*, Paris: Éditions Karthala.

Pineda, J. (2000) "Partners in Women-headed Households: Emerging Masculinities," *European Journal of Development Research* 12 (2): 72–92.

Phillips, A. (2001) "Feminism and Liberalism Revisited: Has Martha Nussbaum Got it Right?" *Constellations* 8 (2): 249–66.

Pradhan, R., F. von Benda-Beckmann and K. von Benda-Beckmann (eds) (2000) *Water, Land and Law: Changing Rights to Land and Water in Nepal*, Kathmandu: FREEDEAL, Wageningen: WAU and Rotterdam: EUR.

Rajagopal, B. (2003) *International Law from Below: Development, Social Movements and Third World Resistance*, New York: Cambridge University Press.

Rodríguez-Garavito, C. (2011) "Un nuevo mapa para el pensamiento jurídico latinoamericano," in Rodríguez Garavito, C. (coord.) *El derecho en América Latina: los retos del siglo XXI*, Buenos Aires: Siglo XXI, pp. 11–22.

Schiff Berman, P. (2009) "The New Legal Pluralism," *Annual Review of Law and Social Science* 5: 225–42.

Serra, C. (ed.) (2008) *Linchamentos em Moçambique I (uma desordem que apela à ordem)*, Maputo: Centro de Estudos Africanos, Unidade de Diagnóstico Social, Universidade Eduardo Mondlane.

Sieder, R., L. Schjolden and A. Angell (eds) (2005) *The Judicialization of Politics in Latin America*, New York, NY: Palgrave Press.

Sierra, M. T. (ed.) (2004) *Haciendo justicia: interlegalidad, derecho y género en regiones indígenas*, Mexico: CIESAS.

——(2007) "Justicia indígena y estado: retos desde la diversidad," in Robinson, S., H. Tejera and L. Valladares (eds) *Política, etnicidad e inclusión digital en los albores del milenio*, Mexico: Porrúa/UAM, pp. 265–93.

Sooriyakumaran, P. (2010) "Gender and Development: Do Men and Masculinities Need to be Reconsidered?" *The Australian Development Review*, http://www.theadr. com.au/wp/?=273 (accessed 6 June 2011).

Tamanaha, B. (2000) "A Non-Essentialist Version of Legal Pluralism," *Journal of Law and Society* 27: 296–321.

——(2008) "Understanding Legal Pluralism: Past to Present, Local to Global," *Sydney Law Review* 30: 375–411.

Teubner, G. (ed.) (1996) *Global Law without a State*, Boston, MA: Dartmouth Publishing.

Twining, W. (2000) *Globalization and Legal Theory*, Evanston, IL: Northwest University Press.

United States Institute of Peace/Peaceworks (USIP) (2010) *Local Justice in Southern Sudan*, Washington, DC: USIP.

UN Women (2011) *Progress of the World's Women*, New York, NY: United Nations.

Vaughan, O. (ed.) (2005) *Tradition and Politics: Indigenous Political Structures in Africa*, Trenton, NJ and Asmara: Africa World Press.

Waldorf, L., R. Shaw and P. Hazan (2010) *Localizing Transitional Justice: Interventions and Priorities after Mass Violence*, Stanford, CA: Stanford University Press.

Walsh, C. (2010) "Development as *Buen Vivir*: Institutional arrangements and (de)colonial engagements," *Development* 53 (1): 15–21.

Whitehead, A. and D. Tsikata (2003) "Policy Discourses on Women's Land Rights in Sub-Saharan Africa: The Implications of the Return to the Customary," *Journal of Agrarian Change* 3: 67–112.

World Bank (2011) *World Development Report 2011: Conflict, Security and Development*, Washington DC: World Bank, http://wdr2011.worldbank.org/fulltext (accessed March 2012).

Young, C. (1994) *The African Colonial State in Perspective*, New Haven, CT and London: Yale University Press.

Young, I. M. (1990) *Justice and the Politics of Difference*, Princeton, NJ: Princeton University Press.

Chapter 1

Gender, human rights and legal pluralities: experiences from Southern and Eastern Africa

Anne Hellum

Introduction

African states, African women's rights organizations and international human rights agencies face major challenges to unmake gender inequalities created and upheld by the plural legal systems originating from the colonial era.[1] Although most postcolonial legal systems in Africa aim to secure legal unification and to be "gender neutral," they are still made up of imported Western law and the customary and religious laws of different ethnic and religious groups. Customary law often takes precedence in areas of personal law concerning marriage, family affairs and inheritance, and conflicts with principles of gender equality, to a large extent trapping women within the colonial legal constructions of unequal gender relations.

In Sub-Saharan Africa, the rapid adoption of international and regional human rights instruments, such as the United Nations (UN) Convention on the Elimination of All Forms of Discrimination against Women (CEDAW) and the Protocol to the African Charter on Human and Peoples' Rights on the Rights of Women in Africa (AfPRW), is shaping the work of national governments, local, national and international women's rights organizations and international development agencies. These international instruments constitute key components in rights-based approaches to development that understand women's poverty and underdevelopment to be a *result* of gender discrimination that in turn causes unequal distribution of resources such as land, water, food and education.[2]

By adding a new normative and institutional layer to existing state laws, these human rights' instruments have clearly opened up spaces for individual women and women's rights organizations who have the social and economic resources to contest male privileges embedded in state law and customary law. These developments are reflected within the growing body of African scholarship on women's rights and gender justice. One stream of literature focuses on women's rights struggles related to the "weak" form of legal pluralism that is embodied in the plurality of legal orders that exist within the state legal system.[3] It shows how discriminatory rules embedded in statutory law and customary laws are changing as a result of constitutional change, law reform and judicial review (Banda 2005; Albertyn 2007). Another stream of scholarship addresses the "strong" form of legal pluralism deriving from the fact that the same social space and the same activities are subject to more than one body of law (Griffiths 1986). On the basis of social actors' experiences and perceptions, this body of literature explores how gender relations are shaped and reshaped in a plural, unsettled and contested terrain where human rights, state law, customary law and local norms coexist and interact in the same social field (Griffiths 1997; Bentzon et al. 1998; Hellum 1999; Hellum et al. 2007; Claassens and Cousins 2008; Tsarga and Stewart 2011).

A number of recent ethnographic studies focus on how the norms and expectations that inform gender relationships are shaped and reshaped in negotiations involving actors including national lawmakers, rights-based development agencies, humanitarian organizations, women's rights organizations and individual women (Derman et al. 2013; Hellum 2013; Hellum and Derman 2013; Ikdahl 2013; Bourdon 2013; Henquinet 2013). Turning from a state-centered notion of governance exclusively tied to the national state towards a more functional conception of governing activities, this body of scholarship engages with questions related to the effects of a multiplicity of governance agents, "who engage in new modes of exercising power, often guided and legitimized by 'alternative' legalities" (Benda-Beckmann et al. 2009a: 2), and on how this exercise of power and governance relates to existing gender, race and class inequalities.

Cognizant of the apparent failure to deliver the projected human rights benefits and protections to people on the ground, women's law researchers, development institutions and human rights agencies are increasingly engaging with the complex legal situations that arise from the coexistence and interaction of international, national and local norms (ICHRP 2009; UN Women 2011). In an attempt to bridge the gap between state law and legal pluralities on the ground, international and national law and policymakers have in recent years turned their attention to the informal justice sector. The UN Commission on Legal Empowerment of the Poor, for example, calls for liberalization of the justice sector and recommends recognition of non-state legal services and informal justice systems (Commission on Legal Empowerment of the Poor 2008). Current trends to recognize religious and customary norms may on the one hand expand the spaces for the exercise of local autonomy by different social, ethnic and religious groups, but may on the other hand reinforce existing inequalities within these groups in terms of gender, status and age. Globalization may therefore affect women's rights to equality under international and national law in complex and contradictory ways. As Christine Chinkin, Shelly Wright and Hillary Charlesworth (Chinkin et al. 2005) have observed, the way in which centralization of power within the sovereign state has been fragmented by globalization is not necessarily supportive of equality between women and men. In their

Introduction to this volume, Rachel Sieder and John-Andrew McNeish have suggested that any consideration of the gendered dynamics of human rights and development-related interventions marrying human rights and legal pluralism must be located within a broader analysis of regimes of governance.

Taking this as a point of departure, this chapter explores how national lawmakers, rights-based development agencies, women's rights organizations and individual women, setting out to promote equal rights, navigate a plural legal terrain where international and national law coexist and interact with local gendered norms and practices. With an overall focus on the effects emerging constellations of governance shaped by history, power structures and legal pluralism have on existing relations of inequality and domination and control, I analyze case studies from South Africa, Tanzania and Zimbabwe. Each of these countries has a complex social field in which human rights, national law, local norms and practices, power structures, and history form the context in which struggles for women's rights take place. Assuming that women suffer hardships and injustices not only because they are women, but also because of their race, class or age, the aim is to uncover how unequal and complex gender relations mediate the relationship between international, national and local law (Hellum et al. 2007: xix).

A basic question posed in this chapter is how the power structures that inform unequal gender relations at the levels of the family, the local community and state law are handled by state and non-state actors involved in law reform, administration of law, mediation of conflicts and provision of legal literacy. Addressing these questions I turn to Lukes' definition of power, which includes the visible power embedded in state law, the hidden power embedded in institutions that are not formally part of government and the invisible power embedded in social and religious norms (Lukes 1974). Visible power pertains to public decision-making processes involving the legislative, executive and judicial branches of power. Hidden power is exercised in institutions that are not part of government, ranging from transnational economic institutions to traditional and religious institutions. Invisible power is embedded in social and religious structures that uphold prevailing perceptions, stereotypes and practices related to gender, race or class. A key question is: what awareness do the different actors that are involved in human rights initiatives at the international, national and local level have of structures of power? And in what ways are they challenging and positioning themselves vis-à-vis power-holders in these spheres? A related question is: how does this awareness translate into measures aimed at assisting women as individuals and as members of local communities?

The chapter unfolds in eight parts. Following this introduction, the second section provides some background, signaling the long-run historical processes that have shaped existing constellations of legal pluralities and governance in Southern and Eastern Africa. The third part shows how the struggle against colonialism and racism in Africa is reflected in international and regional African human rights treaties' protection of the right to self-determination, the right to culture and the right to equality and non-discrimination. With a focus on historical contestations about what constitutes "African values" part four illustrates the slow and uneven process whereby the principle of gender equality was adopted by postcolonial states in Southern and Eastern Africa.[4] With an overall focus on the relationship between state and civil society parts five, six and seven present case studies from South Africa, Tanzania and Zimbabwe that describe and analyze how non-governmental organizations (NGOs) setting out to promote and protect women's right to equality engage with the visible, hidden and invisible structures of power that generate and sustain unequal gender relations at national, local and family levels. The final section concludes that successful interventions to advance gender justice depend on the actors' ability to develop situational and locally appropriate strategies of argumentation and implementation that can bridge gaps between human rights principles and the legal pluralities that operate in women's lives.

The colonial legacy: dual legal systems and race, class and gender

African women's rights struggles epitomize the complex and ambivalent relationships that exist between African norms and values and human rights. In postcolonial laws and policies there is a tense relationship between the principle of gender equality and the protection and promotion of "African culture." An analysis of colonialism's impact on the region's legal development is central to understanding these ambiguities (Derman et al. 2013).

A characteristic feature of the legal systems that were put in place under colonial rule in Southern and Eastern Africa is their dual character. One system of law, the imported Western law, applied to the European settlers, while the system of customary law applied to Africans (Bentzon et al. 1998: 30–9). Through the establishment of native administration and colonial state courts European judicial officers became the main interpreters of African customary law (Woodman 1988). This implied a formal shift away from family- and tribal-based adjudication towards the jurisdiction of state-administered customary courts. Most of the colonial legal regimes established criteria through legislation that directed courts in the choice of law to be applied. In the area of personal law governing marriage, family and inheritance matters, customary law applied to Africans (Bennet 1985). The customary law developed by the colonial administration and the colonial courts viewed African women as legal minors under the guardianship of their husbands or male relatives, although in the light of Western considerations of justice and morality certain attempts were made to modify customary norms that were seen as an inhumane treatment of women. The differential treatment of African men and women was to a large extent upheld according to the dominant view that native women were in a more "primitive" stage of human development than men (Hellum 1999: 139–41). Thus law played an important role in constructing African law and culture as something "other" and less civilized than Western law and culture, and in constructing African women as something "other" and less civilized than African men.

Historical studies that combine political economy approaches with an actor perspective analyze the formation of African customary laws in the light of both external and internal social, economic and legal factors. They show how customary law was shaped in the course of complex struggles involving colonial administrators, elder African men and young women and men. In his classical study of how customary law was created in the early phase of colonialism, Martin Chanock describes how complex struggles where Western colonizers, African tribal authorities and African men and women invoked and manipulated notions of Western and African law merged into a new form of law that was neither customary nor Western (Chanock 1989). Studies of the struggles that shaped these so-called customary laws in different colonies in Southern and Eastern Africa reveal how male elders and colonial administrators formed strategic alliances with the aim of reinstating customs that would keep the unruly and immoral African women in place. One example is the enactment of the Native Adultery Punishment Ordinance in Rhodesia in 1916 (Folbre 1988: 61–91; Hellum 1999: 376–8; Mittlebeeler 1976: 122–35). African chiefs and elders who felt they were losing control complained to the native Commissioners about the increasing infidelity of their wives: "You have taken away our old power to control marriage, but you have done nothing to make the woman stand by her contract which she has entered into by free will" (Mittlebeeler 1976: 126). The colonial administrators, who understood women's increasing promiscuity as a threat to the colony's social order, willingly responded to the male elders' attempt to use custom as a means of social control.

Studies from colonial South Africa, Malawi, Tanzania, Zimbabwe and Zambia show how African women and men from different age and status groups responded to the evolving colonial legal system and, in spite of unequal power relations, manipulated it to serve their own aims and goals (Chanock 1985; Parpart 1988; Walker 1991). Women who were married against their will, for example, turned to the colonial courts in an attempt to have local marriage customs declared as repugnant to natural justice and morality. Barth Rwezaura has described the colonial legal development as a process in which:

> the colonial and post-colonial states had contributed considerably to the transformation of the traditional social and economic system. This development enabled the subordinate members of the society such as sons, daughters and wives to claim autonomy from the male elders. Yet

36 Gender Justice and Legal Pluralities

simultaneously some element of state policy and administrative practices tended to conserve customs and tradition.

(Rwezaura 1990: 17)

From anti-colonial to postcolonial gender and class struggles

Anti-colonial struggles in the wake of the Second World War were human rights struggles for self-determination, self-rule and national independence. The struggle against colonialism and racism in Africa is reflected in international law's protection of the right to self-determination as well as protection against discrimination on the grounds of sex and race. A significant contribution to the development of the international human rights system is the right to petition, which was pioneered by African and Asian states calling for more effective international legal weapons against apartheid.[5] African states were also the driving force behind the preparation of the draft Convention on Consent and minimum Age for Marriage in 1961. While the female UN representative from Togo argued that the Convention was a means of liberating African women from "the yoke imposed on them by custom," the Convention was resisted by many Western states that claimed that such an instrument would be difficult to implement due to the vast range of "cultural and ethnological patterns in various countries" (Burke 2010: 128). In short, the West was raising the cultural relativist argument against moves to improve African women's rights.

The question of freedom and fundamental rights to self-determination were part of African independence movements, as were the multiple promises made by African liberation movements about how democracy, freedom and equality between different races, classes and sexes would replace colonialism. As members of the United Nations, all African States adopted the Universal Declaration of Human Rights as they entered the United Nations once freed from colonial rule. They also participated in and voted for the broad set of international human rights' instruments as they were debated and voted upon in the United Nations. Most African nations signed and ratified international human rights instruments like the 1966 International Covenant on Civil and Political Rights (ICCPR), the 1966 Covenant on Social, Economic and Cultural Rights (ICSECR), the 1979 Convention on the Elimination of All Forms of Discrimination against Women (CEDAW), and the 1989 Convention on the Rights of the Child (CRC).

Africa is one of the three regions in the world today that has its own supra-national system for the protection of human rights. The African Charter on Human and Peoples' Rights adopted by the Organization of African Unity in 1981 came into force in 1986, but with minimal enforcement mechanisms. It included civil, political, social, cultural and economic rights and recognized the right to environment and the right to development.

Protecting both group rights and individual rights, it set the scene for long-standing debates around the appropriate relationship between the state's obligation to protect women against sex discrimination on the one hand and to protect the family as the custodian of custom and culture on the other (Banda 2005; Onoria 2002).

It was CEDAW, with its application in both the private and public spheres, and the globalization of women's rights organizations, which precipitated a major shift in the priorities of governments and human rights organizations in Africa as elsewhere in the world. The World Conference on Human Rights in Vienna and the Fourth World Conference on Women in Beijing facilitated global discussions about which elements of women's rights were "Western" and which were not. Transcending national and continental histories, these World Conferences brought about new forms of cooperation and understandings. For African women's rights NGOs these global events became stepping stones from which to advance basic claims such as equal property rights. All Sub-Saharan African states, with the exception of Mauritania, accepted without reservation to:

> [U]ndertake legislative and administrative reforms to give women full and equal access to economic resources, including the right to inheritance and to ownership of land and other property, credit, natural resources and appropriate technologies.[6]

In response to the new wave of struggles for equality and human rights in twenty-first century Africa, the African Charter was followed by the 1999 African Charter of Rights and Welfare of the Child. Where the African Charter was weak on women's rights these rights were formulated and included in the 2005 Protocol to the African Charter on Human and Peoples' Rights on the Rights of Women in Africa (the AfPRW). The Protocol to the African Charter on the Rights of Women was prompted by the growing body of African women's rights NGOs emphasizing that the norms, expectations and resources deriving from membership in a family, a clan, an ethnic, religious or political group often conflict with women's rights and freedoms as individual citizens. In Article 2.2 the Protocol puts an obligation on states to change gender stereotypes embedded in cultural and religious beliefs.

> 2. States Parties shall commit themselves to modify the social and cultural patterns of conduct of women and men through public education, information, education and communication strategies, with a view to achieving the elimination of harmful cultural and traditional practices and all other practices which are based on the idea of the inferiority or the superiority of either of the sexes, or on stereotyped roles for women and men.

Postcolonial law: a site of gender struggles

These international and regional human rights instruments have clearly made a mark on the development of most Sub-Saharan African legal systems. Yet there is considerable variation in the degree of protection offered by the constitutions and laws of those African states that have ratified existing international and regional human rights treaties. The slow and uneven change speaks to the contested relationship between "African values" and the principle of gender equality that for many African nationalist politicians is associated with Western feminism.

African governments came under pressure to abolish customary law in line with the liberal law and modernization theories that guided international economic development policies in the 1960s. By abolishing the customary laws guiding extended family relationships it was believed that free individuals would emerge who could act independently of the demands of the larger family unit (Hydén 1983: 148). On the other hand new nationalist governments desired to preserve the African extended family and to mold the social, economic and legal order of the new nation-state on the basis of African values and traditions. In the 1960s the African nationalist position was at its peak. This envisioned a new common law based on African customary laws. Underlying this vision was the assumption of an inherent unity of different customary norms and practices. In order to provide continuity with the African legal heritage, a restatement strategy was devised, aimed at compiling legal rules collected from elders, court assessors and chiefs into a comprehensive and unified version of customary law (Allott 1965, 1968). One criticism against these initiatives was that their legal view of the past was ahistorical and excluded the colonial context in which customary law was constructed (Chanock 1985).

The debates about the creation of the legal systems in the newly independent African states illustrate the dilemmas and conflicts that emerged in the attempts to marry "African values" with the demands of human rights principles like freedom and equality for women. The Mozambican FRELIMO government (Frente de Libertação de Moçambique), unlike most other governments, set out to create a unified legal system that was neither customary nor Western but rather based on an amalgamation of people's customs and practices, the principles of the new constitution and socialist ideals and values (Sachs and Welch 1990; Berg and Gundersen 1991; Gundersen 1992). A more typical approach was to accommodate both customary law and received law within a single court system. This was the situation in Zimbabwe, where an attempt was made to combine choice and pluralism with the overall aim of unity and unification (Ncube 1989; Hellum 1999). In the 1980s and early 1990s, before the ratification of CEDAW, the Zimbabwean judiciary enhanced the principle of gender equality through a range of cases that on the basis of the Legal Age of Majority Act struck down a series of customary laws that were seen as discriminatory.[7] In response to the tension between the judiciary and the government in the mid-1990s, the government sought to control the judiciary through appointment of politically loyal judges. The changing composition of the Supreme Court is reflected in the famous *Magaya* case.[8] In this case the claw-back clause in the Zimbabwean constitution, stipulating that customary law in the field of family and inheritance law takes precedence when coming into conflict with national law, was invoked.

The Tanzanian legal system also constitutes an attempt to combine pluralism and choice with the overall aim of unity and unification. Aiming at unification and gender equality, the Tanzanian family law reform was in the forefront of promoting equal rights for women in Southern and Eastern Africa (Rwezaura and Wanitzek 1988). While the Tanzanian Constitution of 1977 protects the principle of gender equality, its status in relation to customary law is contested. The political and legal battles over the discriminatory customary laws that govern inheritance matters epitomize the contested nature of the principle of gender equality as reflected in Tanzanian national law (see Bourdon, Chapter 7 in this volume).

Among the African countries that are examined in this chapter, the most extensive human rights protection is offered by the South African Constitution of 1996 which encompasses the whole catalogue of civil, political, social and economic rights and recognizes customary law only in as far as it is compatible with the principle of gender equality. The gender equality principle embedded in Article 9 of the Constitution forms the legal backbone of South African women's right to equality in general and in the restitution process in particular (Albertyn 2007). By the right to equality is meant substantive equality in terms of "full and equal enjoyment of all rights and freedoms."[9] Towards this end the Constitution prohibits both direct and indirect discrimination on the grounds of race, gender, sex, pregnancy, marital status, social status or sexual orientation.[10] To prevent discrimination and facilitate substantive equality the Constitution allows the state to take proactive measures in order to "promote the achievement of full equality, legislative and other measures designed to protect or advance persons, or categories of persons, disadvantaged by unfair discrimination."[11]

Despite many varied social, legal and economic experiments ranging from socialism in Tanzania and Zimbabwe to South African human rights constitutionalism, the 1980s and 1990s brought a broad disillusionment with African governments. The Western focus on Africa shifted to markets, formal elections, civil and political democracy coupled with structural adjustment programs that attempted to force most African nations into a single economic mold. Since the adoption of the Human Rights Based Approach to Development (HRBA) the disjuncture between the approaches of the multinational economic organizations and the rights-based institutions of the

40 Gender Justice and Legal Pluralities

United Nations has continued to impede a broader adoption of socio-economic human rights as well as civil and political ones (Skogly 2001).

It is against this background that I now turn to the case studies from South Africa, Tanzania and Zimbabwe in order to explore how different constellations of governance and legal pluralities constrain and enable greater gender justice. Overarching questions are under what conditions are complex legal pluralities a factor in producing gendered forms of exclusion, and under what conditions do they constitute a resource for different groups of women to challenge their marginalization?

South Africa – equal rights to land restitution under shifting policy trajectories

The South African Constitution and the Restitution of Land Rights Act were key elements in the fulfillment of the African National Congress (ANC) government's promise to unmake race, class and gender injustices deriving from apartheid's land laws and policies. Given the centrality of the right to equality and non-discrimination the rights-based land reform policy adopted by the ANC government held out great promise for rural women. The initial phase of the land reform process, launched by the newly elected ANC government in 1984, was characterized by a strong emphasis on the political economy of poverty and the need for land redistribution and land restitution. This led the ANC to embrace a new model of restitution that attempted to marry social justice and business interests. The shifting structures of law, policy and governance that defined it makes South Africa's land restitution process a good case to explore how different constellations of governance, legal pluralities and power may constrain or enable greater gender justice. Of particular interest is how the complexities and divided gender and class interests within local communities have been approached by state and non-state actors involved in the restitution process.

In cooperation with Bill Derman I have been involved in a longitudinal study following the legal claims of five dispossessed communities in Levubu in the Limpopo Province since they were launched in 1997. We have examined the disjuncture between the principle of gender equality embedded in constitutional and national law and the gendered effects of the different implementation strategies associated with changes in official policy. The phases of claims-making and claims-verification were informed by a rights-based social justice approach developed by the Mandela administration after 1994. In the settlement and post-settlement phases the ANC government, in line with the adoption of a neo-liberal economic policy, turned to a market-oriented land reform model and a new conceptualization of restitution. Known as the "strategic partner model," this entailed claimant communities forming a joint venture company with a private entrepreneur with the aim of running the restituted land on a commercial basis (Derman et al. 2010).

With an overall focus on the complex relationship between women as individual rights holders and as part of group claims we have explored how the right to equality embedded in CEDAW, the South African Constitution and the Land Restitution Act has been respected, protected and promoted by the state and non-state actors involved in different phases of the land restitution process as played out in Limpopo Province (Hellum and Derman 2010; Hellum and Derman 2013). Since rural women's right to restitution has been accommodated as part of group claims, lodged in the name of the chief, the overall focus of our research concerns local tensions surrounding the pursuit of a fair balance between communities, households and individuals. We analyze how these tensions have been handled by the different actors that have been part of the process, including government and civil society agents, business partners and chiefs.

Our research demonstrates how the social justice approach, which informed the claims-making and claims-verification period, went a long way towards enacting and implementing a legal framework that aimed to ensure justice for all groups, including women and labor tenants. In this phase, between 1997 and 2000, government laws and policies were supported by a network of NGOs that addressed gender inequalities within the claimant communities. The land rights NGO, Nkuzi, provided extensive assistance to communities who wanted to lodge claims. In line with the overall policy "equality for all," Nkuzi adopted a series of measures to include women on an equal basis. Nkuzi's emphasis on equality between community members did not sit well with the traditional leaders' hierarchical notion of status and power within the community. According to Nkuzi's gender advisor, there was a lot of discussion about how they should go about ensuring that all individuals in the community were put on an equal footing.[12] To change patriarchal power relations between the community members and the traditional leaders and between husbands, wives and children within the family, Nkuzi tried to convince traditional leaders and male members of the claimant communities that everyone would benefit from an approach that included women. Nkuzi staff also argued that since women were the ones who catered for the wellbeing of the community members in terms of health, care and food they should be included in the claim on an equal basis.

As a result of the joint efforts made by state and non-state actors, women attained equal membership and ownership rights in the new common property institutions. Our study shows that there is a highly gendered and, to a certain extent, class-based response to how the benefits from rent and grants related to community land should be distributed. Yet the views of women and poorer members of the community on this crucial issue are not articulated in policies or in the constitutions and practices of communal property associations (CPAs). In the planning process in Limpopo the claimant communities were to a large extent seen as undifferentiated, with similar interests, and therefore insufficient account was taken of their complexities and

42 Gender Justice and Legal Pluralities

divisions. The legal content of membership and the rights of members in a group claim were not defined prior to the transfer of land. How to distribute property between different groups or individuals within the community is unspecified despite legislation that aims to "ensure that all the dispossessed members of the community shall have access to the land or the compensation in question on a basis which is fair and non-discriminatory towards any person, including a woman and a tenant."[13] While mandating internal democratic principles of participation and decision-making, the constitutions of CPAs are vague or silent in relation to the sustainable use of resources, individual use rights and allocation of benefits that will flow to the community from rent, profits from the new company, or grants from government.

In the post-settlement phase the government's attempt to marry social justice and business resulted in a new governance model that included state law, administrative discretion, contract and custom (Hellum and Derman 2009). Where existing gender and class hierarchies within the community and the household were regarded as private matters, no measures were taken to ensure equal participation on the board of the new venture companies. While chiefs figure neither in the Communal Property Act nor in the agreements constituting the new venture companies, they are in practice playing a central role determining hiring practices and distribution of eventual profits. Paradoxically this new business model, rather than changing unequal power relations within the claimant communities, is reinforcing the hidden and invisible power embedded in existing hierarchies of status and power upheld by chieftainship.

All in all the South African land restitution study shows how human rights organizations' spaces of operation opened and then closed in the political shift from a social justice to a market-based land policy (Langford et al. 2012). While one such NGO, Nkuzi, was invited by the government to assist the claimant communities in a process aiming at democratic and equal property relations in the claims-making phase, in the post-settlement period it was replaced by business actors who regarded the relationships within the claimant communities as private matters. The disjuncture between the principles embedded in national law and actual practice on the ground, however, speaks to a situation where insufficient attention has been devoted to the hidden power exercised by traditional authorities and the invisible power embedded in the local norms guiding access to power and resources within the communities.

Tanzania – equal protection of property and diverse responses

Tanzania's current land law, which dates from 1999, is known for its efforts to integrate women's rights issues into legislation aimed at the formalization of land rights.[14] In the course of the law reform process, national and international actors ranging from the World Bank to Tanzania's civil society organizations made their mark (Ikdahl 2010; Manji 2006). The existing legislation is on the one hand a response to the widespread confusion and insecurity related to customary rights in land documented by the Presidential Commission, often referred to as the Shivji Commission.[15] Yet the overall aim of the legislation is to facilitate a market in land, in line with the push from the World Bank. The legal framework for land registration constitutes a delicate balancing act that builds on existing local institutions and customary norms, while at the same time prohibiting discriminatory customary practices. As a result of interventions by Tanzania's women's rights organizations, the legislation recognizes women's equal rights to own land, prohibits the application of discriminatory customary law and requires spousal consent as a prerequisite for transactions regarding marital property (Benschop 2002; Ikdahl et al. 2005; Ikdahl 2008). Critics have suggested that these human rights initiatives overestimate the potential of state law as a tool for empowerment (Manji 2006). Such state-centrism, it has been argued, is based on an unrealistic view of the capacity and benevolence of the state, as well as a portrayal of customary or local norms that ignores the role they play in livelihood, security and identity.

The plurality of international, national and local norms and actors at work in the Tanzanian land reform process makes it an ideal case to explore how gender struggles are mediated in the context of globalized lawmaking and governance structures. Within changing constellations of governance Tanzanian women's rights organizations have created a space where they are in a position to influence the content and implementation of women's human rights through expert advice, media campaigns, legal literacy and legal aid.[16] Recognizing that these processes include questions of power, where translation can be dominated by a relatively powerful group who uses rights for their own narrow purposes, I turn to two empirical studies that explore how women's rights embedded in CEDAW are being translated into attainable benefits for individual women.[17]

Diverse responses from differently positioned women

Ingunn Ikdahl's study of individual women's responses to the opportunity to claim formal property ownership during the land titling process in Hanna Nassif in Dar es Salaam reinforces the critique that has been raised against the state-centric women's rights approach (Ikdahl 2010, 2013). According to Ikdahl, in privileging the husband–wife relationship, attempts by both international law and state law to protect women's equal right to a home exclude entitlements and challenges that derive from relationships in the extended family. In line with findings from South Africa, Ikdahl's research points to the fact that the wife is not the only woman with a stake in the family property. The right to a home is often nested in a bundle of rights and obligations among family members from past, present and future generations. Ikdahl argues that in order to promote an inclusive and gender equal property-rights system it is important to consider how different groups of women are positioned in complex chains of relationships between people and property. Her study of individual women's responses demonstrates how lack of such considerations by women's rights NGOs, international and national law and policy makers can influence how registration of individual land rights plays out at grassroots level. In Hanna Nassif widows with a strong position in the local community, due to their significant economic contributions, often opted for formal registration and protection by state law. However, widows in a weaker economic position used the names of their children or their deceased husbands on the documents in order to increase their protection against external threats such as state expropriation and internal threats from intra-family property grabbing. In a situation where state law exercises limited hegemony, the responses of differently positioned women are diverse. Each makes strategic choices with a view to ensuring a secure future for themselves and their children. This nuanced conception of how unequal and complex gender relations mediate the relationship between state law and "local law" challenges the notion of rigid divisions between customary law and state law, and registered and unregistered property. Instead of fitting women's quest for equal property rights into these binary categories, Ikdahl's research supports the case for a broad and dynamic concept of tenure security whereby human rights discourse can respond to complex and situational gender relations on the ground.

Remaking unequal gender relations through appropriation of plural institutions and norms

In order to bridge the gap between state law and legal pluralities on the ground international and national law and policymakers have in recent years turned their attention to the informal justice sector. The UN Commission on Legal Empowerment, for example, calls for liberalization of the justice sector and recommends recognition of non-state legal services and informal justice systems.[18] The ceding of legal space to local groups and practices, such as conflict mediation, provides for solutions beyond the confines of the prescribed rules associated with state law. In a situation where the relationship between women's right to equal status under international and national law and local norms based on gender difference is contested a key question is who within a local community has the power to define, interpret, implement and enforce law at the multiple levels it operates. Natalie Bourdon has researched two Tanzanian NGOs, The Tanzanian Women's Lawyers' Association (TAWLA) and The Women's Legal Aid Center (WLAC) in Dar es Salaam with an overall focus on the possibilities and constraints of the use of Alternative Dispute Resolution (ADR) as a tool for achieving women's rights in Tanzania (Bourdon 2013). Situating the two organizations within their broader national, regional and international networks, her study explores how feminist ideas and human rights principles are perceived, adopted and translated through the day-to-day work of these organizations. In a situation where state law is often unfavorable for women, these legal aid schemes have begun to offer mediation and conciliation with the goal of settling disputes out of court. Bourdon's study explores the normative repertoire that is employed by lawyers acting on behalf of the women. While legal rights are invoked in ADR cases, NGO lawyers also use rights as a moralizing discourse, blending notions of legal rights with religious and customary notions of obligations in order to arrive at what they consider to be a just and acceptable conclusion. Where the law does not meet up with their notions of justice, NGO lawyers go beyond the bounds of state law and devise their own standards for payment of alimony and child support based on what they feel the men in these cases can and will pay. Bourdon demonstrates the importance of attending to the role of language in order to discern what power relationships are at play in guiding the processes and effectuating the outcomes of ADR cases. The rhetorical devices that are employed in negotiations, including "proper" gender roles, the notion of a "good wife" and legal and moral rights and responsibilities, are informed by the way in which gender is constructed in the CEDAW and the African Protocol.

The identity of the African feminist human rights lawyer is central to these processes and outcomes. The lawyers play a key role as mediators, guiding the case away from men's moralizing of women's positions towards a framing discourse premised on African feminist and human rights gender values. How gender is reconstructed through a form of mediation that fuses human rights and custom is illustrated by an incident where the lawyer details the duties and responsibilities of "the good husband." Likewise, NGO lawyers take advantage of the open-ended and flexible ADR process by considering what is just and by asserting their power to reach agreements about remuneration that sidestep the letter of the law. As this study demonstrates, Tanzanian human rights lawyers use ADR to challenge unequal gender relations and make awards to women in ways that would not be possible in other legal settings such as the courts. By means of a blend of human rights norms and local and moral norms, they are often able to reach a consensus that resonates with basic principles of equality and welfare. This study also suggests that the outcome of informal third-party mediation relies heavily on the background and identity of the third party.

Zimbabwe – legal pluralities and the search for legitimacy

Since the late 1990s the Zimbabwean state has gained global notoriety for its fierce resistance to human rights claims, widespread political violence and the breakdown of the rule of law. In response to the growing number of Supreme Court rulings in favor of women,[19] workers, students and journalists that occurred in the 1990s, the ZANU PF (Zimbabwe African National Union – Patriotic Front) government responded by making constitutional amendments that reversed the progressive rulings of the Supreme Court and by changing the court's composition (Gubbay 1997; Madhuku 1999; Magaisa 2010). Women's struggle to secure protection against discrimination in the Zimbabwean Constitution epitomizes the tense relationship between the quest of women's rights activists for gender equality and ZANU PF's nationalist policies embracing what the Minister of Justice has termed an "Afrocentric" worldview.[20] In 1996, prior to its first report to the CEDAW Committee, the ZANU PF-dominated Parliament amended Article 23 of the Constitution in order to prohibit sex discrimination while at the same time exempting matters regulated by customary law in relation to marriage, divorce, adoption, inheritance and other matters of personal law from protection against discrimination. What this amounted to was a ban on discrimination against women and girls in the public sphere but license for its persistence in private arenas (Stewart and Damiso forthcoming). In order to illustrate how women's rights NGOs operating in this contested terrain have been able to secure human rights and change legal and ideological power structures I now turn to the action-oriented research on inheritance undertaken by the Zimbabwean Women and Law in Southern Africa Research Trust (WLSA) research team and the legal aid and empowerment initiatives carried out by the Zimbabwe Women's Lawyer Association (ZWLA).

In the mid-1990s the Zimbabwean WLSA research team set out to describe and understand women's inheritance rights under state law and customary law, with the aim of improving the position of women. Their research and lobbying strategy, which focused on living customary law, illustrates the potential of combining a legal pluralist and human rights approach in a context where the dominant political discourse considers gender equality to be a Western human rights imposition and as such a threat to national sovereignty and African cultural values. The context for the research was the weak position of women as widows and daughters under the customary law applied in the formal courts. In the 1991 Murisa case the Zimbabwean Supreme Court ruled that "[c]ustomary law does not recognize a widow's right to inherit in a direct fashion from her deceased husband's estate. She may be entitled to support from the estate but not to a share therein."[21] Hypothesizing that the state court's version of customary law was out of tune with living customary law, the WLSA researchers turned their attention to inheritance practices at the level of the local community and the family (WLSA 1994; Stewart and Tsanga 2007; Stewart 1998). The research, which made extensive use of anthropological fieldwork methods, indicated a growing preference for the appointment of the widow as an intestate heir to the deceased husband's estate, both at the level of the lower courts and at the family level. It revealed that living customary law was far more nuanced and flexible than the state court's version of customary law, which was based on case law from the colonial courts. This research, which was guided by the notion of living customary law as a dynamic and flexible form of law, was subsequently critical in negotiating legislative reform. Although human rights were not directly invoked in this process, according to the actors involved they were among the background influences that helped drive the process (Stewart and Damiso forthcoming). Based on empirical research and customary argumentation, the ZANU PF-dominated parliament formally recognized the rights of women and all children to inherit on an equal basis from their deceased parents' estates; this in spite of the claw back clauses in the Constitution and increasing state resistance to international human rights.[22]

Implementation of this new law leaves a lot to be desired in a context where state legal institutions have been politicized to defend the interests of the ZANU PF elite. In spite of the notion that the rights of the widow should be protected and that the estate should benefit all the children these rights are, in practice, dependent on the social and religious context where they are pursued. The Zimbabwe Women Lawyers Association has negotiated space to offer legal assistance to women who are disadvantaged in accessing the justice system (Hellum et al. 2012). Its legal aid and empowerment program in urban and rural areas advises women on matters concerning divorce, maintenance, property, inheritance, gender violence and child abuse. In order to enhance women's capacity to use their rights ZWLA is, in dialogue with local women, addressing invisible power structures that are encountered in response to women's mobilization of their rights, such as the belief in spiritual sanctions.[23] Because these attitudes and beliefs often spill over into the courts in terms of gender bias, ZWLA's legal literacy programs target not just the women themselves, but also those who implement the law, particularly police, clerks of court, magistrates and traditional leaders.

In a political situation where political and legal spaces open and close according to power struggles related to national and local elections, ZWLA employs a variety of strategies to make law accessible to women (Hellum et al. 2012). In response to a disruption of activities and gatherings in the rural areas by war veterans, ZWLA have brought women to Harare for workshops.[24] In order to maintain their legal awareness and legal aid programs in rural areas, ZWLA has sought cooperation with community-based organizations whose leaders have been able to achieve permission to operate from the President's office or the police. They also rely on partnerships with those organizations that are less likely to be harassed when holding gatherings, for example church groups. However, access to areas where vital government economic interests are at stake (such as the Marange diamond mining area where ZWLA had started a project that involved dialogue with religious leaders) has not been obtained.

Conclusions

The proliferation of non-state actors involved in human rights advocacy has opened up important spaces for women's rights organizations and individual women who have the social and economic resources to contest male privileges embedded in state law and customary law. With an overall focus on the relationship between state and civil society, the case studies from Tanzania, South Africa and Zimbabwe discussed here exemplify how NGOs seeking to promote and protect women's rights to non-discrimination and equality engage with the visible, hidden and invisible structures of power that create and uphold unequal gender relations at national, local and family levels. Analysis of these struggles for gender equality indicates the normative and institutional complexity of the broadening field of governance in Southern and Eastern Africa. Through the lens of gender struggle the case studies provide a window onto the complex processes whereby the relationship between state and non-state actors is negotiated and renegotiated.

The new governance model set up for the restitution of communal land in South Africa demonstrates how tensions between a rights-based approach and a neo-liberal development approach are reflected in changing relationships between the government, civil society, market actors and traditional authorities. It illustrates how strong rights-based legislation and constitution can coexist with a shift towards neoliberal economic models, and how the latter (in this case at least) in practice tend to trump the former, at least when it comes down to rights that challenge "traditional" African values such as women's rights. The political shift from a social justice to a market-based land policy shows how the space of operation for human rights organizations opened and closed within a shifting and contested international and national political terrain. While one such NGO, Nkuzi, was invited by the government in the claims-making phase to assist the claimant communities in a process aiming at democratic and equal property relations, in the post-settlement period it was replaced by business actors who regarded the structures of domination and power within the claimant communities as private matters. The government's attempt to marry a social justice and a market model thus curtailed both state and non-state actors' ability to deal with power structures that uphold existing gender and class hierarchies within the local community. While notions of equality and participation still figure high in the constitutional and legal framework of South Africa's new mode of governance, developing practice on the ground is quite different. In the negotiation of power and resources within the new venture companies set up to govern the management and distribution of resources on the farms taken over by the claimant communities, it became far more difficult for weakly organized groups like women, poor community members and farm workers to mobilize support for their claims against members of the chiefs' families, businesses and state agents.

In the context of a broadening field of governance institutions and practices, Tanzanian women's rights organizations have been able to claim spaces where through expert advice, media campaigns, legal literacy and legal aid they are in a position to influence both the content and implementation of women's human rights. The two case studies from Tanzania illustrate the options and limits of legal pluralities in a situation where state law lacks legal hegemony. First, legal pluralities may reinforce structures of inequality as the plurality of available norms decreases the power of state law (Benda-Beckmann et al. 2009a: 12). Ikdahl's (2013) study of individual women's responses to the opportunity of claiming formal property ownership during the land titling process in Hanna Nassif in Dar es Salaam shows significant differences between women according to their age and socio-economic status. Ikdahl shows how the limited hegemony of state law generates diverse responses from differently positioned women, who make strategic choices in order to try to secure a future for themselves and their children. Second, in a political situation where the state provides space for civil society interventions, the existence of a plurality of norms and institutions may also open up a space for maneuvering in which women can choose a forum of mediation that they expect to be beneficial (Benda-Beckmann 1981). As Bourdon's study shows, Tanzanian women's rights NGOs have clearly taken advantage of the space provided by out-of-court mediation. As third party mediators, Tanzanian female lawyers are, by means of a blend of human rights norms, state law and local norms embedded in religion and custom, successfully reaching solutions that resonate with basic principles of equality and welfare. In a context where state law is to a large extent out of tune with Tanzania's human rights obligations they have been able to reconfigure socio-legal relationships that constrain women's equal rights by adopting a pluralistic and consensus-oriented approach. What shapes the relationships of power in this forum is Tanzanian women rights lawyers' economic and professional capacity to challenge the invisible power embedded in customary and religious norms and to use it to further their own aims and goals.

How evolving analytical perspectives on legal pluralities under the circumstances may have very real impacts in terms of legislative change is demonstrated by the Zimbabwean study. The research, lobbying and advocacy strategies adopted by Zimbabwean women's rights NGOs illustrates the potential of combining a legal pluralist and human rights approach in a context where the dominant political discourse views gender equality as a Western human rights imposition and a threat to the nation and "African" cultural values. Using the gaps and contradictions between the plurality of formal and informal norms and institutions in the field of inheritance, the WLSA researchers opened spaces for renegotiating the position of women (Stewart and Tsanga 2007). By defining customary law as a dynamic and flexible form of law that was undergoing change, the research team provided a discursive opening for legal reform. The ability to use this possibility

50   Gender Justice and Legal Pluralities

was in turn dependent on the mobilization of the researchers' professional status as national legal experts, university professors and members of the law commission. In a situation where the state has failed to take measures to implement the new law due to the politicization of the legal institutions, women's rights NGOs space has to be renegotiated. Recognizing law's patriarchal underpinnings, ZWLA addresses both the visible power embedded in customary and general laws and the invisible power structures that are encountered as women claim their rights, such as the threat of spiritual sanctions in terms of disease.

As these examples indicate, the role of women's rights NGOs in Southern and Eastern Africa is vital in efforts to secure greater gender justice in contexts of complex legal pluralities. Through expert advice, media campaigns, legal literacy and legal aid such organizations are in a position to influence both the content and the implementation of women's human rights. In some instances these interventions reflect the experiences and problems of the middle-class women who set the agendas of these organizations and fail to deal with conditions of women from other social groups. Successful interventions are ultimately dependent on their ability to develop situational and locally appropriate strategies of argumentation and implementation that are capable of bridging gaps between human rights principles and legal pluralities as they affect different groups of women on the ground. Yet the cases also show how the development of such strategies are constrained by changing constellations of governance whereby claimed spaces close, such as the situation in Zimbabwe and increasingly in South Africa.

Notes

1 As discussed in the second part of this chapter, historical studies, which combine a political economy approach with an actor perspective, understand the formation of African customary laws in the light of both external and internal social, economic and legal factors (Chanock 1985).
2 The UN Convention on the Elimination of All Forms of Discrimination against Women establishes rural women's right to have equal "access to agricultural credit and loans, marketing facilities, appropriate technology and equal treatment in land agrarian reform as well as in resettlement schemes" (Article 16). The African Protocol on the Rights of Women places an obligation on states' parties to "promote women's access to control over productive resources such as land and guarantee their right to property" (Article 19).
3 "Plural legal systems" is a concept that refers to a situation when the official legal order (the state legal system) recognizes a plurality of legal orders. The Tanzanian legal system, for example, recognizes both the customary laws of different ethnic groups within the country and Islamic law (Bentzon et al. 1998: 31). Unlike the centralist notion of plural legal systems, legal pluralism refers to situations that are "characterized by the presence in one social field of more than one legal order" (Griffiths 1986). John Griffiths uses the phrase "weak legal pluralism" about situations where the state legal order recognizes a plurality of normative orders and the phrase "strong legal pluralism" about situations where regulatory

Experiences from Southern and Eastern Africa 51

and normative systems other than the formal state law affect and control people's lives.
4 What constitutes "African" values was and still is central to defining possibilities for framing women's rights claims (Banda 2005).
5 Burke 2010: 74–75.
6 The Beijing Declaration and Platform for Action was the result of the Fourth World Conference on Women in 1995.
7 *Katekwe v Muchabaiwa* 1984 (1) ZLR 117 G-H and *Chihowa v Mangwende* 1987 (1) ZLR 228(S).
8 *Magaya v Magaya* 1999 (1) ZLR 100.
9 Constitution of South Africa, Article 9 (2), 1st sentence.
10 Constitution of South Africa, Article 9 (3) (4).
11 Constitution of South Africa, Article 9 (2), 2nd sentence.
12 Interview Furule Thembani, Tzaneen, 25 July 2009.
13 Restitution Act, Article 35.
14 Land Act 1999; Village Land Act 1999.
15 Presidential Commission of Inquiry into Land Matters, submitted in 1992.
16 A claimed space according to Gaventa is one "claimed by less powerful actors from or against the power holders" while a created space is "created more autonomously by them" (Gaventa 2006: 27).
17 Harri Englund (2006) has demonstrated how elements of the Malawian middle class have turned the language of human rights to their advantage.
18 Commission on Legal Empowerment of the Poor (2008).
19 *Katekwe v Muchabaiwa* 1984 (1) ZLR 117 G-H and *Chihowa v Mangwende* 1987 (1) ZLR 228(S).
20 *The Herald*, 10 February 2002.
21 *Murisa v Murisa* S-41-91.
22 The Administration of Estates Act Amendment Act 6/97 (Chapter 6:01).
23 When mobilizing their rights under state-law, such as the right to inheritance or maintenance, women are often faced with threats that the spiritual ancestors will express their anger in terms of disease or accidents.
24 In 2005 the ZWLA had to withdraw from the Murewa District where it was working with peer educators due to "untenable relationships with local administrators as a result of sensitive political developments" (ZWLA 2005).

References

Albertyn, C. (2007) "Equality," in Bonthuys, E. and C. Albertyn (eds) *Gender, Law and Justice*, Johannesburg: Juta, pp. 82–119.
Allott, A. (1965) "Towards the Unification of Law in Africa," *The International and Comparative Law Quarterly* 14: 366–89.
——(gen. ed.) (1968) *Restatement of African Law, Volume 1, The Law on Marriage and Divorce*, Cotran E. (ed.) London: Sweet & Maxwell.
Banda, F. (2005) *Women, Law and Human Rights: An African Perspective*, Oxford: Hart Publishing.
Benda-Beckmann, K. von (1981) "Forum Shopping and Shopping Forums: Dispute Processing a Mingangkabu Village," *Journal of Legal Pluralism* 30/31: 87–120.
Benda-Beckmann, F. von, K. von Benda-Beckmann and J. Eckert (eds) (2009a) *Rules of Law and Laws of Ruling: On the Governance of Law*, Surrey and Burlington, VT: Ashgate.

52   Gender Justice and Legal Pluralities

Benda-Beckmann, F. von, K. von Benda-Beckmann and A. Griffiths (eds) (2009b) *The Power of Law in a Transnational World: Anthropological Enquiries*, New York, NY and Oxford: Berghahn Books.

Bennet, T. W. (1985) *Application of Customary Law in Southern Africa*, Cape Town: Juta.

Benschop, M. (2002) *Rights and Reality: Are Women's Equal rights to Land, Housing and Property Implemented in East Africa?* Nairobi: UN HABITAT (United Nations Human Settlements Program).

Bentzon, A. W., A. Hellum, J. Stewart, W. Ncube and T. Agersnap (1998) *Pursuing Grounded Theory in Law: South-North Experiences in Developing Women's Law*, Oslo/Harare: TANO/Mond Books.

Berg, N. and A. Gundersen (1991) "Legal Refroms in Mozambique: Equality and Emancipation through Popular Justice," in Stølen, K. A. and V. Mariken (eds) *Gender and Change in Developing Countries*, Oslo: Norwegian University Press.

Bourdon, N. (2013) "Coercive Harmony? Realizing Women's Rights through Alternative Dispute Resolution in Dar Es Salaam's Legal Aid Clinics," in Derman, B., A. Hellum, and K. Sandvik (eds) *Worlds of Human Rights: Ambiguities of Rights Claiming in Africa*, Leiden: Brill.

Burke, R. (2010) *Decolonization and the Evolution of International Human Rights*, Philadelphia, PA: University of Pennsylvania Press.

Chanock, M. (1985) *Law, Custom, and Social Order: The Colonial Experience in Malawi and Zambia*, Oxford: Heinemann, reprinted 1998.

——(1989) "Neither Customary nor Legal: African Customary Law in an Era of Family Law Reform," *International Journal of Law and the Family* 3: 72–78.

Chinkin, C., S. Wright and H. Charlesworth (2005) "Feminist Approaches to International Law: Reflections from another Century," in Buss, D. and A. Manji (eds) *International Law: Modern Feminist Approaches*, Oxford and Portland, OR: Hart Publishing.

Claassens, A. and B. Cousins (eds) (2008) *Land, Power and Custom: Controversies Generated by South Africa's Communal Land Rights Act*, Athens, OH: Ohio University Press.

Claassens, A. and S. Ngubane (2008) "Women, Land and Power: The Impact of the Communal Land rights Act," in Claassens, A. and B. Cousins (eds) *Land, Power and Custom. Controversies Generated by South Africa's Communal Land Rights Act*, Athens, OH: Ohio University Press, pp. 154–84.

Commission on Legal Empowerment of the Poor (2008) *Making the Law Work for Everyone*, Vol. 1, New York, NY: United Nations Development Program.

Derman, B., A. Hellum and K. B. Sandvik (eds) (2013) "Introduction," in *Worlds of Human Rights: Ambiguities of Rights Claiming in Africa*, Amsterdam: Brill.

Derman, B., E. Lahiffe and E. Sjaastad (2010) "Strategic Questions for Claimant Communities, Government and Strategic Partners: Challenges and Pitfalls in South Africa's New Model of Land Restitution," in Walker, C. et al. (eds) *Land, Memory, Reconstruction and Justice: Perspectives on Land Claims in South Africa*, Athens, OH: Ohio University Press, pp. 306–24.

Englund, H. (2006) *Prisoners of Freedom: Human Rights and the African poor*, Berkeley and Los Angeles, CA: University of California Press.

Folbre, N. (1988) "Patriarchal Social Formations in Zimbabwe," in Parpart, J. et al. (eds) *Patriarchy and Class in Africa*, Boulder, CO and London: Westview Press.

Gaventa, J. (2006) "Reflections on the Uses of the 'Power Cube Approach for Analyzing the Spaces, Places and Dynamics of Civil Society Participation and Engagement,'" *CFP Evaluation Series*: 2003–6.

Griffiths, A. (1997) *In the Shadow of Marriage: Gender and Justice in an African Community*, Chicago, IL: University of Chicago Press.

——(2002) "Legal Pluralism," in Banakar, R. and M. Travers (eds) *An Introduction to Law and Social Theory*, Oxford and Portland, OR: Hart Publishing, pp. 289–310.

Griffiths, J. (1986) "What is Legal Pluralism?" *Journal of Legal Pluralism* 24: 1–50.

Gubbay, A. (1997) "The Protection and Enforcement of Fundamental Rights: The Zimbabwean Experience," *Human Rights Quarterly* 19: 227–54.

Gundersen, A. (1992) "Popular Justice in Mozambique: Between State Law and Folk Law," *Social and Legal Studies* 1: 257–82.

Hellum, A. (1999) *Women's Human Rights and Legal Pluralism in Africa: Mixed Norms and Identities in Infertility Management in Zimbabwe*, Oslo: TANO Aschehoug/ Harare: Mond Books.

——(2013) "Introduction to Human Rights in a Gendered, Relational and Plural Legal Landscape," in Derman, B., A. Hellum and K. Sandvik (eds) *Worlds of Human Rights: Ambiguities of Rights Claiming in Africa*, Leiden: Brill.

Hellum, A. and B. Derman (2009) "Government, Business and Chiefs: Ambiguities of Social Justice through Land Restitution in South Africa," in Benda-Beckmann, F. von, K. von Benda-Beckmann and J. Eckert (eds) *Rules of Law and Laws of Ruling: On the Governance of Law*, Surrey and Burlington, VT: Ashgate, pp. 125–50.

——(2010) "The Making and Unmaking of Unequal Property Relations between Men and Women: Shifting Policy Trajectories in South Africa's Land Restitution Process," *Nordic Human Rights Journal* (2): 202–30.

——(2013) "Between Common Community Interest and Gender Difference: Women in South Africa's Land Restitution Process," in Derman, B., A. Hellum and K. B. Sandvik (eds) *Worlds of Human Rights: Ambiguities of Rights Claiming in Africa*, Amsterdam: Brill.

Hellum, A., B. Derman, G. Feltoe, E. Sithole, J. Stewart and A. Tsanga (2012) "Rights Claiming and Rights Making in Zimbabwe: A Study of Three Human Rights NGOs," in Andreassen, B. A. and G. Crawford (eds) *Human Rights, Power and Non-Governmental Action: Comparative Analyses of Rights-based Approaches and Civic Struggles in Development Contexts*, London: Routledge.

Hellum, A., J. Stewart, S. Sardar Ali and A. Tsanga (2007) "Paths are Made by Walking: Introductory Thoughts," in Hellum, A. et al. (eds) *Human Rights, Plural Legalities and Gendered Realities: Paths are Made by Walking*, Harare: Weaver Press, pp. ii–xi.

Henquinet, K. (2013) "Translating Women's Rights in Niger: What Happened to the Radical Challenge to Patriarchy?" in Derman, B., A. Hellum and K. Sandvik (eds) *Worlds of Human Rights: Ambiguities of Rights Claiming in Africa*, Leiden: Brill.

Hyden, G. (1983) *No Shortcut to Progress: African Development Management in Perspective*, London: Heinemann.

Ikdahl, I. (2008) "'Go Home and Clear the Conflict': Human Rights Perspectives on Gender and Land in Tanzania," in Englert, B. and E. Daley (eds) *Women's Land Rights and Privatization in Eastern Africa*, Woodbridge: James Currey, pp. 40–60.

——(2010) *Securing Women's Homes: The Dynamics of Women's Human Rights at International Level and in Tanzania*, Oslo: Unipub.

54   Gender Justice and Legal Pluralities

——(2013) "Mutiple Threats, Manifold Strategies: Women, the State and Secure Tenure at the Interface of Human Rights and Local Practices in Dar es Salaam" in Derman, B., A. Hellum and K. Sandvik (eds) *Worlds of Human Rights: Ambiguities of Rights Claiming in Africa*, Leiden: Brill.

Ikdahl, I., A. Hellum, R. Kaarhus, T. A. Benjaminsen and P. Kameri-Mbote (2005) *Human Rights, Formalisation and Women's Land Rights in Southern and Eastern Africa*, Studies in Women's Law, no. 132. Oslo: Institute of Women's Law, Dept. of Public and International Law, University of Oslo.

International Council on Human Rights Policy (ICHRP) (2009) *When Legal Orders Overlap, Human Rights, State and Non-State Law*, Geneva: ICHRP.

Langford, M., B. Derman, T. Madlingozi, K. Moyo, J. Dugard, A. Hellum and S. Shirinda (2012) "South Africa: From Struggle to Idealism and Back Again," in Andreassen, B. A. and G. Crawford (eds) *Human Rights, Power and Non-Governmental Action: Comparative Analyses of Rights-based Approaches and Civic Struggles in Development Contexts*, London: Routledge.

Lukes, S. (1974) *Power: A Radical View*, Basingstoke: Macmillan.

Madhuku, L. (1999) "A Survey of Constitutional Amendments in Post-Independence Zimbabwe (1890–1999)," *Zimbabwe Law Review* 16: 82–107.

Magaisa, A. (2010) *Negotiating the Path from Mere Constitutionality to Constitutionalism through the Constitutional Reform Process in Zimbabwe*, http://www.osisa.org/sites/default/files/sup_files/Constitutionality%20vs%20constitutionalism.pdf (accessed January 2010).

Manji, A. (2006) *The Politics of Land Reform in Africa: From Communal Tenure to Free Markets*, London: Zed Books.

Mittlebeeler, E. V. (1976) *African Custom and Western Law: The Development of the Rhodesian Criminal Law for Africans*, New York, NY and London: Africana Publishing Company.

Moore, S. F. (1973) "Law and Social Change: The Semi-Autonomous Field as an Appropriate Subject of Study," *Law and Society Review* (7): 719–46.

Ncube, W. (1989) *Family Law in Zimababwe*, Harare: Legal Resources Foundation.

Onoria, H. (2002) "Introduction to the African System of Protection of Human Rights and the Draft Protocol," in Benedek, W. et al. (eds), *Human Rights of Women. International Instruments and African Experiences*, London and New York, NY: Zed Books.

Parpart, J. (1988) "Sexuality and Power on the Zambian Copperbelt: 1926–64," in Stichter, S. and J. L. Parpart, *Patriarchy and Class: African Women in the Home and the Workforce*, Boulder, CO: Westview Press.

Rwezaura, B. (1990) "Researching the Law of the Family in Tanzania: Some Reflections on Method, Theory and the Limits of Law as a Tool for Social Change," in Armstrong, A. (ed.) *Perspectives on Research Methodologies*, Harare: Women and Law in Southern Africa Research Trust, pp. 1–23.

Rwezaura, B. and U. Wanitzek (1988) "Family Law Reform in Tanzania: A Socio-legal Report," *International Journal of Law and the Family* 2: 1–27.

Sachs, A. and G. Welch (1990) *Liberating the Law Creating Popular Justice in Mozambique*, London and New Jersey: Zed Books.

Skogly, S. (2001) *The Human Rights Obligations of the World Bank and the International Monetary Fund*, London: Cavendish.

Stewart, J. (1998) "Why I Can't Teach Customary Law," in Eekelaar, J. and T. Nhlapo (eds) *The Changing Family: Family Forms and Family Law*, Oxford: Hart Publishing.

Stewart, J. and C. Damiso (2013) "Zimbabwe and CEDAW Compliance: Pursing Women's Equality in Fits and Starts," in A. Hellum and H. S. Aasen, *Women's Human Rights: CEDAW in International, Regional and National Law,* New York, NY: Cambridge University Press.

Stewart, J. and A. Tsanga (2007) "The Widow's and the Child's Portion: The Twisted Path to Partial Equality for Widows and Daughters under Customary Law in Zimbabwe," in Hellum, A., J. E. Stewart, S. S. Ali and A. Tsange (eds) *Human Rights Plural Legalities and Gendered Realities: Paths are Made by Walking,* Harare: Weaver Press.

Tsanga, A. and J. Stewart (2011) *Women and Law: Innovative approaches to teaching, research and analysis,* Harare: Weaver Press.

UN Women (2011) *Progress of the World's Women,* New York, NY: United Nations.

Walker, C. (1991) "Gender and the Development of the Migrant Labour System 1850–1930: An Overview," in Walker, C. (ed.) *Women and Gender in Southern Africa,* Cape Town: David Philip.

Women and Law in Southern Africa (WLSA) (1994) *Inheritance Law in Zimbabwe: Law, Customs and Practice,* Harare: WLSA.

Woodman, G. (1988) "How State Courts Created Customary Law in Ghana and Nigeria," in Morse, B. and G. Woodman (eds) *Indigenous Law and the State,* Dordrecht: Foris.

Zimbabwe Women Lawyers Association (ZWLA) (2005) "Evaluation Report for WOMANKIND World Wide International: Legal Assistance and Empowerment program July 2002–June 2005," Harare: ZWLA.

Chapter 2

Indigenous women fight for justice: gender rights and legal pluralism in Mexico

María Teresa Sierra

Introduction

This chapter analyzes indigenous women's strategies to secure gender justice in the context of complex legal pluralism in Mexico. It refers to the obstacles they face to access justice before indigenous and state authorities and underlines indigenous women's efforts to redefine indigenous law. The official recognition of legal pluralism in the country has provoked both a discussion of multicultural forms of justice and of gender rights, with different consequences for indigenous women's demands. The two emblematic experiences of women's organization within collective forms of indigenous justice in Mexico analyzed in this chapter point to the complex realities of women's lives and the ways in which the tensions between individual and collective rights are played out in context of extreme marginalization and gender violence.

The struggle for gender justice is one of the main agendas for indigenous women in Mexico and throughout Latin America today. Indigenous women have not only organized to demand their rights, they are also taking the lead in the redefinition of indigenous law from their own cultural frames of reference. In different forums they have developed a critique that addresses the impunity, gender violence and discrimination they experience as indigenous women, within their communities and in society as a whole. They are determined to confront gender oppression at different scales and levels, drawing on the support of national and transnational networks of human rights organizations. In a recent analysis, Aida Hernández has described how indigenous Meeph'a women living in conditions of extreme marginalization and poverty in Guerrero who were raped by soldiers confronted the Mexican state at the Inter-American Court of Human Rights, and achieved a historic legal victory against a regime that had denied them justice (Hernández 2011). The Inter-American court's ruling resulted in the case being transferred from a military to a civilian court, an unprecedented occurrence in Mexico.[1] At the same time Meeph'a women from the mountain region of Guerrero are fighting to ensure that their community-based systems of justice reflects a vision of gender equity, something that would have been unthinkable only a few years ago.[2] This dual process of appealing before state and indigenous authorities reveals the new conjunctures and contexts that indigenous women now confront, placing them center-stage in the struggle for their rights. By analyzing such processes I intend to demonstrate indigenous women's active role in the building of their own agendas particularly their effort to fight for their rights in different institutional settings without leaving aside their own cultural frameworks. Indigenous women's rights are in fact at the center of a major controversy regarding culture and rights, one which becomes particularly relevant in the context of legal reforms to recognize indigenous law.

In fact, the new context of legal pluralism in Mexico – established via constitutional reforms on indigenous issues approved in 2001 – has opened up the possibilities for women to discuss the nature and limits of both state and indigenous justice systems.[3] Perhaps more than in other countries in Latin America, in Mexico the recognition of indigenous rights has generated considerable concerns about gender inequalities and the observance of human rights standards in indigenous regions. In fact state officials refer to these topics in order to justify a limited recognition of indigenous rights, voicing fears that "savage" indigenous customs may violate human rights, and particularly those of women. Rather than expressing legitimate worries about women's rights, such political uses of human and gender rights discourses reproduce colonial strategies of power and restrict the recognition of indigenous jurisdictions and rights to autonomy.[4] Thus, the recognition of indigenous peoples' collective rights and indigenous women's rights occurs in a context of strong tensions that reveal the structural racism of the state and the preeminence of universalist discourses about rights; these discourses tend to disqualify culture as oppressive for women.

Women's active role in ethnic mobilizations and the politicization of their rights have created alternatives for their participation in different areas of social life, permitting them to hold positions from which they were previously barred. This process is particularly notable within the spaces of community justice. Not only in Mexico, but in Ecuador, Peru, Bolivia, Guatemala, the USA and Canada, indigenous women are actively defending their peoples' collective rights and at the same time introducing changes in key institutions within their communities and organizations (Sieder and Sierra 2010). Women are attempting to redefine their rights from a gender perspective, something that triggers off diverse reactions and challenges within and outside their communities.[5] Within this process global discourses of gender and law are being activated and redefined by local actors; they are imbued with new meanings, incorporating local knowledge and a critical reflection about traditions and justice. This process of vernacularization of gender rights (Merry 2006) is one of the principal challenges indigenous women confront when having to discuss and legitimate their demands in face

58 Gender Justice and Legal Pluralities

of their communities. It is therefore critical to study indigenous women's concrete efforts to promote gender justice and the challenges they encounter.

In this chapter I first discuss how the recognition of indigenous rights came about in legal reforms in order to signal the specific characteristics of legal pluralism in Mexico. I will then refer to the particular ways in which indigenous women are discussing gender rights and access to justice, stressing gender ideologies and the consequences of women becoming organized. In order to illustrate these processes I analyze two contrasting experiences in Mexico: the case of Nahua women in Cuetzalan, in the state of Puebla, and that of the Na'savi, Meeph'a and *mestiza* (non-indigenous) women of the *policía comunitaria* in the state of Guerrero. These are two emblematic experiences demonstrating indigenous women's contribution to local dynamics of law and gender justice, as well as the ways in which local power structures permit or impede the exercise of women rights. In both cases the politicization of gender and ethnic identities pose new challenges for justice practices. The contrast between these two experiences furthermore reveals the importance of both context and legal consciousness when analyzing gender rights, as well as pointing to the impact of neoliberal governance in the definition of law and autonomy. Lastly I discuss the challenges in conceptualizing gender justice from a perspective of cultural diversity and plural legal rights within the contemporary context of legal pluralism in Mexico.

Legal pluralism in Mexico and indigenous women rights: paradoxes of legal recognition

In contrast to other Latin American countries, the official establishment of legal pluralism in Mexico in 2001 implied a limited recognition of indigenous normative systems and their subordination to the hegemony of state law. This in effect signaled what might be termed an "additive" form of legal pluralism that does not recognize full indigenous jurisdiction.[6] In fact, Mexico represents one of the less developed poles in the continuum of multicultural constitutionalism in Latin American countries that ranges from a limited version of legal pluralism to the recognition of the plurinational character of the state.[7]

In spite of having the largest indigenous population in the Americas and a long tradition of indigenist state policies, reforms to recognize indigenous rights in Mexico were limited. The Mexican Constitution was first amended in 1991 to recognize the pluricultural character of the nation. But it was not until 2001 that constitutional reform recognized the collective rights of indigenous communities. In terms of legal pluralism the changes to Article 2 of the Mexican Constitution explicitly acknowledge indigenous authorities and their right to apply their own normative systems within their communities.

Although limited, these reforms implied a major shift away from nearly two centuries of legal monism in constitutional law (Stavenhagen 2002; Sieder 2002).

As in other Latin American countries, Mexico's multicultural reforms are part of neoliberal structural reforms that promoted decentralization and deregulation of the state with the rollback and restructuring of social policies. Along with reforms recognizing the pluricultural character of the nation and certain rights for indigenous peoples, others, such as the reform of Article 27 of the Constitution, opened collective land ownership up to the market and paved the way for access to natural resources by transnational capital. What was presented as a response of the Mexican state to settle a historical debt with indigenous peoples actually meant a *neo-indigenist* policy reproducing a new form of state control without responding to the autonomy claims of indigenous peoples (Hernández et al. 2004). Neoliberal policies increased marginalization, insecurity and poverty in indigenous areas including transnational migration. In fact the material basis for the reproduction of the indigenous and rural economies was severely hampered by neoliberal globalization, which in turn limited the implementation and practice of indigenous rights (Speed et al. 2009; Harvey 2001).

Indigenous legal reforms thus occurred in a structural context that has deepened inequality and in a political conjuncture where the Mexican elite and transnational interests view indigenous peoples' demands to autonomy with suspicion, as granting these would affect their privileges. This is the broader context that frames Mexican reforms to recognize indigenous rights. In terms of justice this has implied a reduced scope for indigenous legal systems, which are seen as a kind of auxiliary to state jurisdiction, useful for dealing with minor offenses and crimes. Furthermore, the reforms follow the logics of neoliberal multiculturalism (Hale 2005) and distinguish between "legitimate" and "illegitimate" forms of indigenous justice. The state retains the power to name and categorize the domains of indigenous jurisdiction; in consequence, it officializes what has become known as "multicultural justice."

The reforms reveal the process of state formation in Mexico and the long political tradition of negotiation and control in rural areas (Joseph and Nugent 1994). Ambiguity and a certain margin of recognition characterize the reform of indigenous rights as part of a larger process of modernization of the Mexican judiciary. New indigenous courts created by official decree in different states of Mexico were established without considering the existing traditional forms of justice.[8] These reforms fragmented and restructured the field of indigenous justice, generating new kinds of ethnic authority that affected indigenous-state dynamics (Chávez and Terven forthcoming).

Thus, the Mexican reforms entail differentiated forms of state control within a new frame of legal pluralism and define a highly limited scope for autonomy in the field of justice. They reveal the regulatory power of the multicultural reforms, which nevertheless have been appropriated and contested by indigenous actors. Other important institutions practising de facto indigenous autonomy, such as the *"policía comunitaria"* (community police) in Guerrero (Sierra 2010) and the Zapatista *"Juntas de Buen Gobierno"* (Councils of Good Governance) in Chiapas (Mora forthcoming) go far beyond the new legal framework, challenging the official multicultural order. Such instances of indigenous organization are deemed illegal and in consequence are constantly menaced by government authorities.

In sum, the new forms of regulation and surveillance imposed by legal reforms in the field of indigenous justice in Mexico emerged in a context of tensions and contradictions that have involved legal changes and local responses. On the one hand, the state recognizes certain rights that do not question the existing institutional order (considering certain de facto autonomies to be illegal). On the other, indigenous organizations have attempted to appropriate the new judicial institutions within their own cultural terms of reference, disputing the definition and practice of indigenous law and justice with the state. Within this context human rights and women's rights have become important weapons used by state officials to restrict indigenous jurisdictions, while indigenous authorities and organizations have also turned to the language of rights to legitimate their demands, particularly their collective rights. It is also within these spaces that indigenous women take advantage of the new language of rights in order to question established gender relations and claim justice inside and outside their communities.

Indigenous women, rights and access to justice

Given the weight of gender ideologies that justify the subordination of women to male decision-making and power differentials, it has been very difficult for indigenous women to gain access to state and community justice. A patriarchal vision prevails both in the state legal system and in indigenous law.[9] Studies in indigenous regions have documented the conditions of disadvantage, racism and exclusion that women encounter within state justice institutions, as well as the difficulties they face when dealing with their own local authorities (Hernández 2002; Barragán and Solís 2011; Chenaut 2007; Sierra 2004).

Mistreatment, sexual abuse, marital abandonment and abandonment of parental responsibilities as well as other forms of gender violence are revealed when women approach justice institutions at community or state level. It is difficult to talk about rights in a context where women have many obligations and very restricted possibilities to take personal decisions about their domestic life. These conditions are aggravated by poverty and marginalization, which complicate the survival of women and their families. Community norms tend to naturalize gender subordination, forcing women to

Gender rights and legal pluralism in Mexico 61

accept their assigned roles according to the idea that customs cannot be questioned. It is not easy to confront a violent husband when women have no guarantees that they will not be additionally punished or expelled from their home, particularly if they have nowhere else to go. This was the experience of Rosa, a Na'savi woman in Guerrero; when she complained about maltreatment she was forced by her partner to abandon the family home.[10] It is usual that women look first to their communal authorities when seeking justice. Even if their husband is aggressive they prefer to negotiate a solution with him in the presence of communal authorities, rather than following the labyrinthine processes of justice through the state courts (Sierra 2004). Only in extreme situations do women demand state intervention to sanction violent men. It is also true that women are not only victims but also important actors in domestic and community social life, and their presence has increased due to socio-economic dynamics and changes impacting local life, particularly because of migration. Women act as midwives, *curanderas* (healers), and partners to their husbands in a number of ritual and collective activities. They also play an active role in local productive endeavors, such as agriculture and handcrafts. The very fact that many women seek justice reflects their social agency (Chenaut 1999, 2004; Sieder and Macleod 2009; Sierra 2004, 2009).

Gender oppression has become a focus of discussion amongst indigenous women's organizations and of public policy intervention due to the high levels of violence that both indigenous and non-indigenous women suffer.[11] Nevertheless gender violence cannot be isolated from the structural and political violence women suffer due to their conditions of ethnicity and social class. For indigenous women, their circumstances of extreme poverty, marginalization, lack of access to health care and education, as well as the racism prevalent in their relations with the state and dominant society, are all characteristics that affect them and their families, men and women alike (Sieder and Sierra 2010). Furthermore, these conditions shape the ways that violence is materialized and experienced. For these reasons, the Foro Internacional de Mujeres Indígenas (International Forum of Indigenous Women) (FIMI) has appealed for an intersectional perspective when analyzing violence against indigenous women, in which violence is seen "in relation to aspects of identity beyond gender, using an approach that accounts for the ways that identities and systems of domination interact to create the conditions of women's lives" (FIMI 2006: 12). The forum also insists that full recognition of indigenous peoples' collective rights is the key to reducing violence against indigenous women.

Indigenous women's organizations in Mexico and Latin America have attempted to create alternative approaches to confront patriarchal views of justice and gender violence from their own cultural perspectives. They are not only discussing rights, but are determined to influence the practice of law inside and outside their communities. Many different experiences have

62 Gender Justice and Legal Pluralities

emerged linking indigenous women's initiatives to official or non-official institutions supporting indigenous women's legal defense: these include women's human rights commissions, defense councils or human rights and non-governmental organization (NGO) networks, as well as indigenous women's institutions. At the same time, the new context of legal pluralism and the renewal of community-based justice in Mexico, albeit limited, have opened new forums for indigenous women to participate and to promote discussion about indigenous rights and traditional justice. Women seek appropriate formulas to talk about gender subordination and a more adequate way of living based on ideas of *"el buen trato"* (literally "good treatment"), reaffirming their relationship with their collectivity.[12] In fact, they are contributing to theorize the very conception of gender equity by appealing to complementarity and "cosmovision" (or indigenous worldviews).[13]

A cultural climate that favors women's rights can therefore be observed. A number of external factors play an important role, such as the legitimation of a gender discourse within federal public policies, international legislation, mass media and the discourse of NGOs on human and gender rights. These discourses are invigorated by indigenous women's organizations (Cunningham 2003; FIMI 2006). New laws that penalize violence against women on the national and international levels undoubtedly imply significant advances. However, they also create other problems since public policies tend to impose liberal models of rights and gender without taking into account cultural contexts and indigenous women's worldviews. Official discourses therefore produce a series of contradictions and tensions that hamper the very practice of rights (Hernández 2006). Within the context of legal changes and the opening of new institutions of indigenous justice or the official recognition of existing ones – such as occurred in the state of Oaxaca[14] – the participation of indigenous women has become a central focus.

Towards an intercultural justice: the case of Nahua women in Cuetzalan, Puebla[15]

The experience of the *juzgado indígena* in Cuetzalan in the eastern Sierra Norte of Puebla reveals the possibilities and limits that Nahua women face to build indigenous justice with a gender perspective.[16] The creation of an indigenous municipal court was part of official multicultural policies in a region where indigenous communities have had a long presence and where local organizations involving men and women have mobilized to defend indigenous rights (Terven 2009). Indeed, local indigenous activists were able to appropriate the new indigenous court, disputing its legitimacy with state authorities. Although limited in its legal competences, the Indigenous Court has promoted new alternatives to indigenous justice. At the same time, the longstanding tradition of organizing amongst indigenous women in the region has provided important spaces for the defense of women's rights, such as the Indigenous Women's Center (CAMI – see below), also with the support of state institutions (Terven 2009; Mejía 2010). Both the *juzgado indígena* and CAMI illustrate the central role that women play in contributing to indigenous justice with gender equity. They reflect women's abilities to appropriate state-created institutions, investing them with new meaning.

The *juzgado Indígena* of Cuetzalan opened in 2002. It is one of five Indigenous Courts created by the judiciary in the highlands of the state of Puebla in response to legal reforms regarding indigenous rights (Terven 2009).[17] The *juzgados indígenas* (indigenous courts) are officially considered an alternative form of justice; they are in fact part of the state legal system's modernization policies that promote the *justicias de mediación* (alternative dispute resolution) and oral court proceedings.[18] The *juzgado indígena* was imposed on indigenous communities' traditional authorities, the *jueces de paz* (justices of the peace, also known as auxiliary judges), who were not formally recognized as indigenous authorities by the new law.[19] This has provoked continuous tensions in the relations between the *juzgado indígena* and the *jueces de paz*. Nevertheless, indigenous organizations have successfully appropriated the *juzgado indígena* and transformed it into an institution that goes beyond the official framework (Chávez 2008; Chávez and Terven forthcoming).

In spite of its limited legal attributes, the Indigenous Court has become a central point of reference for indigenous peoples in Cuetzalan. The court can only deal with minor crimes, which are solved by mutual agreements based on "customary law." Most of the issues dealt with in the *juzgado* relate to problems between neighbors, domestic violence, debts, demands surrounding custody of children, inheritance, land boundaries and water disputes, as well as other claims regarding everyday lives in the communities. Crimes like homicides, rape and felonies are turned over to the jurisdiction of the state (Terven 2009). In fact, the Indigenous Court now deals with most of the problems that were previously solved by indigenous local communal authorities, but the Court also deals with cases that were previously taken to the *mestizo* municipal court in the city of Cuetzalan. The Indigenous Court operates within the municipality as a kind of second-tier legal forum to attend to cases within indigenous jurisdiction. However, the legal status of the new *juzgado indígena* remains ambiguous, affecting the practice of justice. The fact that this novel judicial forum was a product of a top-down decision and was not discussed with the local indigenous authorities, the *jueces de paz*, has also affected its legitimacy. For this reason, the *Consejo del Juzgado* (Legal Council), a reinvention of local traditions within indigenous communities, has become a new instance created by indigenous organizations to advise the *juez indígena*. The *consejo* has made great efforts to improve relations with local authorities in the communities. Indigenous women have been very active in this process as members of the *consejo*. This has offered an important opportunity for women to promote a gender perspective in the practice of justice.

The Indigenous Women's Center (CAMI Maseualcalli) was created in 2003. Led by indigenous women, CAMI has become a widely recognized and respected paralegal institution in the region and an important reference point for the provision of legal defense and the promotion of women's human rights (Terven 2009). With the strong support of *mestizo* women who have worked in the region for many years (Mejía 2010), CAMI developed an integrated methodology involving legal and therapeutic interventions to deal with domestic violence and discrimination. It has also become an alternative instance of dispute resolution at the municipal level. Women from the CAMI have developed a solid relationship with the *juzgado indigena*. This support, however, does not mean a non-critical acceptance of the customary legal order. Some members of CAMI have also accumulated considerable experience in accompanying women involved in legal processes within the state legal system and are aware of the discrimination and obstacles they face seeking justice (see Figure 2.1).

Gender ideologies in the practice of justice: between customs and rights.

It has not been easy for Nahua women to influence the practice of justice in the new Indigenous Court. The indigenous authorities, the *juez indígena* and the *mediador*,[20] are both creating styles of administering justice based on "uses and customs" as defended by the law. They do not necessarily share the priorities of indigenous women. For this reason, women from CAMI, as members of the *consejo*, promote a continuous dialogue with indigenous authorities in order to convince them to consider gender rights when imparting justice. This is the case, for example, when dealing with domestic violence or spousal abandonment. Nevertheless, it is difficult to question naturalized ideologies and longstanding customs that subordinate women (Sierra 2004; Vallejo 2004). The Nahua women of CAMI have learned to reframe their own discourses of women's rights taking local cultural models into account in order to influence these institutionalized spaces. For example, they have tried to convince the indigenous judge that it is not a good resolution to accept that a woman loses the custody of her children just because she needs to go out to work and migrate temporarily to the city. Men are not used to accepting women's counsel, not even to discuss with them their style of doing justice. Women's intervention within such legal forums implies patience, respect and a capacity to negotiate and to accept that cultural changes are very slow and require agreements with men. This conflicts with some feminist positions that consider that indigenous women suffering violence need to confront custom in a much more direct way. In fact, liberal feminism tends not to contemplate context or cultural values when referring to indigenous women's subordination (Hernández 2006).

Figure 2.1 Poster for International Women's Day in CAMI, Cuetzalan, which reads: "Violence towards women is not something natural, nor is it part of our custom. Don't keep quiet – ask for help!" (photo: Rachel Sieder)

66 Gender Justice and Legal Pluralities

The following case illustrates changes in the practice of justice and the active role that indigenous women are playing within it. Ocotlán, a Nahua woman from San Miguel Tzincapan, a community in the municipality of Cuetzalan, Puebla, was badly beaten by her husband and her father when she returned home after selling handicrafts in the village.[21] After being informed by Ocotlán's young son about the beating, the justice of the peace and the subaltern agent,[22] local authorities of Tzinacapan, summoned both men to explain their actions. The father explained that Ocotlán was punished because she disobeyed custom, that she did not have permission to leave home and walk alone. Ocotlán subsequently disappeared. The authorities decided to imprison Ocotlán's father until she was found. In fact after being hurt she had first sought help in the hospital of Cuetzalan, and then she went to CAMI, where she received emotional support. The justice of the peace of San Miguel demanded that she present herself at the community court. She arrived there accompanied by women from CAMI. With the presence of Ocotlán's family, her parents, her husband and children, the judge sought negotiation. Although Ocotlán and her husband arrived at an agreement that allowed her to work, her father was not convinced and it seemed he still thought the beating he had administered was justified. The women from CAMI therefore insisted on establishing a commitment between Ocotlán and her family within the *juzgado indígena* in the city of Cuetzalan in order to guarantee her physical integrity. It was only when the *juez indígena*, Don Alejandro, called for an extended dialogue with the whole family that he finally convinced Ocotlán's father to respect her decision to work. Don Alejandro insisted that times have changed and women now have the right to work and to help with the family economy. But he also stressed that Ocotlán's physical integrity had to be respected. Finally a written agreement was established between the family and Ocotlán. At the same time Ocotlán and her husband were recommended to participate in CAMI's workshops on gender rights and domestic violence, which they in fact did.

The case reveals different facets of justice practices in a Nahua community and the impact of women's rights and legal innovations. First, it indicates the preeminence of customary law at the local level, when the authorities tried to convince Ocotlán's father to let her work and to forgive her. This clearly shows the predominant masculine order, even though women are able to accuse men of domestic violence. Different cases taken to local courts confirm these practices and the ways that women manage to deal with violence without challenging male domination (Sierra 2004; Vallejo 2004). Second, the role played by women of CAMI supporting Ocotlán stands out, as well as the *juez indígena*'s legitimacy in convincing her father. His intervention was particularly relevant as it posed the defense of gender rights. Members of CAMI not only accompanied Ocotlán during the process, but also provided oversight and insisted on an agreement established within the framework of the *juzgado indígena*, looking for a more formal agreement. Nahua women from CAMI have won recognition in the region and have achieved a leading role in improving gender rights and rights consciousness, but they do not have the legitimacy of the *juez indígena* nor his capacity to negotiate with male actors in the same terms and languages. Finally, CAMI's representatives also managed to incorporate the couple into their workshops where other indigenous men and women participate to promote awareness of gender rights and respect within the family.

CAMI's capacity to transform justice practices by incorporating a gender perspective within the *Juzgado Indígena* is also noteworthy. These achievements may seem minor but are gradually becoming part of indigenous authority discourse; indigenous authorities now believe that women have rights and must not be abused. While not all cases are resolved with due respect for gender equity, in Cuetzalan indigenous women know that there are places where they can go to seek solutions to their problems. Given the limited formal scope of the indigenous court, members of CAMI are aware that not all cases can be resolved there: the most serious cases still have to be taken to state judicial forums. Members of CAMI therefore use state law and international legislation whenever necessary. However, they are also contributing to an integral strategy to deal with domestic violence beyond legal forums, where conflicts are not always resolved. Indeed, they are creating interlegal proposals with the aim of promoting intercultural justice with gender equity (Terven 2009).[23]

Indigenous women's claims within the community police of Guerrero: the fight for rights and community jurisdiction

The political project of the indigenous community police in the state of Guerrero aims to secure autonomous indigenous jurisdictions, something which goes far beyond the legal pluralism recognized in the Mexican constitutional reform of 2001. This experience evidences the strength and legitimacy of pluri-ethnic organizing in the region (dating from 1995), which has at its heart a project to build an autonomous legal order that is not subordinated to the state. Within this context, indigenous women from different ethnic origins – Na'savi, Meeph'a and *mestizo*[24] – are promoting the discussion of custom and gender norms within the practice of justice, with the aim of opening spaces for women's participation in the communitarian system, something which in turn generates tension and resistance within the communities themselves.

The *policia comunitaria* have maintained their demands for regional autonomy in the exercise of security and justice. This has meant they are subject to continuous surveillance and aggression from the state, which, nonetheless, has been obliged to tolerate their existence. Women have participated in the community police in a number of different ways since its inception. As the male leaders acknowledge, without women's support it

68 Gender Justice and Legal Pluralities

would not have been possible to create the organization. Above all, women have benefited most from the new security system which now guarantees their safety on the roads, making them feel free of the fear of rape or robbery when travelling to the city. As women and their male partners put it, "the *comunitaria* changed our lives."[25] In a region characterized by acute inequality, poverty, violence and racism, the participation of women can only be understood as part of a collective and community-based project.

The communitarian security and justice system incorporates two separate bodies: the Regional Community Police, and the Regional Coordinator of Community Authorities (CRAC) (Sierra 2010). The system exercises jurisdiction over about 100,000 people living in 80 communities distributed in an extensive territory stretching from the coast to the mountains in the south west of Mexico. In terms of justice, it incorporates the traditional local authorities of communities, who are subordinated to regional authorities in a new justice and security system. The CRAC administers regional justice, dealing with all types of crimes not solved within communities. They also have a re-education system where people who are found guilty after undergoing a justice process are subject to control and collective work in communities. The re-education process is one of the features distinguishing the *comunitaria* from other experiences of community justice in Latin America (such as the *rondas campesinas* in Peru, or the *guardia indigena* in Cauca, Colombia), which normally sanction people involved in crimes *in situ*, but do not detain them for long periods (Sierra forthcoming). This in fact implies extensive organization among communities and authorities in order to sustain the re-education process.

As is the case with most indigenous justice systems, community justice within the CRAC is strongly marked by gender ideologies that subordinate women. The results of a collaborative research project with women of the *comunitaria* indicate the difficulties and problems women face in order to access justice.[26] A lot of cases presented to the CRAC refer to naturalized customs that subordinate women to the decisions of men within their family and communities. The revision of the judicial records of cases taken to the CRAC and the observation of dispute resolution confirm a gender bias in the practice of justice. Nevertheless women prefer to attend community courts rather than the state courts located in San Luis Acatlán, the same mestizo city where the regional offices of the CRAC are located. They fear corruption, impunity and discrimination if they take their claims to the official authorities and are confident that the CRAC will attend their cases in their mother tongue and secure some degree of redress (see Figure 2.2).

In recent years various attempts have been made to open spaces for women and to recognize the particularity of their justice claims. In 1997, when the CRAC was formed, a women's commission was created to accompany the CRAC when dealing with detained women.[27] Since 2006, women have also been elected as authorities within the CRAC. These developments are a response to the need to incorporate a female perspective

Gender rights and legal pluralism in Mexico 69

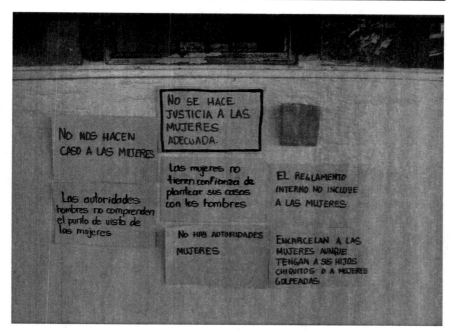

Figure 2.2 Exercises in a workshop organized by promotoras de justicia in Santa Cruz del Rincón, Malinaltepec, Guerrero (photo: María Teresa Sierra)

on justice practices, given the significant amount of cases involving women presented to the CRAC, some of them highly complex issues, such as cases of domestic violence, rape and infanticide.[28] The presence of women in the institution is not by itself enough to guarantee appropriate access to justice for women. However, it does respond to a pending debt community justice has with women. But women's participation has not been constant, nor have they received sustained support from men in order to promote their own vision of justice and rights. This is a highly complex task, but women are determined to continue with their project.

The opportunity to promote gender rights within the *comunitaria* has provided a privileged vintage point to see at first hand the enormous challenges facing women in their everyday lives.[29] It is not easy to discuss deep-rooted customs surrounding practices of courtship, matrimonial alliances, access to land, male authority, or domestic violence in societies where women's subordination structures life worlds and social representations. It is even more difficult to speak about women's rights in situations where the material conditions of life are marked by such strong social inequalities, which in turn affect the exercise of those rights. For many women in the communities it is a new experience to talk about these subjects; most of them do not even know that they have rights or they consider them as duties: that is for

70 Gender Justice and Legal Pluralities

example what a Na'savi woman said when, during a workshop, she stated that she has the "right" to take care of her children and to prepare food for the family. Some women do not dare to lodge a demand against their husband because they are afraid of being punished by their in-laws. The weight of community regulation and social control through gossip and defamation, which affect women's honor, is notable, and this can also expose women to threats and witchcraft. Many of these problems are revealed in the cases that women take to the instances of local community justice, and ultimately to the CRAC in San Luis Acatlán.

In contrast to Cuetzalan, the women of the community police are in the initial stages of an organizational process, which is still very embryonic. They do not have the support of productive projects like handicrafts, which could provide them with economic guarantees of survival and a certain level of autonomy, as was the case for Nahua women in Cuetzlan. Initiatives to build an organization of women are still weak, and normally are not supported by men; but these attempts are important because of the scope of the community police of Guerrero. Even if the presence of women taking decisions or applying justice is still limited, the fact that they are already participating and promoting their rights as women has important symbolic implications. In particular, it visibilizes the presence of women in all public and community events. Women have won a place in the *comunitaria* and in this process women have learned to prioritize the collective rights of their institution even more than their own rights as women.[30] They are aware that the defense of autonomy and jurisdiction is a condition for the existence of the communitarian justice and security system, so they are committed to defending it, as they have done in different confrontations with the state and the army.[31] Women's demands within the *comunitaria* are in fact a new topic of discussion. As is the case with other indigenous women's organizations in Mexico and Latin America, women are building their agenda according to their needs rather than in line with strategic gender agendas that do not necessarily resonate with their context (Mejía 2010). Nevertheless they are also discussing fundamental issues of gender rights.

The circulation of gender rights discourses promoted by federal government programs and feminist NGOs impact local processes, even if they endorse an individual vision of gender rights. Through their practices, women of the *comunitaria* translate the language of rights to their own realities in order to help women when they seek justice. The following case illustrates some of the complexities involved.

Transforming community justice: women's efforts to redefine indigenous law

> Mateo (the *comandante* of Espino)[32] began to flirt with me and I responded. I also did it out of spite because my husband never visited

me while I was in jail. Mateo come into my cell on three occasions in the middle of the night, it's very cold there in the mountain and I was afraid because I was alone. As a result of those three times that I was with the *comandante*, I got pregnant. The problem right now is that I gave birth [by caesarian section] in a hospital and I need money to pay for my medical attention and also I am ashamed for having a child that is not my husband's.[33]

María, a monolingual Mixtec woman held in the CRAC for "re-education", was found guilty as her husband's accomplice in a case of livestock theft. Her husband fled. María tried to escape but was detained again. For that reason she was sent to another detention site, the CRAC offices in Espino Blanco in the mountain. Here she could no longer be visited by her children, which had been possible in the CRAC offices in San Luis Acatlán, where she was previously held. She was finally released after three months of detention. Later, when she was in the clinic giving birth, Paula – a *promotora de justicia* (community justice promoter or auxiliary) – then found out that the baby's father was a *comandante* in Espino Blanco. María wanted to give her child up at birth, so a women official from the Department of Family Protection (DIF) intervened. The CRAC was subsequently accused of allowing María to be abused while she was in detention, but the official also accused María of wanting to sell her baby. Paula informed the CRAC of the facts of the case and the *comandante* was detained, accused of having taken advantage of María.

During the proceedings, participation by *doña* Asunción (the only woman authority in the CRAC at the time) and Paula was fundamental in supporting María and seeing that she be treated fairly. María admitted that the *comandante* had not forced her; she had willingly had sex with him. What she asked was that he helped to support the child and that he give her his name. The *comandante*, who had been detained, assumed his responsibility and agreed to María's requests (although this implied a conflict with his own family). Nevertheless, the CRAC decided to send him for "re-education" since he also had been accused of abusing his authority. María was unable to return either to her home or to her community and she now lives in the city of San Luis, where her brother supports her. However, the interventions of *doña* Asuncion and Paula gave her the strength to demand her daughter back and she feels that justice has been done.

Maria's experience reveals various aspects of the drama that many women expenses when they are involved in criminal offenses. It also highlights some of the changes going on in communal justice, especially because of the role women are playing in following cases. On the one hand it should be pointed out that women are vulnerable in the re-education process and there are no guarantees for their personal integrity; this in fact is an important weakness of the communitarian justice system. The question of women in re-education

72 Gender Justice and Legal Pluralities

is a recurring issue that has motivated women to participate in supporting the system. From the beginning of the CRAC in 1997, they were invited to follow the cases of detained women. Re-education has been designed mainly for men and the fact that very few women have been involved in serious crimes has not produced an adequate response in cases involving women. On many occasions women committed to the communitarian process, many of whom are actually *promotoras de justicia*, have volunteered to accompany female detainees, sleeping in the office with them and finding productive activities for them to participate in. María did not have that kind of support, and her transfer to the office in the mountain made her more vulnerable and finally exposed her to sexual abuse. The CRAC offices are primarily masculine spaces and there is insufficient control over what goes on at various sites.

This case also shows how important it is for indigenous women to participate in the communitarian institution: one of them has a position of authority at the CRAC (as a regional coordinator) and the other assumed her role as *promotora de justicia*. Both of these women supported María and helped her confront her situation; to counter the mistreatment and accusations from the DIF official, and guarantee that the CRAC would intervene and pass judgment on the *comandante*. It was also important in compelling the *comandante* to pay child support and give his daughter his name. It was due to these women's influence that the CRAC decided that the *comandante* should be sent to "re-education," because he had abused his authority and as a form of exemplary punishment.

No doubt the main change that has taken place in the CRAC's communitarian justice is that women now participate as authorities at the CRAC. Although it is very recent, this space was gained as a result of women's engagement and because of the legitimacy of their demands. There are still few *promotoras de justicia* and their long-term project is not yet defined, but the importance of their participation is clear: to accompany women seeking justice and to promote their rights. It is not easy to open spaces in processes so strongly marked by *machista* ideologies which pose obstacles for women and ultimately question masculine privilege. Some men do not agree that women should participate or that they be called *promotoras de justicia*. Others concede them recognition but are extremely critical of any mistakes they might make, and there are others who strongly support them. Until a few years ago women's participation was not visible and was considered as some sort of appendix. Today it is accepted and even encouraged. The Indigenous Women's Center recently established in San Luis Acatlán,[34] run by indigenous women from the region to deal with health and violence problems, offers new possibilities that can strengthen women's work in the area of justice. Although the Center's main objective is in the field of women's health and in supporting traditional healing practices it incorporates an integral procedure to deal with these topics and this implies consideration of gender violence, one of the most common causes of women seeking justice. In the future hopefully *"promotoras de justicia"* (justice promoters) and *"promotoras de salud"* (health promoters) will develop common strategies to promote women's rights.

Indigenous women's commitment to the communitarian process and the defense of their system of justice has become clearer and clearer. Fewer women are turning to the state judicial system and increasingly more prefer the CRAC's intervention. This is the case of María who, in spite of having been detained and the drama of her case, recognizes how important it is for women to participate in the communitarian justice system since they understand each other's perspectives; she also appreciated being spoken to in her own language and not being charged for justice services, as occurs frequently in official state justice institutions.

These are daily processes that signal changes in the *comunitaria* justice system in Guerrero. Although – in contrast to Cuetzalan – this is not the case of a consolidated group of organized women with a well-defined gender agenda, women's participation in the *comunitaria* is enhanced because of the overall impact of this institution. The fact of being a regional justice and security system that exercises jurisdiction over a vast territory without state legal recognition is particularly relevant. In this process women are opening spaces within their institution; they are constructing their own language for speaking about rights and obligations and they are already playing an important role in the practice of justice.

Women's experience in the communitarian system reveals their commitment to the collective project and their unconditional defense of this institution, because they know that it belongs to them as indigenous peoples, and particularly because the communitarian police guarantee them the security and access to justice that the Mexican state has been unable to offer. Beyond the tensions, limitations and mistakes made by the communitarian justice and security system, this institution has generated hope and gives them, men and women, dignity. Nonetheless these women still have a long way to go in order to ensure that their rights as women are taken into account within the system.

In sum, the analysis of both experiences of indigenous women seeking justice in Mexico – the case of Nahua women of Puebla and that of indigenous women in Guerrero, confirms the importance of context and organization when discussing gender rights. Indigenous jurisdictions per se – as in the case with the *comunitaria* – are insufficient to guarantee indigenous women's rights. The goal of increasing an awareness of gender issues appears to be more feasible when there is a strong indigenous women's organization. This has been the case in Cuetzalan, Puebla, where indigenous women have built a longstanding network to defend their rights. Nevertheless, the officialization of indigenous justice, as exemplified by the *juzgados indigenas* and the controls imposed on indigenous law, affect the possibilities women have

74 Gender Justice and Legal Pluralities

to solve disputes within local indigenous courts. For this reason, organized Nahua women in Cuetzalan have developed alternative strategies to support women involved in legal disputes within both indigenous and state justice systems: at the same time they have built paralegal institutions to help women to cope with gender violence, such is the case of CAMI. In contrast, the embryonic organization of women belonging to the Communitarian Justice and Security System of Guerrero cannot yet respond fully to the difficulties women face when trying to find their way through the system. In fact it is the legitimacy of the *policia comunitaria* that makes indigenous women's participation so relevant to the communitarian institution. Women's engagement in the collective project in order to strengthen indigenous jurisdiction vis-à-vis the state is of particular importance. However, there is still a long way to go until gender equity really becomes a goal within the *policía comunitaria*. Both of these experiences reveal different subordinations where gender intersects with ethnicity and class, signaling the role women play in effecting social and legal change. They also underline the complex realities that frame the tensions between individual and collective rights in practice.

Conclusions

In this chapter I have analyzed the ways in which the new context of legal pluralism and legal pluralities in Mexico has opened alternatives for indigenous women to access justice. Legal reforms in Mexico recognizing indigenous jurisdiction, even if restricted, as well as the new international framework of women's rights, have motivated discussions on gender inequalities within and outside indigenous communities. Women play an active role questioning entrenched customs and gender orders that naturalize violence and women's subordination. Women are not only discussing rights and promoting gender consciousness, they are participating in local courts trying to influence legal proceedings in marital disputes and cases involving women. They are also aware of their identity as indigenous women and their engagement with their collectivities, thus they are committed to redefining their own institutions taking into account their cultural values and cosmovision or worldview. In this process women take advantage of the globalized languages of human and gender rights, imbuing them with their own meaning (Merry 2006). These dynamics are particularly important within specific institutional spaces, as is the case in the judicial field.

Multicultural legal changes in Mexico have assumed the form of an additive legal pluralism that recognizes a limited version of indigenous jurisdiction. This has generated new official categorizations to distinguish "official" indigenous legal systems and institutions, like the *juzgados indígenas* in Puebla, from others considered to be non-official and illegal, like the Communitarian Justice and Security System, in the state of Guerrero. In fact, the existence of institutions such as the *comunitaria*, practicing a de facto jurisdiction, constitutes a significant challenge to the national state legal order and reveals its inability to recognize indigenous peoples' demands. In sum, additive legal pluralism in Mexico promotes an official form of governance framing indigenous justice possibilities, with important consequences limiting the exercise of indigenous collective rights, what has been referred to here as "multicultural justice." In contrast, new forms of contra-hegemonic governance, developed in the margins of the state, go beyond official law, reproducing a condition of ambiguity and illegality, which means they are subject to state surveillance and menace. Both of these experiences materialize the contrasting effects of neoliberal legal reforms in Mexico have had on indigenous justice systems. This new constellation of governance affects the dynamics of gender justice with contradictory consequences.

The resort to the language of rights help women confront male authority and limit gender violence, but gender rights per se cannot guarantee better outcomes for women. Gender ideologies are the principal obstacles to women's claims for justice. For this reason women clearly insist on the need to involve men in their process so as to provoke a deeper cultural change in gender relations and open new opportunities for women's participation in local and regional settings.

Both experiences analyzed here show the vernacularization of gender rights within indigenous justice systems. These spaces respond to indigenous cultural logics and offer women better options to frame and solve their disputes. They are also important sites to discuss dominant conceptions of indigenous law and understandings of justice. Through their practice women confirm that customary law can be transformed without losing its cultural value; they also show that gender rights are shaped by cultural and ethnic identity and need to be understood in the intersection between individual and collective rights. Indigenous women distance themselves from universalistic visions of rights and gender justice that do not respond to their claims. In spite of the important progress of the recognition of women's rights in indigenous courts there is a long way to go to guarantee greater gender justice.

These processes are similar to experiences indigenous women are living in other Latin American countries where they are also opening local, regional, and national legal spaces. Women's demands, in fact, are at the forefront of debates regarding recognition of plural legal orders and collective rights at the national and international level.

Acknowledgements

I want to thank Rachel Sieder, Florencia Mercado, Morna Macleod and Mariana Mora for their comments and support on earlier versions of this chapter. I am also grateful to the Center of US-Mexican Studies of the University of California in San Diego for their support during my sabbatical stay at the Center as a Visiting Fellow (2011–12) where the writing was completed.

Notes

1 The case of Valentina Rosendo and Inés Fernández, indigenous *meeph'a* women from the state of Guerrero raped by soldiers of the Mexican army, is an emblematic case of indigenous women seeking justice in national and international courts: http://www.tlachinollan.org/Ines-y-Valentina/ines-y-vale.html (accessed 30 November 2011); see also Hernández and Ortíz Elizondo 2010.

2 Only in recent years have indigenous women's demands been expressed in terms of specific gender rights. The voices of Zapatista indigenous women in Chiapas after the indigenous uprising in 1994 were fundamental to opening space for the expression of women's rights awareness within indigenous collective claims for justice.

3 In August 2001, Article 2 of the Mexican Constitution was reformed to recognize indigenous rights to autonomy and self-determination within their communities. A subordinated version of legal pluralism was established recognizing local normative systems of law and indigenous authorities.

4 For an example of the ways in which Mexican state authorities use the defense of indigenous women's rights to discredit customary law, see http://www.jornada. unam.mx/2008/01/19 (accessed 30 November 2011).

5 For a comparative view of these processes in Mexico, Guatemala and the USA, see Speed et al. 2009; for a perspective on Latin American experiences of women accessing justice, see Lang and Kucia 2009; Sieder and Sierra 2010.

6 André Hoekema distinguishes between an egalitarian formal legal pluralism – where indigenous legal systems are recognized at the same level as state legal system – and additive legal pluralism, where indigenous legal systems remain subordinated to state law and institutions (Hoekema 1998).

7 Raquel Yrigoyen Fajardo refers to this process as the pluricultural horizons of constitutional reform in Latin America, most advanced in the constitutions of Bolivia (2009) and Ecuador (2008): Yrigoyen Fajardo 2011.

8 Different legislation in Mexico created new indigenous courts of justice as a response to the federal reform on indigenous rights; for example in Puebla, Michoacán, Hidalgo and Quintana Roo.

9 For a critical overview on indigenous women's access to justice in Latin America, see Sieder and Sierra 2010; see also Nostas and Sanabria 2009 on Bolivia.

10 These claims were made by Rosa, a Na'savi woman, during a workshop to elaborate a report on women's ideas on rights and customs, held in the community of Buenavista, Guerrero, in January 2009.

11 See, for example, in Mexico the General Law on Women's Access to a life without violence (*Ley General de Acceso de las Mujeres a una vida libre de violencia*). Federal Government, Mexico, approved 1 February 2007, http://www.diputados. gob.mx/LeyesBiblio/pdf/LGAMVLV.pdf (accessed 30 November 2011).

12 A similar reference is the Andean principle *"el buen vivir"* ("good living") as a guide for living in family and community for women and men alike (Walsh 2010).

13 The relation between gender and cosmovision has been particularly developed by Maya women in Guatemala (see Macleod 2011).

14 Legal reforms in the state of Oaxaca (1995) – the state with the highest indigenous population in Mexico – have recognized indigenous normative systems in a broader way than other state legislations in Mexico (see Anaya 2006; Martínez 2012).

15 This section is based on Adriana Terven's PhD thesis (2009), Susana Mejía's PhD thesis (2010), and Claudia Chávez's master thesis (2008), and on my personal research in the region (Sierra 2004, 2009).

16 The Sierra Norte of Puebla, where the *juzgado indigena* of Cuetzalan is based, is an inter-ethnic region located in the central-east highland of Mexico inhabited by Nahuas, Totonacas and *mestizos*.

17 The *juzgado indígena* in Huehuetla, a Totonaco region also in the state of Puebla, is an important contrast to the implementation of officialized indigenous courts (see Maldonado 2011).

18 The *justicias de mediación* (mediation justices) respond to the alternative dispute resolution model developed in the USA in the 1970s. The model has been transplanted to Latin American countries as a part of the modernization policies supported by international institutions, a process that represents the transnationalization of law (Sieder 2006; de Sousa Santos and Villegas 2001). In Puebla the judicial reform received funding from the World Bank (Terven 2009).

19 The *juez de paz* (justice of the peace), is a legal figure recognized by the law to administer justice within municipalities and local courts. In indigenous communities they function as local authorities and are part of a traditional system of community authorities (*sistema de cargos*). In 2004 the state of Puebla recognized the faculty of the justices of the peace to apply customary law; nevertheless their recognition as indigenous authorities remained ambiguous (see Chávez 2008).

20 The *juez mediador* is also a new legal figure created by the same judicial reform in the state of Puebla. He is responsible for the new *centro de mediación* (mediation center) and acts as an auxiliary member of the Indigenous Court (see Terven 2009).

21 This case was followed by Adriana Terven as part of her PhD research on gender justice in Cuetzalan, Puebla (Terven 2009). I am grateful to her for letting me use her data to build this case.

22 The *agente subalterno* (subaltern agent) is the name of a representative of the *Ministerio Público* (District Attorney or public prosecutor's office) in indigenous communities. This authority has been incorporated to the traditional community authority system (*sistema de cargos*) and is usually exercised by a neighbor without receiving any salary.

23 CAMI's integrated program to deal with intrafamilial conflicts, developed over nine years, involves emotional support, legal or paralegal procedures, and men's reflection groups.

24 The *comunitaria* has a regional jurisdiction involving indigenous and peasant communities from different ethnic origins including poor *mestizos* (non-indigenous). These *mestizos* share with indigenous people a history of marginalization and style of living based on communal life.

25 Such is the testimony of women, like Carmen, who are strongly engaged with the communitarian project.

26 Since 2009 I have been involved in a project on women's rights and access to justice with indigenous women of the *comunitaria* who are interested in discussing community justice and violence against women.

27 The community police was initially created in 1995 to provide surveillance and security on the roads. Offenders were detained and handed over to the state judicial authorities. However, given the lack of will to prosecute them, in 1998 it was decided to create the Regional Coordinator of Indigenous Authorities (CRAC) as a specialized body to apply justice.

28 Infanticide, the killing of a newborn baby, is a serious crime. Normally these cases involve young women. Abortion is not permitted and is considered a form of infanticide.

29 As part of this project we carried out a participatory diagnosis with women in order to gain information regarding issues of customs, rights and access to justice affecting women (Sierra et al. 2010).

30 Shannon Speed describes something similar in the experience of Zapatista women of Chiapas when confronting individual and collective rights (Speed 2007).

78 Gender Justice and Legal Pluralities

31 Carmen, a *promotora de justicia*, referred to confrontations with the state when women were at the forefront of demonstrations to support their regional authorities.
32 Espino Blanco in Malinaltepec is one of the three regional offices of the CRAC; the others are in San Luis Acatlán (the original office) and Zitlaltpepetl in the municipality of Metlatónoc.
33 Paula Silva, justice promoter at the CRAC, recorded this testimony.
34 The center in San Luis is similar to the CAMI established in Cuetzalan; it is hoped it will play a similar role in promoting women's rights.

References

Anaya, A. (2006) *Autonomía indígena, gobernabilidad y legitimidad en México: la legalización de los usos y costumbres electorales en Oaxaca*, Mexico: Universidad Iberoamericana.
Barragán, R. and C. Solís (2011) "Etnografía de la justicia estatal. La violación como prisma de las relaciones de género," in Chenaut, V., M. Gómez, H. Ortíz and M. T. Sierra (eds) *Justicia, diversidad y pueblos indígenas en tiempos de globalización*, México: CIESAS/FLACSO, Ecuador, pp. 313–35.
Chávez, C. (2008) "Del deber ser a la praxis. Los jueces de paz en el renovado campo judicial de Cuetzalan. ¿Hacia un fortalecimiento de la jurisdicción indígena?" Unpublished master thesis in social anthropology, Mexico: CIESAS.
Chávez, C. and Terven, A. (forthcoming) "Prácticas de justicia indígena bajo el reconocimiento del estado. El caso poblano desde la experiencia organizativa de Cuetzalan," in Sierra, M. T., A. Hernández and R. Sieder (eds) *Estado, derecho(s) y violencia. Pueblos indígenas frente a la justicia en México y Guatemala*, Mexico: CIESAS/FLACSO.
Chenaut, V. (1999) "Honor, disputas y usos del derecho entre los totonacas del Distrito Judicial de Papantla, Veracruz," unpublished PhD Thesis in Social Sciences, Zamora, Mexico: COLMICH.
——(2004) "Prácticas jurídicas e interlegalidad entre los totonacas de Papantla," in Sierra, M. T. (ed.) *Haciendo justicia. Interlegalidad, derecho y género en regiones indígenas*, Mexico: CIESAS/Porrúa.
——(2007) "Indigenous Women and the Law: Prison as a Gender Experience," in Baitenmann, H., V. Chenaut and A. Varley (eds) *Decoding Gender: Law and Practice in Contemporary Mexico*, New Brunswick: Rutgers University Press, pp. 109–24.
Cunningham, M. (2003) "Las mujeres indígenas en el derecho internacional," *Memoria* 174: 22–25.
de Sousa Santos, B. (1998) *La globalización del derecho. Los nuevos caminos de la regulación y la emancipación*, Bogota: ILSA.
de Sousa Santos, B. and M. Villegas (2001) *El caleidoscopio de las justicias en Colombia. Análisis socio-jurídico*, Bogota: Colciencias, ICAH, Universidad Nacional de Colombia, Siglo del Hombre.
Foro Internacional de Mujeres Indígenas (FIMI) (2006) *Mairin Iwanka Raya: Indigenous Women Stand Against Violence*, New York, NY: FIMI, http://www.fimi-iiwf.com (accessed 30 November 2011).
Gómez, M. (2011) "En busca del sujeto perdido: los pueblos indígenas bajo el signo de la privatización," in Chenaut V., M. Gómez, H. Ortíz and M. T. Sierra (eds)

Gender rights and legal pluralism in Mexico 79

Justicia, diversidad y pueblos indígenas en tiempos de globalización, Mexico: CIESAS/FLACSO, Ecuador.

Hale, C. (2002) "Does Multiculturalism Menace? Governance Cultural Rights and Politics of Identity in Guatemala," *Journal of Latin American Studies* 34: 485–584.

——(2005) "Neoliberal Multiculturalism: The Remaking of Cultural Rights and Racial Dominance in Central America," *PoLAR Political and Legal Anthropology Review* 28 (1): 10–16.

Harvey, N. (2001) "Globalization and Resistance in Post-Cold War Mexico," *Third World Quarterly* 22 (6): 1045–61.

Hernández, R. A. (2002) "National Law and Indigenous Customary Law," in Molyneux, M. and R. Shahra (eds) *Gender Justice, Development and Rights*, Oxford and New York, NY: Oxford University Press.

——(2006) "Between Feminism Ethnocentrism and Ethnic Essentialism: The Zapatista demands and the National Indigenous Women's Movement," in Speed, S., R. A. Hernández and L. Stephen, *Dissident Women: Gender and Cultural Politics in Chiapas*, Austin, TX: University of Texas Press.

——(2011) "Entre la justicia comunitaria y el litigio internacional: El Caso de Inés Fernández ante la Corte Interamericana," paper presented at the workshop "Mujeres y Derecho en América Latina: Justicia, Seguridad y Pluralismo Legal," Cuetzalan, Puebla, November 2011.

Hernández, R. A. and H. Ortíz Elizondo (2010) *Caso Inés Fernández vs. Estados Unidos Mexicanos: Informe Pericial Antropológico*, Document on file with the author.

Hernández, R. A., S. Paz and M. T. Sierra (2004) *El Estado y los Indígenas en tiempos del PAN: neoindigenismo, legalidad e identidad*, Mexico: CIESAS/Miguel Angel Porrúa.

Hoekema, A. (1998) "Hacia un pluralismo jurídico formal de tipo igualitario," *América Indígena* LVIII (1–2): 261–300.

Joseph, G. and D. Nugent (eds) (1994) *Everyday Forms of State Formation: Revolution and Negotiation of Rule in Modern Mexico*, Durham, NC: Duke University Press.

Lang, M. and A. Kucia (comp.) (2009) *Mujeres indígenas y justicia ancestral*, Quito, Ecuador: UNIFEM.

Macleod, M. (2011) *Nietas del fuego, creadoras del alba. Luchas político-culturales de mujeres mayas*, Guatemala City: FLACSO.

Maldonado, K. (2011) "El Juzgado Indígena de Huhuetla, Sierra Norte de Puebla," in Chenaut, V., M. Gómez, H. Ortíz and M. T. Sierra (eds) *Justicia, diversidad y pueblos indígenas en tiempos de globalización*, México: CIESAS/FLACSO, Ecuador, pp. 487–506.

Martínez, J. C. (2012) *La nueva justicia tradicional: Interlegalidad y campo judicial en Oaxaca*, Mexico: UABJO-CIESAS.

Mejía, S. (2010) "Resistencia y Acción Colectiva de las Mujeres Nahuas de Cuetzalan. ¿Un feminismo Indígena?" Unpublished thesis in Rural Development, Mexico: Universidad Autónoma Metropolitana.

Merry, S. (2006) *Human Rights and Gender Violence: Translating International Law into Local Justice*, Chicago, IL: The University of Chicago Press.

Molyneux, M. and R. Shahra (eds) (2005) *Gender Justice, Development and Rights*, Oxford and New York, NY: Oxford University Press.

80 Gender Justice and Legal Pluralities

Mora, M. (forthcoming) "La politización de la justicia zapatista frente a la guerra de baja intensidad en Chiapas," in Sierra, M. T., R. A Hernández and R. Sieder, *Estado, derecho(s) y violencia. Pueblos indígenas frente a la justicia en México y Guatemala*, Mexico: CIESAS/FLACSO.

Nostas, A. and C. Sanabria (2009) *Detrás del cristal con que se mira. Órdenes normativos e interlegalidad. Mujeres quechuas, aymaras, Sirionó, tinitarias, chimane, chiquitanas y Ayoreas*, La Paz: Coordinadora de la Mujer.

Sánchez, M. (coord.) (2005) *La doble mirada. Voces e historias de indígenas latinoamericanas*, Mexico: UNIFEM.

Sieder, R. (2002) *Multiculturalism in Latin America: Indigenous Rights, Diversity and Democracy*, Basingstoke and New York, NY: Palgrave Macmillan.

——(2006) "El derecho indígena y la globalización legal en la posguerra guatemalteca," *Rev. Alteridades*, 16 (31): 23–37.

Sieder, R. and M. Macleod (2009) "Género, derecho y cosmovisión maya en Guatemala," *Desacatos* 31: 51–72.

Sieder, R. and M. T. Sierra (2010) *Indigenous Women's Access to Justice in Latin America*, Chr. Michelsen Institute working paper, Bergen: Chr. Michelsen Institute.

Sierra, M. T. (1995) "Customary Law and Indians Rights in Mexico: A Study of the Nahuas of the Sierra de Puebla," *Law and Society Review* 29 (2): 227–54.

——(2004) (ed.) *Haciendo justicia: Interlegalidad, derecho y género en regiones indígenas*, Mexico: CIESAS/Porrúa Editores.

——(2009) "Las mujeres indígenas ante la justicia comunitaria. Perspectivas desde la interculturalidad y los derechos," *Desacatos* 31: 73–88.

——(2010) "Indigenous Justice Faces the State: The Community Police of Guerrero Mexico," *NACLA Report of the Americas*, Sept–Oct: 34–38.

——(forthcoming) "Desafiando al Estado desde los márgenes. Justicia y seguridad en la experiencia de la policía comunitaria de Guerrero," in Sierra, M. T., R. A Hernández and R. Sieder (eds) *Estado, derecho(s) y violencia. Pueblos indígenas frente a la justicia en México y Guatemala*, Mexico: CIESAS/FLACSO.

Sierra, M. T., J. Corzo and I. Cruz (2010) *Sobre costumbres, derechos y acceso a la justicia: Diagnóstico participativo con enfoque de género en comunidades mixtecas y tlapanecas de la Montaña de Guerrero*, Document on file with the author.

Speed, S. (2007) *Rights in Rebellion: Indigenous Struggle and Human Rights in Chiapas*, Palo Alto, CA: Stanford University Press.

Speed, S. M., R. A. Blackwell, J. Hernández, M. Herrera, R. Macleod, R. Ramirez, R. Sieder and M. T. Sierra (2009) "Remapping Gender, Justice, and Rights in the Indigenous Americas: Towards a Comparative Analysis and Collaborative Methodology," *Journal of Latin American and Caribbean Anthropology* 14 (2): 300–31.

Stavenhagen, R. (2002) "Indigenous People and the State in Latin America: An Ongoing Debate," in Sieder, R. (ed.) *Multiculturalism in Latin America. Indigenous Rights, Diversity and Democracy*, New York, NY and Basingstoke: Palgrave Macmillan, pp. 24–44.

Suárez Návaz, L. and R. A. Hernández (2008) *Descolonizando el feminismo. Teorías y prácticas desde los márgenes*, Valencia: Ediciones Cátedra.

Terven, A. (2009) "Justicia Indígena en tiempos multiculturales. Hacia la conformación de un proyecto colectivo propio. La experiencia organizativa de Cuetzlan," Unpublished doctoral thesis in Social Anthropology, Mexico: CIESAS.

Vallejo, I. (2004) "Relaciones de género, mujeres nahuas y usos de la legalidad en Cuetzalan, Puebla," in Sierra, M. T. (ed.) *Haciendo justicia: Interlegalidad, derecho y género en regiones indígenas*, Mexico; CIESAS/Porrúa eds.

Yrigoyen Fajardo, R. (2011) "Derecho y jurisdicción indígena en la historia constitucional: De la sujeción a la descolonización," in Rodríguez-Garavito, C. (ed.) *El derecho en América Latina: los retos del siglo XXI*, Buenos Aires: Siglo XXI, pp. 139–59

Walsh, C. (2010) "Development as *buen vivir*: Institutional Arrangements and (De) Colonial Entanglements," *Development* 53 (1): 15–21.

Chapter 3

The gender of law: politics, memory and agency in Mozambican community courts

Bjørn Enge Bertelsen

Arguably, the postcolonial world is an apt empirical (as well as conceptual) context for exploring novel understandings of crime, law and justice. Indeed, one may argue that postcolonial Africa is prefiguring global developments generally as well as in the context of law, as argued recently by Comaroff and Comaroff (2009, 2012). Following this argument, it may be instructive to analyze gendered dimensions of the various legal orders in operation in Africa – the influence of the 1979 UN Convention for the Elimination of Discrimination against Women (CEDAW) being a case in point. In a recent short assessment on CEDAW's impact in south and eastern Africa, Glady M. N. Mutukwa notes that a number of legal, administrative and political instruments have been implemented (Mutukwa 2010: 81). However – and speaking from a gender advocacy point of view – Mutukwa points out that these reforms "do not appear to have brought about commensurate changes in the lives of women." To some extent Mutukwa's view stands in contrast to an assessment made by legal scholar Johanna Bond who claims that work towards the implementation of CEDAW in African contexts has both downplayed women's agency and is "dismissive of culture" (Bond 2010: 428). Coming from the camps of advocacy and academia respectively, both Mutukwa and Bond, however, recognize that African contexts are complex and frequently contested. They also suggest that there are conceptual alternatives to positions that counterpose multicultural group rights and gender equality – alternatives that may be captured by the notion of plural legalities proposed by the editors of this volume.

This chapter scales down Mutukwa's and Bond's differing macro-analyses to look specifically at Mozambique – a country that Boaventura de Sousa Santos (2006) calls a "heterogeneous state." Further, given Mozambique's wide range of state-sanctioned legal orders, entities and systems of law, not only may Mozambique be seen as a "heterogeneous state" but it can also be characterized by what Benda-Beckmann, Benda-Beckmann and Griffiths call "state legal pluralism" – an order where legal pluralism exists within state legal structures (Benda-Beckmann et al. 2009b: 4). The focus of this chapter, the so-called community courts (CCs), illustrates such pluralism: existing in all urban and rural contexts, CCs are state-sanctioned tribunals where ordinary citizens with little or no legal training act as judges. Being the most widely used Mozambican court, CCs employ various combinations of codified state law, traditional notions of justice and common sense in solving petty crimes, neighborhood quarrels, domestic disputes, and so forth.

I argue here that the institution of CCs constitutes a highly dynamic and polysemic field of legality and I explore in particular how these courts deal with notions of justice, law and gender. The ways these notions are related to in court are not only informed by codified state law, but must rather be seen as simultaneously produced by past legal orders that are embedded in local communities as well as informed by relational and reciprocal aspects of sociality and individual and collective recall.[1] Based on fieldwork in CCs in the city of Chimoio, central Mozambique, I will focus on the ways in which such different strands of legalities – past and present – are invoked and remembered. Further, I will argue that such memories are central to the constant, dynamic and gendered creation of oratories of defense, accusation and arbitration in evidence in these forums.

Such a focus is especially salient as Mozambique's socialist past strongly emphasized emancipatory ideals for women, whereas the current processes of recognition of "traditional" domains under the auspices of the new state legal pluralism appears to contradict or undermine such past political and legal orientations. Using CCs as a vantage point, the chapter further aims to disentangle certain strands of legal pluralist dynamics, identifying key historical trajectories and points of contestation where different positions are undergirded by past and present legal orders. As such, my analysis of the CCs argues for the centrality of what one might call legal fragments rather than legal corpi. Rather than linear history, I emphasize the role of social and individual memory as a living practice, pointing to the importance of a "politics of memory" rather than idiosyncratic individuated recall, and signaling the perpetual emergence of legalities that are socially embedded, transformed and negotiated. This perspective also opens up for probing what has been called "idiom shopping" in legal settings. By showing how legal dynamics and agency in community courts are socially and historically constituted, such a perspective emphasizing how memory and socio-political processes affect gendered differentiation in court stands in contrast to the literature on legal pluralism that emphasizes the importance of differing legal corpi.[2]

Post-independence law

Any analysis of the current complexities of Mozambican legal orders must signal some key characteristics of legality in the Portuguese colonies. First, one needs to appreciate that the Portuguese colonial legal system, to a much higher degree than in the French and British, dominated African populations

84 Gender Justice and Legal Pluralities

through upholding violent regimes of forced labor (O'Laughlin 2002). Even though slavery was formally abolished in 1869, its de facto practice continued well into the twentieth century in many areas of Mozambique. A new labor code was promulgated in 1899 that tied the civilizing of Africans to the obligation to work (Capela and Medeiros 1987). As Roberts and Mann note in a comparison of French, British and Portuguese colonial legal systems, this made Africans:

> liable to compulsory labor either for the colonial state or for the private sector. Failure to work in Portuguese Africa was thus a legal offense, contributing simultaneously to the criminalization of the bulk of the African population and to the emergence of myriad forms of resistance to colonialism.
>
> (Roberts and Mann 1991: 30)

A second important feature of the Portuguese colonial regime was the legal separation into metropolitan and native law – one for Portuguese citizens and another for African subjects not yet civilized enough to take part in the fineries of Portuguese law, protection and citizenship. Despite the complex colonial history of Afro–Portuguese interaction (Zamparoni 2008) and the ideological smokescreen in part provided by Salazarian ideologue Gilberto Freyre (1961) through the term *lusotropicalism* (a term emphasizing the intimate, well-functioning and benevolent interaction between the Portuguese colonial state and the Africans), the category of the *indigenato* (native group) was legally upheld throughout colonial rule (Cabaço 2010). The *indigenato* regime effectively bifurcated Mozambican inhabitants into civilized citizens (*civilizados*) and native subjects (*indigenes*) and provided administrators and *régulos* (chiefs) of the latter with wide-ranging authorities to judge, sentence and punish, often physically, their native subjects (O'Laughlin 2000; see also Mamdani 1996). Thus, this legal regime was intimately tied to the violent enforcement of Portuguese colonial law, a feature persistently noted by scholars (Pélissier 2004). In particular, corporal punishment was widespread and the dreaded *chamboco* (a whip originally made from rhinoceros hide) or the *palmatória* (a wooden paddle-like instrument) were both used by administrators, police and Portuguese citizens for penal purposes (see also Bertelsen 2011).

Following independence in 1975 the Mozambican liberation movement Frelimo (*Frente de Libertação de Moçambique* – Liberation Front of Mozambique), having fought a very violent liberation war (1964–74) to dismantle the Portuguese system of colonial rule, embarked on a revolutionary path of development with a particular socialist orientation. Instituting itself as a vanguard movement in government, Frelimo set out to radically transform the structural inequalities generated by the colonial era and lead *o povo* – the people – to a new era of prosperity and equality. From the late

The gender of law in Mozambican community courts   85

1970s onwards, the economy and markets became a key area for revolutionary transformation: the new postcolonial ideology decreed collectivization and opposed individual profiteering. Yet despite these efforts, the latter persistently posed challenges and the black markets (*candongos*) were regularly described as challenging the Revolution and, more importantly, being inimical to *o povo*. Frelimo's post-liberation efforts towards collectivization and revolution were, however, increasingly hampered by a civil war that began in 1976 and increased in violence and scope until finally ending in 1992. The civil war saw the emergence of an opposition movement, Renamo (*Resistência Nacional de Moçambique* – Mozambican National Resistance), initially orchestrated, funded and trained by the racist regimes of Rhodesia and thereafter South Africa, that capitalized on popular antipathy with Frelimo's radical politics by waging what they called "a war of the spirits" against the Frelimo state (Bertelsen 2009b). In so doing, Renamo appropriated and re-defined key elements of what they saw as "tradition" by installing chiefs in the areas it controlled and thereby effectively assumed and instituted ritual and factual dominance (Geffray 1990).

In Frelimo-led public meetings these two ills – black market profiteers and Renamo rebels – were often jointly displayed to the public. Frelimo rhetoric in such meetings also emphasized time and again the similarities between economic predation (as personified in black market profiteers, smugglers or in general non-contribution to collective enterprises) and the counter-revolutionary warfare waged by Renamo and its foreign supporters. An example from an article in the national newspaper *Notícias de Moçambique* dated 17 February 1983 is instructive in this regard.[3] Its headline (translated from the Portuguese) reads: "With the same revolutionary violence: Punish bandits, punish black-marketers." According to a report from a public meeting held a few days earlier, Mozambique's legendary president Samora Machel (1975–86) took an active role in establishing the links between *bandidos armados* ("armed bandits," a common term for Renamo guerrillas) and economic predation. Crucially, Machel recalled both the violence meted out to criminals under colonial rule, as well as the extensive use of forced labor undergirded by the dreaded *palmatória* (wooden paddle).

> [In order] to exercise popular power, there need to be measures that one can take to suppress those that commit crimes against the people. There has to be revolutionary violence. The power needs to be exercised.[4]

Machel's endorsement of revolutionary violence against the specter of enemies of the Mozambican revolution, which was also produced (and reproduced) in government-controlled newspapers, radio programs and television broadcasts (Loforte 2007), was also significantly implemented in other areas of radical social and political transformation: i.e. the ascendance, formation and implementation of a new socialist legality of popular justice (*justiça*

86 Gender Justice and Legal Pluralities

popular) (Sachs and Welch 1990).[5] As a concrete expression of popular justice so-called popular courts (*tribunais populares*) were established from the 1980s onwards. These five member committees addressed issues ranging from petty theft to political deviants, in line with Machel's warning to enemies of the people. Such popular courts were introduced to replace, for instance, chiefs' courts, which, Frelimo argued, had functioned in the interests of the colonial administration (Isaacman and Isaacman 1982). As made clear by Mozambican law in 1978, popular courts were to act as "a permanent arm pointed at the class enemy, against reactionaries and traitors, against saboteurs of the economy and scrupulous exploiters, against criminals and marginalized bandits in the whole country" (Gomes et al. 2003: 189, n2). Informed by a socialist and revolutionary orientation, female participation in the popular courts was crucial to Frelimo's political project. Therefore, each popular court was supposed to have at least one female judge selected by Frelimo's women's movement OMM (*Organização da Mulher Moçambicana* – Mozambique's Women Organization) (see also Gundersen 1992). The popular courts were, in other words, integral to the socialist project of not only refashioning the administrative, productive and economic sectors of Mozambican society but also to transforming the role of women (Casimiro 2004).

The popular courts assumed particular importance during the so-called *Operação Produção* (Operation Production, OP) that was initiated in 1983 (Jenkins 2006). A state-driven urban–rural reconfiguration, the OP entailed the ousting of parasitic elements from the cities in sweeping campaigns of social cleansing. In practice, OP meant that many urban people who were found to be lacking various forms of identification proving grounds for residency (as students, workers or residents) were deemed parasitic. This construction of the parasitic urbanite affected both genders but arguably niches with many women were targeted: traditional healers (*curandeiros*) was one of these categories that was susceptible to be seen as "unproductive" as were market women – cast as black marketers – in addition to prostitutes.

In vast campaigns in Mozambique's major cities, women and men were apprehended on the streets, judged in "verification posts" (*postos de verificação*) under the popular courts and frequently airlifted to agricultural "production centers" in the Northern Province of Niassa (Buur 2009). However, OP did more than cleanse the urban landscape; it was effectively a state apparatus for capturing elements of the labor force that were seen to parasitically feed off the productive rural population. Alcinda Honwana details how OP in Maputo was also used to forcibly oust traditional authorities from the city by relocating these for work in the rural areas (Honwana 1996: 42). Rulings on traditional healers (*curandeiros*), for example, are contained in transcripts of court cases, some of which were reproduced in the journal *Justiça Popular* published by the Mozambican ministry of law.

Case no. 374/83 of the *Tribunal Popular da Cidade de Maputo* (Popular Justice Court of Maputo), for instance, deals with a traditional healer that under OP was to be forcibly relocated from Maputo to Niassa. The healer had brought his case before the court on the grounds that until 1981 he had been a textile factory worker and, hence, had been productive (Justiça Popular 1984: 39–42). The Popular Justice Court's verdict expressed the prevailing state antagonism towards traditional healers at the time.

1. There is no recognition on the part of the State for the activities of *curandeiros* [traditional healers].
2. With *Operação Produção* the *curandeiros* are equated with unemployed and odd-job men.

A similar argument was given during a 2009 interview with an informant in Chimoio, a former judge on a popular court, when I asked her about whom they targeted during OP. Being then a woman in her mid-fifties, she recalled that a particular focus was the "problem of the *curandeiros*."

> Many of these *curandeiros* were women who just tricked men! They claimed to be able to heal but were just parasites. Sending them to Niassa taught them to work properly and produce food – although life was hard there.

The weeding out of "unproductive elements" – and its undercurrent of a radical egalitarian ethos – also affected the many enterprising women who, during the civil war, initiated businesses of making and selling bread and trading and marketing goods. A female informant I interviewed in 2011 recalled that it was very dangerous to be a market woman during the era of OP: "[T]hey could suddenly come and take you by force. And then you would be gone – sent to the bush without anything!"[6]

Based on such a partly gendered understanding of parasitic behavior, OP cleansed urban spaces of dangerous non-modernity: making ready its landscape for the inscription of socialist meaning at the same time as it made that landscape susceptible to surveillance (West 2005), Frelimo's political argument for introducing popular justice was, of course, a widespread popular skepticism towards the courts, police, law and legal system of the Portuguese colonial era. Capturing the spirit of the time (and written in the early 1980s when Apartheid South Africa was a significant threat to Mozambican stability), Sachs and Welch's (1990: 10) work on popular justice exhibits some of the rationale behind its introduction and trajectory.

> [If] people lose respect for the legal system – the people feel that it is not protecting them, it's protecting the parasites, it's protecting the crooks and the black marketers, it's protecting the people who'd be only too

88 Gender Justice and Legal Pluralities

happy if apartheid came to their country, then there is no legality, there is an absence of legality.

Informed by such analyses under Machel's presidency (1975–86) the Mozambican state also introduced in 1983 the public flogging of thieves as a measure to achieve a popular and socialist legal order (Sachs and Welch 1990). Replicating or, at least, re-shaping the overt violence of the colonial state, the public demonstration of the state's (and the people's) power was directed against different individual and corporeal expressions of enemies of the revolution. However, as these cases developed in popular courts across the country, they neither necessarily conformed to the strict logic of popular justice that Machel outlined, nor did they unfold exactly as described in the neat records of the journal *Justiça Popular*, as exemplified above.

Pluralizing law and authority: retaining the one party

In my research in Chimoio the discordance between official rhetoric and popular law in practice was abundantly clear. In the work I have undertaken on similarities and differences between community courts and popular courts, a revealing account was provided in August 2011 by a man we can call Rui, a former judge at a popular court in Chimoio and a person I have known since 1999. We talked of courts and law in general and I broached the sometimes difficult subject of how witchcraft (*uroi*) was dealt with during Machel's era.

RUI: We solved the problem of witchcraft (*uroi*) very often through beatings. What we did first was to use public criticism – in the street or in the market place – against the accused. After he or she was convicted, they were often beaten (*chambocado*) in the market place as well.

B: So, how did you decide whether the person was guilty or not?

RUI: Well, after someone came to us in the popular court with the accusation – we were normally eight people – we went to a *curandeiro* (traditional healer) to confirm the accusation or not. After the *curandeiro* confirmed the accusation, we took the accused and beat him or her until they confessed. As punishment, a normal sentence was being beaten 15 times on the buttocks with a *palmatória* [wooden stick or paddle] in a public square and then taken to another public sphere where this was repeated.

This recollection of legal practice during the early postcolonial era demonstrates both the importance of looking at practice as well as analyzing how many aspects coalesce and were continued under popular justice. For one, it underlies the rather mundane aspect of not only using official records (such as *Justiça Popular*) when exploring past and present legal orders, in particular the importance of collecting oral accounts of cases

The gender of law in Mozambican community courts 89

and experiences. Also, the concern with witchcraft and the popular court's use of a *curandeiro*, officially in disrepute as we saw in the case from 1983 above, demonstrates the use of a colonial instrument of physical punishment as well as the court taking seriously the existence of witches despite their denial in socialist rational thought. As such it indicates how law under the legal regime of popular justice became in practice a hybrid arrangement drawing on various understandings of punishment, authority and cosmology.

As many community court judges in Chimoio are fond of demonstrating by referring to photocopies of legal documents, the system of popular justice was abandoned in 1990 with Mozambique's new constitution. In a new law passed in 1992 (*Lei no., de 6 de Maio*, printed in *Boletim da Republica*, 1 serie, numero 19, 1992) CCs (*tribunais comunitários*) were to replace the popular courts (Gomes et al. 2003). However, the new courts were often comprised of the same members of the popular courts and distinctions between the two systems have been, in my informants' view, sometimes difficult to ascertain. The current situation is thus one in which justice at the CC level is dynamic and complex exhibiting colonial, early postcolonial and current legal corpi and institutions. As notions of "community" and ideas about decentralization transformed the local courts, the new system clearly contradicted ideologies of "popular power" and ideologies of emancipation – also gendered – which was integral to post-independence politics in the 1980s.[7] Although Mozambique has been subjected to various forms of Washington-led programs of economic, social and political restructuring since the mid-1980s (Adam 1996), it was especially in the period after the World Bank's 1999 adoption of the so-called Poverty Reduction Strategy Papers (PRSP) that a radical shift toward large-scale decentralization occurred (Tan 2011). In Mozambique, noticeable effects of this include the increasing focus on CCs, the introduction of so-called community policing during the 2000s, as well as political developments to recognize so-called "traditional authorities" and legal understandings (Bertelsen 2010b). The recent process of official recognition of so-called "traditional authorities," has meant that chiefs (*régulos*), once imperative for Portuguese colonial administration, have again become important politically, legally and administratively (Florêncio 2005).

These reforms are expressions of new discourses of legality that have emerged in the post-war era, also internationally, and accordingly in 1990, the Mozambican constitution was changed from the radicalism of a socialist legality to fit "a new imagined order of liberal democracy" (O'Laughlin 2000: 5). This new order provides legal recognition for non-state legal and administrative entities and has produced a legal plural context wherein common conflicts between men and women in poor urban and peri-urban areas over land, marriage arrangements, domestic violence and so forth are negotiated in communal courts. Such a development, which Weilenmann

90 Gender Justice and Legal Pluralities

(2009; see also Merry 2009) identifies as an effect of what he calls "project law," is increasingly visible in many contexts across Africa: "project law" denotes the range of legal orders and laws instigated by non-governmental organizations (NGOs), international non-governmental organizations (INGOs) and transnational bodies that undermine, transform and challenge state law, comprising what he terms "legal pluralistic actors."

In Mozambique a number of organizations have been working to promote gender rights through the creation, selection and/or presentation of various law-related matters. A concrete example of this is the 28-page leaflet *Legislação aplicavel a resolução do conflitos* (Monteiro 2005), distributed during a 2009 state-organized course for community courts judges. This was a compilation made by Women and Law in Southern Africa-Mozambique (WLSA-M). Part of the regional organization Women and Law Southern Africa (WLSA), WLSA-M is a feminist NGO that works towards gender justice and to identify and rectify the plight of women through various action-research projects.[8] In CC settings I have observed over the last few years, documents such as that produced by WLSA-M function in practice as law books: they are cited extensively, judges use them to assume authority, and they are sometimes also referred to by both judges and female parties in court. However – and this is crucial to my argument about the creative and generative components of legal formation at the local level – there are also constant modifications and adaptations. For instance, an article on violence contained in the above-mentioned leaflet (which condemns in very general terms instances of violence) is translated in CC cases I have observed into a legal practice where the person found guilty of beating another is fined MZN 100 per blow. "Project law" in thereby both materially present and dynamically transformed in the workings of these Mozambican low-level courts.[9]

As indicated by the ethnographic snippets in the sections above, through fieldwork from 1999 onwards I have grappled extensively with the dramatic and complex effects of colonial and postcolonial history as well as current cir-cumstances. Working in the urban and peri-urban contexts of Chimoio, the provincial capital of the central province of Manica (a town of approximately 200,000 inhabitants), a significant aspect of my research has been to analy-tically disentangle the structures and practices of law and authority. This process can be exemplified by the creation of so-called "community autho-rities" (*autoridades comunitárias*) that are meant to be local-level representatives vis-à-vis the state apparatus. The 1992 law mentions party secretaries, *régulos* or "other legitimate leaders." At the same time, the decree does *not* revoke any powers vested in authorities of the formal state apparatus, such as party secretaries. Therefore, the seemingly straightforward process of "recognition" of de facto authorities set out in the law may rather be described as a process of *sedimentation* wherein an increasing number of overlapping and structurally adverse authorities derive potency from present as well as past political regimes, cosmologies and violent conflicts (see also Bertelsen 2004, 2009a).

Such ambivalence as to who wields authority and power after the present restructuring is particularly problematic at the grassroots – in the everyday world of often dangerous *bairros* where rape of women, for instance, is a major fear. Complicating this situation, however, is that in several Chimoio *bairros* community authorities are generally understood as being integral to the apparatus of the Frelimo-dominated state apparatus. As a consequence, a great number of women and men neither consult nor trust these alleged representatives of the community. They turn instead to representatives of Renamo (the guerrilla movement that after the civil war became a major political opposition party), criminal networks, traditional authorities or other formations of authority. For *bairro* inhabitants, these complex sediments of overlapping and conflicting state and non-state authority structures create dramatic situations of insecurity where fundamental needs for protection, justice and conflict resolution are at stake. These historical trajectories of violent transformation of legalities and present uncertainties make up a very complex legal landscape. Several formations are notable in such a landscape, including the rise of lynchings (see Bertelsen 2009a; Serra 2008), but here I want to analyze the CC and its workings in one urban and one peri-urban context, as this is a crucial empirical entry point into gendered dynamics. This is also so in a formal sense, as many of the CCs cases – especially those pertaining to domestic violence and divorce – are transferred from the so-called "Women's Offices" (*Gabinete de Atendimento no Mulher*) at major police stations. Thus, community courts are crucial sites where gendered dimensions of protection and justice are addressed.

Two Wednesdays in community courts

As described above, the CCs were institutionally born from the remains of the popular courts and comprise key aspects of Mozambican plural legalities. CC members are, predominantly, senior members of the community and when adjourned the court is supposed to have no less than five members (eight in total where three are substitutes), although I have attended many sessions with as little as three judges present. Supposedly there should be at least one female judge and often this person is recruited through the women's organization, OMM, as occurred during the era of popular courts. Also, as was the case during the era of popular justice, the majority of judges are male and the head is normally an elderly man. Typically, the court is held in a Frelimo party building or a house associated with Frelimo rule. For those who oppose Frelimo rule, such a localization of the court is politically problematic (see Figure 3.1).

The jurisdiction of the courts is limited to minor conflicts that arise, such as boundary conflicts (the so-called *mugano* between plots of land), quarrels and abuse between two people or groups of people, accusations of witchcraft, theft, robbery or fraud, cases of sexual abuse, and so forth. The 2010

Figure 3.1 Local urban community courts sometimes have designated buildings but are more commonly held in the offices of organizations such as, for instance, the building in this photo that was alleged by most to be a Frelimo party office, doubling as a community court every Wednesday, Chimoio, 2005 (photo: Bjørn Enge Bertelsen).

annual report from one of the largest CCs in Chimoio that I acquired during my 2011 fieldwork illustrates a typical distribution of cases: of a total of almost 90 cases that were not transferred from the CCs to the ordinary provincial system (always a possibility if one of the parties wishes so or does not recognize the authority of the CC), the cases were categorized by the head judge in the following way: 27 cases of drunkenness/disorderliness; 25 cases of debt; 13 cases of adultery; nine cases of defamation; five cases of threats; five cases of violence and three cases of conflicts over ownership of land. While this broad categorization may obscure some issues that are recurrent – as we will also see below in a case involving witchcraft accusations – the overview nonetheless gives a general impression of the types of cases that are dealt with.

Cases are brought before the court at the request of the so-called *queixosa/o* (plaintiff) who will approach either the head of the local CC directly or go via the community authority or party secretary in the area. If the head of the CC deems the case within its jurisdiction, he (or she) will call for the *acusada/o* (defendant) to appear in court, usually the immediately following day it convenes. If the *acusada/o* refuses to have the case heard by the CC, it is automatically transferred to the police and, pending their treatment and investigation, transferred to a higher court, often the provincial court. The vast majority of conflicts in Mozambique are, however, resolved by the thousands of CCs in operation. As a general rule, all Mozambican CCs convene each Wednesday and usually the court is set between nine a.m. and ten a.m.

Honde, 30 October 2005

In this rural context, the court is held in what are the local Frelimo party headquarters, a mudded building with iron sheet roofing and earth floor with the Frelimo flag flying on a pole outside. The defendant and the plaintiffs have all been informed by the court that their cases will appear on that day, so together with them, witnesses and other interested parties, I waited from eight to ten a.m. before the judge appeared together with two co-judges. With little further ado (the judge and co-judges knew me from consecutive fieldworks), the court opened. The first case concerning a theft was postponed until the following week because of a death in the family of the accused. The importance of attending to death was accepted without any discussion.

The next case was a complex issue of land tenure: the male *acusado* was accused of "*abriou a terra*" (literally, "opening the ground/earth") in the area and his right to do so was contested by the *queixosos* who outside the court are recognized as (and refer to themselves as) "owners of the land" (*aridzi wo nhika* in the local language of chiTewe). According to the "owners of the land" the *acusado* had not asked them for the piece of land he is farming and had therefore violated local custom. The *acusado* claimed in his defense that the land was not theirs as it pertained to an international NGO that had acquired it from the state to develop for an aid project but had then proceeded to abandon it. After explanations from both parties, the co-judges acknowledged that all land is state land. However, recognizing the long historical line of land ownership belonging to a specific kin group, the co-judges also claimed that this land belongs to the "owners of the land" and that the accused should ask permission from them. The *acusado*, knowing this would involve some annual payment in terms of maize meal, chickens or money, reluctantly agreed to this. The case was settled in about ten minutes.

The third case was discussed in a heated atmosphere and involved a male *acusado* who was accused of repeatedly threatening to kill his mother-in-law with a machete. The *acusado* explained that his relationship with his mother in law was difficult and that she constantly complained about him. His wife – the *queixosa* – explained that her husband always drunk too much *nipa* (local homemade liquor) and that he verbally abused both her, her children and her mother. After hearing the initial statement of the case by the two, the head judge asserted that both would be heard. However, he also added, pointing a finger at the *acusado*, that "you should not be a brute! Women are not things to be thrown away [*coisas para deitar*]. They are equal – and they walk with strength [*anda com força*]." After this he asked the *queixosa* to give

94 Gender Justice and Legal Pluralities

her version. The *queixosa* got up and eagerly provided an example of this by vividly recollecting and recounting a communal party when, in a drunken stupor, her husband had swung his machete around threatening people. On hearing this, the *acusado* interrupted and exclaimed "but I was not going to use it!" The CC head dismissed his excuse and said "You do not walk around with a pistol in your hand without using it! You need to start thinking, think as a man (*pensa bem, como um homem*)." As the *queixosa*'s memories of his actions were energetically conveyed by his wife for a good 30 minutes or more, the *acusado* became increasingly agitated as different instances of his drunken behavior were invoked. Significantly, the *queixosa*'s oral testimony also drew links between his drunken and violent behavior and how unproductive and antisocial he was, also hinting at how people who exhibit such features were treated during "the time of Samora [Machel]" (*o tempo da Samora*). Finally, during the woman's extensive testimony, the man jumped up, grabbed his machete (which has been confiscated by the CC) and ran out of the court room declaring loudly "I do not have a wife anymore!" The person who was assigned the role as court police officer (most CCs have one) gave pursuit but failed to catch up with the *acusado*. The head judge sighed, looked at me and said "These cases cost [i.e. are time and energy-consuming]. Now we have to get relatives to talk to him and get him to visit his mother-in-law to apologize."

The fourth case involved marihuana (*soruma*) and the *acusado*, a boy of around 16 years of age, appeared before the court. When asked to explain himself he claimed he had recently been beaten up and that he did not know why. A court officer showed the judges a roll of paper carrying marihuana and the judges all shook their heads in sadness. The boy tried, again, to explain that he was innocent but was cut short by the judge: "You think you are very smart. But watch out! Look into my eyes! I know that you are also smoking *soruma*! And we have ways to put people like you straight here!" He then showed the boy a so-called *chamboko* – in this case a 60 cm long hard rubber tube. (In this rural CC, the *chamboko* is used for repeated offenders who do not "listen to reason" and a typical sentence is 15 to 20 lashings on the buttocks on top of the fine payable to the *queixosa/o*.) The boy looked intensely at the *chamboko* and nodded slowly. The judge ruled that the court would, nonetheless, try to catch those who had beaten up the boy and see to the case the following week.[10]

After attending to these cases, the court adjourned and lunch was served for the co-judges consisting of *sadza* (maize meal porridge) and beans, a meal purchased with money from the MZN 50 (approx. USD$1.5) paid by the *queixosos* in order to have their cases heard in court.

Chimoio, 16 November 2005

Together with the *queixosa/o, acusada/o*, witness, family and co-judges, I waited outside the *bairro* headquarters of Frelimo from eight a.m. to around

9:45 a.m. before a key could be produced that worked in the rusty padlock. After the five judges (four men and one women), together with one male police officer, opened proceedings in the room, the first case was postponed due to illness. A note from the local community authority explaining the illness was passed around between all the judges and accepted.

The second case involved a complex set of bad relations between two female neighbors. First, the *queixosa* presented a lengthy explanation that revolved around an alleged manipulation of the boundary between the plots the houses were sitting on, a very serious accusation. Further, the *queixosa* also claimed that when confronting the accused with this issue, the neighbor (the *acusado*) had said "I will get someone with a bigger head than you and you will see." On hearing this accusation, several people in the court room exclaimed in horror and shook their heads as this is a common metaphor for eliciting the nebulous services of a *curandeiro* (traditional healer, also called *n'anga*) in order to harm someone by witchcraft. The *acusada's* version was somewhat different: while acknowledging the bad relations, she claimed that this was due to the *queixosa's* husband who, on several occasions, had come to her compound, drunk and disrespectfully *descamisada* (literally "without a shirt"), and created problems. The judge seemed to mistrust the latter version and interrupted several times, also saying to both of them "is it not good to live as neighbors?" The case was deemed too complicated to be solved in the CC and was referred to the local *bairro* authorities; in this case deemed to be the party secretary of the area where they live.

The next case revolved around a man dressed in rags, who had been sleeping outside the court house when we arrived in the morning. He – the *queixoso* – was very thin, looked ill and was visibly uncomfortable within the court context. In a very low voice he explained to the court that his complaint concerned a *profete* (a prophet healer from the African charismatic churches) who, he claimed, had bewitched him. Further, the *queixoso* said that he wanted the case to be referred to the so-called AMETRAMO institution, a state-run body for organizing *profete* and *n'anga* (traditional healers) that sometimes mediates cases where witchcraft is involved and that may have cases referred to it by both police authorities and CCs. The head judge brushed this request away, saying "Here we want a solid case! This will not go to AMETRAMO if this has happened here and it is a case of witchcraft." A friend of mine, also in court that day, with a smile whispered into my ear his version of the case: "The man wanted to get rich and therefore went to a *profete* in order to obtain money-making magic. Instead he became mad and now wants to get treated." The judge suggested that the *queixoso* go and bring the *profete* to the court room, a suggestion the man was clearly uncomfortable with. The judge then decided that they could go with the police officer and wrote a court order (*notificação*) on a slip of paper to the *acusada* instructing her that she should come to court immediately.

96 Gender Justice and Legal Pluralities

After an hour and a number of minor cases, the *profete* entered the room. She was a statuesque woman of around 40, well-dressed and confident. She sat in the back of the court room. The judge asked her to come forward and told her that her customer (*sua cliente*) was now feeling ill and whether she could explain this. The *acusada* said that the *queixoso* had come to her for help and paid her MZN 20 (approx USD$0.70) for her services, acknowledging no blame in his misery. In the same deferential stuttering manner as before, the man claimed he had paid MZN 150 for her services in addition to providing her with commodities such as, notably, tins of Nestlé condensed milk. In addition, he claimed she had bewitched him: "She made me eat *sadza* with snake meat in – as well as eating this with snakes coiled around my neck," he said and displayed a particular rash on his legs that, he alleged, was a result of the *profete*'s witchcraft. He also pulled out some paper slips that were almost falling apart, claiming these were receipts she had given him for the amounts he paid her. The notes were hard to decipher and the judges dismissed their importance while the *profete* remained silent and aloof. The *queixoso* recalled how he went to see the *profete* as he had felt bewitched by a neighbor and after starting treatment, claimed she "then started also to treat my body but bewitched my penis as well." In response to this revelation, the whole courtroom giggled, including the judges. One judge, however, stopped the man's recollections short and addressed the *profete*: "If you pay the man MZN 150, the case is closed. Is this OK?" The woman nodded and left the court room in order to get the money, return and pay the man.

Cosmologies of gender, legal fragments and speech genres

It is commonplace to both identify and analyze women as related to food and cooking in African households, and often the analysis emphasizes their gendered roles as related to foodstuffs and nurture within the household (see for example Moore et al. 1999).[11] Insufficient attention is given to the fact that gendered practices stretch beyond the household's confines, extending into the surrounding society. Metaphorically, the reproductive and nurturing capacity of women as central to household food production is expressed and underlined in cases of witchcraft. The previous case shows how community courts in Mozambique relate to female capacities in terms of reproduction and production, features also evident in the *profete*'s actions: she had appropriated a range of resources from the marginalized man in question: money, (sexual) energy and boxes of very fatty condensed milk. Her actions were interpreted as illicit appropriation of such vital resources, as she had not in reciprocal fashion provided him with the protection that he had required, as a benevolent *profete* would do. The predatory way in which she had appropriated such capacities from her client was thus seen in light of her actions bordering that of the *muroi*: the witch.

There are then at least two dimensions present here that pertain to the central argument of this chapter: first, it is clear that the way in which the court construes its legal subjects is highly influenced by thoroughly gendered cosmologies of production and accumulation, redistribution and healing. Interestingly, in the case of the *profete*, such understandings of gender did not conform to a simplified image of women being victims (or likely victims) of predominantly male violence and transgression, as is, arguably, the dominant tenor of some human rights discourse (see Merry 2009). Crucially, such a structural positioning of women as (likely) victims may be argued to be the case in two respects in the CCs under research: first, this is procedurally or structurally reflected by the above-mentioned "Women's Office" (*Gabinete de Atendimento no Mulher*) at the police station, where women by definition are defined as especially vulnerable. Second, the wide circulation of the leaflet "*Legislação aplicavel a resolução do conflitos*" (mentioned above and argued to be an instance of the implementation of project law at the hands of the NGO WLSA-M) also underlines the vulnerable position of women in terms of protection. The 2009 distribution of the leaflet by WLSA-M was just one instance in which feminist and human rights NGOs had attempted to influence the court system through seminars and publications since the early 1990s.

Interestingly and conversely, in this CC and in the case of the *profete*, the resolution of the case was informed by a particular customary or traditional cosmology of gendered capacities of production and reproduction. Furthermore, the transgressional figure of the witch was evoked indirectly several times and the female *profete* was recognized by all judges (as well as most of the audience) as particularly dangerous. Empowered by her gender as well as her profession, she was therefore viewed (and judged) as having transgressed the boundaries of the social and having exploited a marginal person. As such, the case illustrates also that it is not always the case, as Weilenmann argues (Weilenmann 2009) based on a case study from Burundi, that the implementation of transnational project law undermines local involvement and application through pre-ordaining conditions for participation by donors. To the contrary and against such a view of representing the local as purely receptive and mouldable, the case above also illustrates how project law was seen as irrelevant to the case of the *profete* and, indeed, other cases. It therefore constitutes an argument for neither overstating the impact of a global diffusion of project law nor making generalized assumptions about its implementation.

However, the features characterizing the case of the *profete* – where resolution drew heavily on cosmologically conditioned views of women and men – were not always in evidence. In the case from Honde, for instance, the woman living with a violent husband was recognized as a victim in a more conventional sense. In that case, on the one hand, the court appeared to draw on both the radical gender politics of popular justice of old. It did so by allowing the *queixosa* to draw on the idioms of the era of popular justice in terms of being "unproductive" and "anti-social" and even hinting at the consequences of that which could be either to be subjected to public flogging or being forcibly relocated during OP. On the other hand, there were also references to gender justice and gender rights in this case: prior to hearing the two parties, the head judge chastised the *acusado* and reminded him that women both had "force," should not be seen as things and are to be treated as equals. Such a rhetoric is reminiscent of the era of popular justice and socialism in which women were, in theory if not necessarily in practice, objects of politics of emancipation ("de-entifying" women by construing them as agents was a key component of such policies). However, it also speaks to 2005 being a time of change when a rights-based rhetoric increasingly made its way into the workings of community courts at the expense of notions of popular justice and local understandings of justice. The fact that 2005 was such a time of transformation was also, of course, evidenced by the fact that the threat of corporal punishment – officially banned since 1989 (Gundersen 1992: 282) – was then (and still as of 2011) a part of the court's administering of justice.

Second, there is also a continued emphasis on sociality and the CC's role in that respect. In the case of the *profete*, for instance, her exploitation of the marginalized young man did not only relate to the gendered capacities of women combined with the nefarious intentions of the *muroi*. Moreover, her being nurtured (in the form of condensed milk) and paid without reciprocation assumes the form of the classic denial of the gift – a *sine qua non* in terms of undermining sociality. Likewise, in the case of the abusive and machete-wielding husband, his escape from court did not mean the dispute was automatically transferred to a higher court or to the police. Rather the court assumed the role of mediator and mender of relationships, starting the slow and laborious process of persuading the *acusado* to come to terms again with his wife and, importantly, his mother-in-law. In the head judge's appeal to him to "start thinking like a man," there were also appeals to gendered ideals of comportment and sociality. In a similar vein, the case of the two female neighbors quarrelling was seen as a social and not a criminal case and was returned to the *bairro* authorities for resolution there.

A third dimension was also evident, in particular in the case of the young man with marihuana where there was a history of prior cases that were vividly recalled by the court. The case illustrated there was clearly a limit to the extent to which the court was able to accept recurrent behavior that was socially threatening and undermining of the community. At that point, the vehicle of punishment that was integral to both colonial and postcolonial regimes of law was produced: the *chamboko*. The threat of physical punishment – in this and also other cases I have witnessed in 2010 and 2011 – remains a crucial aspect of the court's authority in a sometimes violent and often insecure context.

What Feldman (2004) calls "the social being of narrative truth" is central to the CC's constantly emerging legalities through its focus on oratory. These are in turn informed by social dynamics and social imaginaries, as in the understandings of female bodies' re-productive and productive capacities and the appropriative potentialities of the *profete* in question. Crucially, in this case, the context of the CC may be interpreted as a way to address potentially violent accusations against women in a city where witches are sometimes lynched (Serra 2008). If we are to make such an argument, this does *not* mean subscribing to functionalist claims of courts acting as "gauges" for what is often described as "social pressure." Instead of relying on such a mechanical metaphor of the social, the CCs in many cases express the profound capacity and dynamics of the social to address, reterritorialize and transform threats emanating from within, or from without, its social realities.

Furthermore, in all the cases cited and given the profoundly oral nature of CCs, the above-described dimensions – the legal fragments from popular justice, cosmologies of gender or appeals to (and practices) of sociality – may all be seen to be integral to the work of navigating and producing multiple *speech genres*. As Bakhtin has asserted:

> [a]n utterance is defined not only by its relation to the object and to the speaking subject-author (and its relation to the language as a system of potential possibilities, givens) but – for us most important of all – by its direct relation to other utterances within the limits of a given sphere of communication.
>
> (Bakhtin 1986: 122)

Certain types of knowledge and narratives of the past talking to the present, such as in a court case that is dependent on the stories and narratives of all involved, may therefore be seen to reflect one another. Bakhtin understands such stories (or "utterances") as an excerpt from a continuum: "There can be no such thing as an isolated utterance; it always presupposes utterances that precede and follow it" (Bakhtin 1986: 136). It is this complexity, where stories interface and are informed by others that Bakhtin (1986: 60) terms a *speech genre* where "[e]ach separate utterance is individual, of course, but each sphere in which language is used develops its own *relatively stable types* of these utterances."

If we employ Bakhtin's well-known concept of *dialogue* to the court room setting, we can see how meaning is created and re-negotiated in the dialogical process. More concretely, it is precisely around individual and collective recall that meaning condenses and is created. Within the Bakhtinian view of speech genres and the interrelation of utterances, different oral practices dealing with the presence of the past indicate profoundly social processes of construction. In settings such as the court rooms of Honde and Chimoio different speech genres are invoked, contested, created and fused. For instance, we see that a speech genre of witchcraft accusations against the *profete* was fused with neoliberal understandings of a client that had suffered fraud, where the specter of the neoliberal discourse of individual responsibilization looms (see also Merry 2009). Furthermore, in his reasoning the marginalized man invoked ideas of a socialist legality past: the ideals of popular courts and their role as weapons against "unscrupulous exploiters" of all kinds. Within the CCs we can discern an ongoing and vibrant process of creating speech genres, some embryonic and novel (emergent), and some more informed by memories of past legalities, ideological convictions or fragments of legalities as these are envisioned (socialist, liberal, neo-traditional, and so forth). As such the speech genres of the courts capture both ongoing struggles in terms of conflicting notions of (gender) justice and must be seen as reflecting a range of sedimented regimes of justice: from the colonial era or notions of traditional justice through to popular justice or novel rights-based approaches.

With Spiertz (1991), we can argue that recall and invocation of such regimes of justice as part of the constant creation of and navigation between speech genres comes close to comprise what he sees as instances of "idiom shopping." These can be understood as transactional processes where plural legal orders – and memories of them – are invoked and vocalized in the course of a case. The particular way in which what is termed idiom shopping is performed here, however, also constitutes an argument against simplified versions of dynamics of legal pluralism which seems to be constrained by an underlying *presentist* orientation – an accentuation of the confluence of different normative and legal orders creating hybridity, ambivalence and spaces for negotiation in the present (see, for example, Griffiths 2009). Instead, what these cases demonstrate is that what may be termed idiom shopping – and, indeed, the dynamics of agency in the CCs – are afforded and circumscribed by *both* historically preceding regimes (i.e. that of popular justice in the 1980s) *and* the broad discursive potential for naming, claiming and blaming that is socially produced and which reflect gendered cosmologies. Put differently and informed by Merry's (2009: 404) distinction, in the CCs there is apt discursive room for the agency of the "relational self" and not merely space for a "responsibilized agentic [individual] self" as celebrated by, for instance, human rights discourses.

As we saw in the cases from both Honde and Chimoio, memories and speech genres are important in a predominantly *oral* legal setting in which few or no documents, besides the verdict (usually a one-liner stating A pays B reparation for the case or noting that the case will be transferred to the regular court system), are involved. Conversely, how things are remembered and conveying these facts in court settings are both integral to oratory and rhetoric. The result in specific community courts are highly localized dynamics of legality that evade simple typologies. On the other hand, being extremely dynamic, staffed by local people and attuned (to some extent) to local realities, the experience of the CCs also underlines the social embedd-edness of such legal forms (Hellum 1999; Hellum et al. 2007). In terms of gender justice, then, the weight of history and the sedimentation of various legal regimes propelling such localized dynamics make difficult an evaluation of the degree to which the legal practise of the CCs conform to ideals set down, for instance, by WLSA-M. Furthermore, such difficulty is also com-pounded by the fact that the Frelimo government in recent years is increas-ingly concerned with "recognizing tradition," a reflection also of its political intent of sapping the power and traction of the main opposition party Renamo (Bertelsen 2010b). However, while the government has repeatedly stated that such recognition should be consistent with state law, there are worries that a politics of including traditional notions of justice, sociality and conflict resolution will, necessarily, hamper the implementation of universal rights for both women and men. A long-standing member of the official women's organization, OMM, said to me in an interview in August 2011: "The problem is not tradition [*tradição*]. The problem is the men sitting and deciding what is tradition – making laws of it. We used to have an open tradition with room for all – both women and men. This new recognition is not good for women."

While the OMM member may be right in fearing the codification of tra-dition in courts – a fear that is not fully supported by the current lack of political support for this – it seems, however, that the cases referred to above point to a somewhat different reality. This is one in which numerous his-torically, politically and relationally informed understandings of justice intersect to create various and localized – and sometimes polysemic – understandings of what gender justice means in Mozambican community courts.

Conclusions

> The law intervenes in the "homogeneous" stability of our pleasure-oriented life as the shattering force of an absolute destabilizing "heterogeneity."
>
> (Žižek 2008: 54)

Following independence in 1975, the emancipatory hopes for women expressed in the popular justice of the revolutionary period failed to fully materialize. If we endorse the early postcolonial Mozambican view of seeing "tradition" merely as a repository for patriarchal socio-cultural structures executing gendered domination, then the recourse to "common sense" (Gundersen 1992) at the base of the emergence of a new socialist legality seemed inadequate to obtain a transformatory or emancipatory impetus of any worth. The effect for many women was that justice as it was carried out in these courts represented a re-confirmation of gendered positions within the selfsame patriarchal framework that the new legal formations initially set out to eradicate (Arnfred 2011). The manner in which the socialist legality unfolded after some duration furthermore turned it into an apparatus of the state and its objectives, as illustrated by the active use of courts for attacks on peddlers and other "parasites" as well as the large-scale social cleansing project of OP in which the courts were effectively clearing houses. Viewed critically, in the community courts (despite having been given new legal documents recently), the use of "common sense" reflects a non-transformational stance vis-à-vis gendered positions without even the rhetorical trimmings of emancipation for women that characterized the era of popular justice. It is in this way we may say that law is gendered in the Mozambican context of CCs.

However, what is clear from the above cases from CCs is that the ongoing reconfigurations of legalities they produce and reflect are embedded in the social. Nevertheless, such a process is also steeped in the ongoing formation of antagonistically posed sovereign entities, such as instances of lynching, police violence and criminal gangs. In such a landscape of violence and power struggles, crime and threats to life, the forms of legality and how it is practiced within a setting such as the CC is largely shaped by orally expressed memories, aspirations and longings. Such a fragmented or, more positively, perpetually emergent and dynamic encapsulation and institutio-nalization of such orally expressed notions of legality is not constrained administratively, politically and legally by either state administration or NGOs (such as WLSA-M) in any coherent and unequivocal way. There are therefore considerable pitfalls in macro-oriented analyses of legality in Mozambique (and, indeed, elsewhere and everywhere) if one allocates cer-tain qualities or assumes the uniform functioning of such a great multiplicity. This is not to say, of course, that any typology or generalization is impos-sible. Rather, it means, as always, that one needs to pay attention to what has been called "the cultural life of law" in general (Engel 2010) and the local socio-historical composition and trajectory of single community courts.

A further aspect of importance in this context is the conspicuous absence of a direct *language* of rights: neither in Honde nor Chimoio were explicit claims made to ideas of individual rights. Such non-subordination to a legal regime of liberal rights underscores, in yet a different way, the social embeddedness of legal processes as these are negotiated within the CCs. Based on the Mozambican material, one may thus claim that it is in the intersection of sometimes conflicting visions and memories of legality, the collective and communal, the social and the plural that the tangents of leg-ality are found. As is clear in the case of the *profete*, this suggests that if we are to pursue gendered dimensions in contexts of plural legalities one point of access are the social cosmologies and imaginaries at work in particular locations. These underpin and inform the everyday production of legal forms and legalities in postcolonial contexts such as Mozambique. Another point

The gender of law in Mozambican community courts   103

of access is also, however, the historically conditioned relations between law, violence and the state and how these impinge on the unfolding of law as practiced in community courts, with gendered effects.

Acknowledgements

This text has been long in the making and has benefited greatly from a number of people, most importantly those connected to the Norwegian Research Council-funded project *Poverty Reduction and Gender Justice in Contexts of Legal Pluralism*, which has also funded fieldwork and research visits to Mozambique. I would therefore like to extend my gratitude to all participants in the project. These include the editors of this volume, Rachel Sieder and John-Andrew McNeish, who have both given me valuable, extensive and critical feedback on various earlier versions of this text, as well as Liv Tønnesen, Maria Teresa Sierra, Natalia de Marinis, Ana Cecilia Arteaga Böhrt and Eyolf Jul-Larsen. I am also grateful to the Department of Anthropology and Archaeology, Universidade Eduardo Mondlane in Maputo for co-hosting the workshop Afro-Latin American perspectives on poverty, gender justice and legal pluralities with us in relation to the project in Maputo on 17 February 2011. In that context, the work and goodwill of Elísio Jossias and Alexandre Mate should be mentioned especially.

Notes

1 As is well-known across human society in time and space, there is great variation as to how justice and law is thought and executed and how crimes are defined. Following Malinowski's 1926 seminal work *Crime and Custom in Savage Society* (Malinowski 1976 [1926]), from the 1950s onwards and led by the likes of Paul Bohannan (1967), Max Gluckman (1967 [1965]) and Laura Nader and Harry F. Todd (Nader and Todd 1978), later contributions within an arguably increasingly re-invigorated legal anthropology have often encompassed such variation and complexity in the phrase "legal pluralism." Such a conceptualization has lately been complemented by a return to a radical probing – and perhaps a global panning out from the local contexts – of crime, law and the state, often inspired by the works of the political philosopher Giorgio Agamben (see, e.g., Agamben 1998 [1995], 2011 [2007]). In anthropology and other social sciences, this has meant a return to questions of crime, punishment, the state's capacity for violence, the intricate relationships between illegality and legality, and the nature of law itself (Comaroff and Comaroff 2006; Harris 1996; Mattei and Nader 2008; Moore 2001; Nader 2009; Nordstrom 2007; Parnell and Kane 2003).
2 For a recent treatment of the notion and importance of legal pluralism, see also Griffiths 2009, where notes 16 and 17 contain a highly useful and extensive overview of recent literature on the subject.
3 *Notícias de Moçambique*, "Com a mesma violência revolucionária: Punir bandidos, punir candongeiros" (Maputo, 17 February 1983).
4 For an interesting yet somewhat unbalanced analysis of Frelimo's use of violence against its enemies during the 1980s, see Igreja 2010.

104 Gender Justice and Legal Pluralities

5 See also Nader 2009 and Humphreys 2010 for incisive analyses of law's colonial, postcolonial and imperial geopolitcs.
6 War-time female entrepreneurship in urban and peri-urban Chimoio was extensive as Chingono 1994 documents and analyzes.
7 Boaventura de Sousa Santos, a renowned scholar of legalities and their multiple forms, has in a two-volume work (de Sousa Santos and Trindade 2003) given a broad overview of the Mozambican "landscape of justice" (*Uma paisagem das justiças em Moçambique*) which is his metaphor for a socially informed analysis of legal formations within the country. While being a comprehensive, multi-disciplinary and very solid contribution to understanding the complexity of legal forms, precisely given its broad number of themes and purportedly nationwide span, as I have argued elsewhere (Bertelsen 2009a, 2009b) the ongoing conflicts pertaining to established (and establishing) legal forms as well as emergent violent non-institutional forms of legality are downplayed. Further, the basic social embeddedness of what one might call "legal creation at the local level" – a notion of the social that is not entifying or consensus-oriented – is also lacking in the collection, perhaps given its nationwide scope (see also Obarrio 2007 for a similar argument).
8 WLSA is funded by a range of sources, including George Soros's Open Society Southern Africa, Oxfam Canada and UN Women, which underlines the transnational dimension of project law. See also Fineman 2011 for a recent treatment of feminist legal thought.
9 See Tan 2011: 84f on the rise of NGOs backed by INGOs and their influence in reshaping law, governance and legalities in Third World countries.
10 See Bertelsen 2011 for an exploration of the corporality of punishment in Mozambique.
11 This is, of course, not restricted to African contexts. Taylor 2002: 241 cites an ethnographic work by Agnes Murgoci in 1926 that presents an ethnographic example of a Romanian woman whose bread was so delicious that a large part of the village consumed it: "The rumour spread that she knew how to take bread-making power away from other women and she was accordingly considered a vampire, sucking vitality from others." Similar beings that suck out the energy or substances from others are widely known, such as the *pishtaco* figure from the Andes region (Weismantel 2005).

References

Adam, Y. (1996) "Trick or Treat? The Relationship between Destabilisation, Aid and Government Development Policies in Mozambique 1975–2000," unpublished PhD thesis, Roskilde University.

Agamben, G. (1998 [1995]) *Homo Sacer: Sovereign Power and Bare Life*, Palo Alto, CA: Stanford University Press.

——(2011 [2007]) *The Kingdom and the Glory: For a Theological Genealogy of Economy and Government (Homo Sacer II, 2)*, Palo Alto, CA: Stanford University Press.

Arnfred, S. (2011) *Sexuality and Gender Politics in Mozambique: Rethinking Gender in Africa*, London: James Currey.

Baker, B. (2003) "Policing and the Rule of Law in Mozambique," *Policing and Society* 13 (2): 139–58.

Bakhtin, M. M. (1981) *The Dialogic Imagination*, Austin, TX: University of Texas Press.

——(1986) *Speech Genres and Other Essays*, Austin, TX: University of Texas Press.

Benda-Beckmann, F. von, K. von Benda-Beckmann and J. Eckert (eds) (2009a) *Rules of Law and Laws of Ruling: On the Governance of Law*, Surrey and Burlington, VT: Ashgate.

Benda-Beckmann, F. von, K. von Benda-Beckmann and A. Griffiths (2009b) "Introduction: The Power of Law," in Benda-Beckmann, F. von, K. von. Benda-Beckmann and A. Griffiths (eds) *The Power of Law in a Transnational World: Anthropological Enquiries*, New York, NY and Oxford: Berghahn Books.

Benda-Beckmann, F. von, K. von Benda-Beckmann, and A. Griffiths (eds) (2009c) *The Power of Law in a Transnational World: Anthropological Enquiries*, New York, NY and Oxford: Berghahn Books.

Bertelsen, B. E. (2004) "'It Will Rain until We are in Power!' Floods, Elections and Memory in Mozambique", in Englund, H. and F. Nyamnjoh (eds) *Rights and the Politics of Recognition in Africa*, London: Zed Books.

——(2009a) "Multiple sovereignties and Summary Justice in Mozambique: A Critique of Some Legal Anthropological Terms," *Social Analysis* 53 (3): 123–47.

——(2009b) "Sorcery and Death Squads: Transformations of State, Sovereignty, and Violence in Postcolonial Mozambique," in Kapferer, B. and B. E. Bertelsen (eds) *Crisis of the State: War and Social Upheaval*, New York, NY and Oxford: Berghahn Books.

——(2010a) "Securitisation of the Social and State Transformation from Iraq to Mozambique," in McNeish, J. A. and J. H. S. Lie (eds) *Security and Development*, Oxford and New York, NY: Berghahn Books.

——(2010b) "Violent Becomings: State Formation and the Traditional Field in Colonial and Postcolonial Mozambique," unpublished PhD thesis, University of Bergen.

——(2011) "'Entering the Red Sands.' The Corporality of Punishment and Imprisonment in Chimoio, Mozambique," *Journal of Southern African Studies* 37 (3): 611–26.

Bohannan, P. (ed.) (1967) *Law and Warfare: Studies in the Anthropology of Conflict*, Garden City, NY: The Natural History Press.

Bond, J. (2010) "Gender, Discourse, and Customary Law in Africa," *Southern California Law Review* 83 (425): 425–90.

Buur, L. (2009) "Xiconhoca: Mozambique's Ubiquitous Post-independence Traitor," in Thiranagama, S. and T. Kelly (eds) *Traitors: Suspicion, Intimacy, and the Ethics of State-building*, Philadelphia, PA: University of Pennsylvania Press.

Cabaço, J. L. (2010) *Moçambique: Identidades, colonialismo e libertação*, Maputo: Marimbique.

Capela, J. and E. Medeiros (1987) *O Tráfico de Escravos de Moçambique para as Ilhas do Índico, 1702–1902*, Maputo: Universidade Eduardo Mondlane.

Casimiro, I. M. (2004) "'Paz na terra, guerra em casa.' Feminismo e organizações de mulheres em Moçambique," Maputo: Promédia.

Castoriadis, C. (1987 [1975]) *The Imaginary Institution of Society*, Cambridge: Polity Press.

Chingono, M. (1994) "Mulheres, guerra e transformacão na Província de Manica. Uma heranca ambígua." *Arquivo: Boletim do Arquivo Histórico de Moçambique* 16: 95–134.

Comaroff, J. and J. L. Comaroff (eds) (2006) *Law and Disorder in the Postcolony*, Chicago, IL and London: The University of Chicago Press.
——(2012) *Theory from the South, or, how Euro-America is Evolving towards Africa*, Boulder, CO and London: Paradigm Publishers.
Comaroff, J. L and J. Comaroff (2009) "Reflections on the Anthropology of Law, Governance and Sovereignty," in Benda-Beckmann, F. von, K. von Benda-Beckmann and J. Eckert (eds) *Rules of Law and Laws of Ruling: On the Governance of Law*, Surrey and Burlington, VT: Ashgate.
Cramer, C. (2007) *Violence in Developing Countries: War, Memory, Progress*, Bloomington and Indianapolis, IN: Indiana University Press.
de Sousa Santos, B. (1984) "From Customary Law to Popular Justice," *Journal of African Law* 28 (1–2): 90–98.
——(2006) "The Heterogeneous State and Legal Pluralism in Mozambique", *Law & Society* 40 (1): 39–77.
de Sousa Santos, B. and J. C. Trindade (eds) (2003) *Conflito e Transformação Social: Uma paisagem das justiças em Moçambique*, Vol. 1, Porto: Afrontamento.
Engel, D. M. (2010) *Tort, Custom, and Karma: Globalization and Legal Consciousness in Thailand*, Palo Alto, CA: Stanford University Press.
Feldman, A. F. (2004) "Memory Theaters, Virtual Witnessing, and the Trauma-aesthetic," *Biography* 27 (1): 163–202.
Fineman, M. A. (ed.) (2011) *Transcending the Boundaries of Law: Generations of Feminism and Legal Theory*, Abingdon and New York, NY: Routledge.
Florêncio, F. (2005) *Ao Encontro dos Mambos: Autoridades tradicionais vaNdau e estado em Moçambique*, Lisboa: Imprensa de Ciências Sociais.
Freyre, G. (1961) *Portuguese Integration in the Tropics: Notes Concerning a Possible Lusotropicology which Would Specialize in the Systematic Study of the Ecological-Social Process of the Integration in Tropical Environments of Portuguese, Descendants of Portuguese and Continuators of Portuguese*, Lisbon: Gráfica Santelmo.
Gastrow, P. and M. Mosse (2002) "Mozambique: Threats Posed by the Penetration of Criminal Networks," paper presented at ISS regional seminar "Organized Crime, Corruption and Governance in the SADC region," Pretoria.
Geffray, C. (1990) *La Cause des Armes au Mozambique: Anthropologie dune guerre civile*, Paris: Karthala.
Gluckman, M. (1967 [1965]) *Politics, Law and Ritual in Tribal Society*, Oxford: Basil Blackwell.
Gomes, C. et al. (2003) "Os tribunais comunitários," in de Sousa Santos, B. and J. C. Trindade (eds) *Conflito e Transformação Social: Uma paisagem das justiças em Moçambique*, Vol. 2, Porto: Afrontamento.
Griffiths, A. (2009) "Anthropological Perspectives on Legal Pluralism and Governance in a Transnational World," in Freeman, M. and D. Napier (eds) *Law and Anthropology*, Oxford and New York, NY: Oxford University Press.
Gundersen, A. (1992) "Popular Justice in Mozambique: Between State Law and Folk Law," *Social and Legal Studies* 1 (2): 257–82.
Harris, O. (ed.) (1996) *Inside and Outside the Law: Anthropological Studies of Authority and Ambiguity*, London and New York, NY: Routledge.
Hellum, A. (1999) *Women's Human Rights and Legal Pluralism in Africa: Mixed Norms and Identities in Infertility Management in Zimbabwe*, Harare and Oslo: Mond Books and Tano Aschehoug.

The gender of law in Mozambican community courts 107

Hellum, A. et al. (eds) (2007). *Human Rights, Plural Legalities and Gendered Realities: Paths are Made by Walking*, Harare: Southern and Eastern African Regional Centre for Women's Law (SEARCWL) and Weaver Press.

Honwana, A. M. (1996) "Spiritual Agency and Self-renewal in Southern Mozambique," unpublished PhD thesis, School of Oriental and African Studies.

Humphreys, S. (2010) *Theatre of the Rule of Law: Transnational Legal Intervention in Theory and Practice*, Cambridge: Cambridge University Press.

Igreja, V. (2010) "Frelimo's Political Ruling through Violence and Memory in Postcolonial Mozambique," *Journal of Southern African Studies* 36 (4): 781–99.

Isaacman, A. F. and B. Isaacman (1982) "A Socialist Legal System in the Making: Mozambique before and after Independence," in Abel, R. (ed.) *The Politics of Informal Justice*, New York, NY: Academic Press.

Jenkins, P. (2006) "Image of the City in Mozambique: Civilization, Parasite, Engine of Growth or Place of Opportunity?" in Bryceson, D. F. and D. Potts (eds) *African Urban Economies: Viability, Vitality or Vitiation?* New York, NY: Palgrave Macmillan.

Justiça Popular (1984) "Jurisprudência: Sala de operações do Tribunal Popular da cidade de Maputo," *Justiça Popular* 8–9: 39–42.

Loforte, L. (2007) *Rádio Moçambique: Memórias de um doce calvário*, Maputo: CIEDIMA.

Malinowski, B. (1976 [1926]) *Crime and Custom in Savage Society*, Totowa, NJ: Littlefield, Adams and Co.

Mamdani, M. (1996) *Citizen and Subject: Contemporary Africa and the Legacy of Late Colonialism*, Princeton, NJ: Princeton University Press.

Mattei, U. and L. Nader (2008) *Plunder: When the Rule of Law is Illegal*, Malden, MA, Oxford and Victoria: Blackwell.

Merry, S. E. (2009) "Relating to the Subjects of Human Rights: The Culture of Agency in Human Rights Discourse," Freeman, M. and D. Napier (eds) *Law and Anthropology*, Oxford and New York, NY: Oxford University Press.

Monteiro, A. C. (2005) "Legislação aplicavel a resolução do conflitos," Maputo: Women and Law in Southern Africa-Mozambique.

Moore, H. L., T. Sanders and B. Kaare (eds) (1999) *Those Who Play with Fire: Gender, Fertility and Transformation in East and Southern Africa*, London and New York, NY: Continuum.

Moore, S. F. (2001) "Certainties Undone: Fifty Turbulent Years of Legal Anthropology, 1949–99," *Journal of Royal Anthropological Institute* (N.S.) 7: 95–116.

Mutukwa, G. M. N. (2010) "Scope of Regional Instruments: A Perspective on the Southern and East Africa Region," Shivdas, M. and S. Coleman (eds) *Without Prejudice: Cedaw and the Determination of Women's Rights in a Legal and Cultural Context*, London: Commonwealth Secretariat.

Nader, L. (2009) "Law and the Frontiers of Illegalities," in Benda-Beckmann, F. von, K. von Benda-Beckmann and A. Griffiths (eds) *The Power of Law in a Transnational World: Anthropological Enquiries*, New York, NY and Oxford: Berghahn Books.

Nader, L. and H. F. Todd (eds) (1978) *The Disputing Process: Law in Ten Societies*, New York, NY: Columbia University Press.

Naudé, C. M. B., J. H. Prinsloo and A. Ladikos (2006) *Experiences of Crime in Thirteen African Countries: Results from the International Crime Victim Survey*, Turin: United

Nations Interregional Crime and Justice Research Institute (UNICRI) and United Nations Office on Drugs and and Crime (UNODC).

Nordstrom, C. (2007) *Global Outlaws: Crime, Money, and Power in the Contemporary World*, Berkeley, CA, Los Angeles, CA and London: University of California Press.

Obarrio, J. M. (2007) "The Spirit of the Laws in Mozambique," Unpublished PhD thesis, New York, NY: Columbia University.

O'Laughlin, B. (2000) "Class and the Customary: The Ambiguous Legacy of the Indigenato in Mozambique," *African Affairs* 99: 5–42.

——(2002) "Proletarianisation, Agency and Changing Rural Livelihoods: Forced Labour and Resistance in Colonial Mozambique," *Journal of Southern African Studies* 28 (3): 511–30.

Parnell, P. C. and S. C. Kane (eds) (2003) *Crime's Power: Anthropologists and the Ethnography of Crime*, New York, NY and Basingstoke: Palgrave Macmillan.

Pélissier, R. (2004) *Les Campagnes Coloniales du Portugal: 1844–1941*, Paris: Éditions Pygmalion.

Roberts, R. and K. Mann (1991) "Law in Colonial Africa," in Mann, K. and R. Roberts (eds) *Law in Colonial Africa*, Portsmouth, NH and London: Heinemann and James Currey.

Rodgers, D. (2006) "The State as a Gang: Conceptualizing the Governmentality of Violence in Contemporary Nicaragua," *Critique of Anthropology* 26 (3): 315–30.

Sachs, A. and Welch, G. H. (1990) *Liberating the Law: Creating Popular Justice in Mozambique*, London and New Jersey: Zed Books.

Serra, C. (ed.) (2008) *Linchamentos em Moçambique I (uma desordem que apela à ordem)*, Maputo: Centro de Estudos Africanos, Unidade de Diagnóstico Social, Universidade Eduardo Mondlane.

Spiertz, H. L. J. (1991) "The Transformation of Traditional Law: a Tale of People's Participation in Irrigation Management on Bali", *Landscape and Urban Planning* 20 (1–3): 189–96.

Tan, C. (2011) *Governance through Development: Poverty Reduction Strategies, International Law and the Disciplining of Third World States*, Abingdon: Routledge.

Taylor, T. (2002) *The Buried Soul: How Humans Invented Death*, London and New York, NY: Fourth Estate.

Weilenmann, M. (2009) "Project Law – a Power Instrument of Development Agencies: A Case Study from Burundi," in Benda-Beckmann, F. von, K. von Benda-Beckmann and A. Griffiths (eds) *The Power of Law in a Transnational World: Anthropological Enquiries*, New York, NY and Oxford: Berghahn Books.

Weismantel, M. (2005) "White," in Kulick, D. and A. Meneley (eds) *Fat: The Anthropology of an Obsession*, New York, NY: Jeremy P. Tarcher / Penguin.

West, H. G. (2005) *Kupilikula: Governance and the Invisible Realm in Mozambique*, Chicago, IL: The University of Chicago Press.

Zamparoni, V. (2008) "Colonialism and the Creation of Racial Identities in Lourenço Marques, Mozambique," in Sansone, L., E. Soumonni and B. Barry (eds) *Africa, Brazil and the Construction of Trans-Atlantic Black Identities*, Trenton, NJ: Africa World Press.

Žižek, S. (2008) *Violence*, London: Profile Books.

Chapter 4

Sexual violence and gendered subjectivities: indigenous women's search for justice in Guatemala

Rachel Sieder

Introduction

As Anne Hellum and other authors have emphasized, "gender relations are shaped and reshaped in a plural, unsettled and contested terrain where human rights, state law, customary law and local norms coexist and interact in the same social field" (Hellum, Chapter 1 in this volume; see also Griffiths 1997; Hellum et al. 2007; Merry 2006). In this chapter, I attempt to locate the discussion of gender (in)justice and legal pluralities within a broader analysis of regimes of governance, or patterns of rule, that are shaped by history and power, and to consider the effects that emerging forms of interlegality have on relations of inequality and domination.[1] Specifically, I examine the ways in which indigenous women's rights to physical integrity and protection from sexual violence are – or are not – addressed within the state justice system and indigenous community justice in postwar Guatemala.[2] My aim is to explore how such issues are framed in the interplay between these different legal spheres, and by different ontologies or understandings of personhood. As this analysis will show, individual and collective agency is shaped by the diverse and mutually constitutive discourses of rights, entitlement, protection, obligation, responsibility and identity at play in the postwar period.

Contemporary constellations of governance determine the prospects for indigenous women's access to justice and redress in the case of sexual violence. These, in turn, are shaped by the histories and relations of power which have determined the nature of state and non-state justice systems and the relationship between them. In order to analyze the impact of legal pluralities on women's access to justice we cannot simply analyze how women fare within different justice forums or how they "forum shop" between them. Instead we should seek to understand different configurations of interlegality and the forms of personhood they reveal as the consequences of histories of colonialism, racism, discrimination, violence and of different counter-hegemonic actions.

The chapter is structured as follows: first, by way of background, I provide some brief details on gender inequalities and violence in Guatemala, locating

110   Gender Justice and Legal Pluralities

these within the broader context of impunity and past and present human rights violations. I then discuss two key features of the country's complex legal pluralities in the postwar period: first, the advance of rights-based discourses and instruments, including new legislative provisions concerning gender equality and gender violence; and, second, the ambiguous recognition by the state of community-based indigenous law. In the third section I adopt an actor-centered perspective to explore recent transformations in Guatemala's complex legal pluralities, exploring their consequences for women's access to justice in cases of sexual violence. I do this through examination of two specific cases of rape and attempted rape that occurred in the department of Quiché, drawing on ethnographic fieldwork I have carried out in and around the departmental capital of Santa Cruz del Quiché since 2006.[3] In the concluding section I reflect on the dynamics of interlegality in the postwar period, the relation between these and new configurations of governance, and the implications for protection of indigenous women from sexual and physical violence.

Violence, inequality and gender

State formation and patterns of development in Guatemala have been deeply marked by colonialism, racism, economic exploitation and multiple forms of violence. The armed conflict between the insurgent Unidad Revolucionaria Nacional Guatemalteca (URNG) and the Guatemalan state, which dates from 1960 and officially ended in December 1996, left more than 200,000 dead, including approximately 50,000 "detained-disappeared," most of them civilians killed as a result of official counterinsurgency policies (for documented cases, see CEH 2000; REMHI 1998). Significant sectors of the population, particularly indigenous people, rural dwellers and women, suffer acute social, economic, cultural and – until relatively recently – political exclusion.[4] The geographic areas with the highest concentration of indigenous population have some of the worst human development indicators in the country.[5] As has often been observed, indigenous women suffer discrimination not only on the basis of their gender, but also because of their race or ethnicity and class. The historical marginalization of indigenous people has reinforced patterns of discrimination against women, meaning that their access to the means to defend their most basic human rights is severely limited. Overall some 77 percent of all indigenous women in Guatemala are poor (DEMI 2007: 28). Although literacy rates for women have improved since the early 1990s, the government-run Defensoría de la Mujer Indígena (DEMI) in its second report, published in 2007, estimated that 58 percent of indigenous women were illiterate, compared to 38 percent of indigenous men (DEMI 2007: 28). Women in general also occupy more precarious and less well-paid jobs: in 2006, 75.7 percent of all women in Guatemala worked in the informal sector, and 53.4 percent of these earned less than the basic minimum wage (PNUD 2008); these employment and income figures are much worse for indigenous women.

In addition to these forms of structural violence, physical violence is also an everyday reality for the majority of Guatemalans, and especially for the poor. The country has one of the highest homicide rates in Latin America and suffers from extremely high levels of crime and gender-based violence. Impunity is routine and systemic, with those responsible for criminal acts rarely prosecuted. On average more than 5,000 murders are carried out every year, yet typically less than 350 murderers are convicted during the same period.[6] While men – and particularly young men – figure disproportionately amongst the victims of homicide, the increase in violent murders of women during the 2000s led Guatemalan human rights campaigners to talk about "femicide" – women killed because they are women, a term which was subsequently accepted even within official circles. Between 2003 and 2008 there was a 179 percent increase in the number of women dying violent deaths. In total, 720 women were violently killed in 2009, an average of 60 a month or two a day (PDH 2009: 11). Women also suffer many different kinds of gender violence, including physical and psychological abuse (most often from male partners), incest, sexual assault and rape. Intra-familial and sexual violence is notoriously underreported and very few cases ever reach trial. Indigenous women have minimal recourse to justice within the official justice system and are particularly vulnerable to the ethnic discrimination suffered by the indigenous population as a whole. Far more indigenous women than men are monolingual, speaking no Spanish at all, and in many parts of the country they still have extremely limited access to state justice services in their own languages.[7] Even if they do speak Spanish, they invariably lack the economic means and the support of family, friends or non-governmental organizations (NGOs) or civic society associations that would enable them to pursue their claims before the courts.[8] Taking a complaint to state prosecution services or to court invariably requires multiple trips to the nearest municipal center, involving time away from families and the expense of travel. Progress is notoriously slow and successful outcomes very far from guaranteed. Even when women do secure a judgment in their favor, for example ordering their former partners to pay child maintenance, based on my observations state authorities make little or no efforts to ensure compliance.

Systematic discrimination and the inability of the state to provide justice and security for the majority of the population have generated complex legal pluralities, with indigenous people relying on their own "customary" or "traditional" forms of community authority. Before independence in the early nineteenth century, indigenous customary law formed part of the bifurcated structure of colonial administration (Hessbruegge and Ochoa García 2011: 80). Following the end of colonial rule indigenous custom was both tolerated and repressed by the non-indigenous state authorities. After the liberal revolution of 1871, the dominant state ideology was one of formal legal equality. In practice, however, indigenous people continued to look to their own alternative legal order to regulate most aspects of daily life, although they were subject to the national penal system in the case of serious crimes. They were also subject to national laws that mandated their forced labor in the agroexport coffee sector, such as the Ley de Vagancia or vagrancy law, which required indigenous people to work for wages for a given number of days a year or be sentenced to labor on the plantations or public works (Hessbruegge and Ochoa García 2011: 81; McCreery 1996). Such exploitative rural relations were challenged during the reformist administrations of Juan José Arevalo (1944–51) and Jacobo Árbenz Guzmán (1951–4), which abolished the vagrancy law and introduced a labor code and a radical program of agrarian reform. However, the democratically elected Árbenz government was overthrown in 1954 in a US-backed coup aimed at protecting the interests of the rural elites and US companies. Efforts to integrate the rural indigenous population into national constructions of citizenship were effectively curtailed, and in practice the bifurcated, racialized system of law and governance continued to operate throughout the countryside: local indigenous self-governance was tolerated to the extent it did not challenge the economic logics of the plantation system. During the armed conflict in the 1980s, indigenous systems of authority were severely disrupted; many community authorities were the direct targets of government repression and highly militarized forms of "law and order" were imposed in indigenous settlements in the rural areas as part of the military's counterinsurgency strategies against the guerrilla. Civilian "military commissioners" were appointed by the army to maintain surveillance and order within villages, and all men between the ages of 16 and 60 forced to take part in paramilitary civil patrols (CEH 2000; REMHI 1998).

Since the early 1990s indigenous community justice practices have been revitalized as part of wider national claims by the indigenous movement for autonomy rights. At the same time, common crime has increased since the end of the armed conflict, posing tough challenges for indigenous authorities and generating new, more violent, forms of "self-help justice," such as vigilante killings and lynchings of suspected criminals that have become a common occurrence (MINUGUA 2002; Snodgrass Godoy 2006). Recent literature on Latin America and beyond has pointed to the dynamic interplay between multiple forms of legality and illegality in the constitution of regimes of governance (Arias and Goldstein 2010; Comaroff and Comaroff 2006, 2009; Goldstein 2004; Goodale 2008; Poole 2004). Many of these authors argue that supposedly "peripheral" para-legal phenomena, such as manifestations of community justice or vigilantism, should not be seen as somehow external to official legality but rather as constitutive of hegemonic and highly racialized and stratified systems of governance. Within these fragmented configurations of governance and legality, transnationalized discourses of rights and the identity-based tropes and imaginaries of indigenous peoples' community-based forms of law have come to represent alternative conceptions of human dignity and routes to obtain justice.

Rights-based paradigms

Rights discourses, particularly those concerning the collective rights of indigenous peoples but also those referring to women's rights and gender equality, are affecting justice practices in postwar Guatemala in multiple and complex ways. Human rights were at the heart of indigenous social movements' organizing during the late 1980s and 1990s; notable examples include CONAVIGUA (The National Coordination of Guatemalan Widows), which was formed by indigenous widows in Quiché during the late 1980s to seek justice for those killed or disappeared, and the organization CERJ, Comunidades Etnicas Runujel Junam, that also originated in Quiché and which organized throughout the highlands in the late 1980s and 1990s to protest against the forced recruitment of indigenous men into the paramilitary civil patrols (Brett 2008). As part of the pan-Mayan movement that emerged during the peace negotiations, a multiplicity of indigenous organizations throughout the country have continued to demand guarantees for the collective rights of indigenous peoples *and* for individual human rights, including, increasingly, gender rights. This is in large part due to the increased participation of Mayan women in social and political organizing.

The peace accords aimed to guarantee fundamental human rights for all Guatemalans and also set out a charter for addressing the historic marginalization of the indigenous population, and particularly of indigenous women. The Agreement on the Identity and Rights of Indigenous Peoples (1995) established specific commitments to protect and promote women's political and social participation within broader guarantees to respect indigenous peoples' collective rights to greater autonomy. The Agreement on Socioeconomic Aspects and the Agrarian Situation (1996) also committed the government to promote gender equity and indigenous women's economic participation. Transnationalized discourses of human rights permeated every aspect of the peace settlement and profoundly shaped its implementation. This was in part because of the rights-based approaches of many of the national and international intergovernmental and nongovernmental organizations involved in "post-conflict" peace-building and development and Guatemala's high degree of dependence on external development cooperation. Issues of gender violence and gender justice have become a key area of concern for development efforts in the postwar period. Guatemala has ratified the UN Convention on the Elimination of all forms of Discrimination against Women (CEDAW). It was also one of the first countries to ratify the 1994 Inter-American Convention to Prevent, Sanction and Eradicate Violence against Women, known as the Belem do Pará Convention, which was approved by the Guatemalan congress in 1995. As a direct consequence of this ratification, a national Law to Prevent, Sanction and Eradicate Intra-Familial Violence was passed.

Various initiatives have emerged aimed at increasing women's participation and reducing violence against them, including the Coordination for the Prevention and Eradication of Intra-familiar Violence and Violence against Women (Coordinadora Nacional para la Prevención y Erradicación de la Violencia Intrafamiliar y contra las Mujeres, CONAPREVI), a collaboration between civil society organizations and government, and the Network for Survivors of Violence (Fundación Red de Sobrevivientes de la Violencia). The peace accords led to the setting up of the Office for the Defence of Indigenous Women (Defensoria de la Mujer Indigena, DEMI) that was intended specifically to address the discrimination and marginalization faced by indigenous women and improve their access to justice. DEMI has offices throughout the country and is staffed by indigenous women professionals, including lawyers and social workers, although it remains so underfunded that it is often unable to pay their salaries. The most common cases it deals with are those of interfamilial violence and claims for child support, and despite its limited budget its caseload has increased every year since it was established. In addition, international development agencies have run campaigns to try to raise public awareness about discrimination and violence against women. For example, in 2008 UN General Secretary Ban Ki-moon launched the international campaign "Sign up to put an end to violence against women" in Guatemala, chosen for the launch because of its appalling record of violence against women.[9] In a local manifestation of such efforts, in 2010 various Spanish governmental and non-governmental agencies paid for billboards and stickers placed in the motorcycle-taxis in Santa Cruz del Quiché, which stated "in Quiché we respect all women" (see Figure 4.1).

The ambiguous recognition of non-state indigenous law

The legal status of non-state forms of justice in Guatemala became a matter of national political debate during the peace negotiations. The 1995 Agreement on Indigenous Identity and Rights, signed by the government and the URNG, committed the state to reforming the 1985 constitution in order to formally recognize indigenous peoples' rights to exercise their own forms of law. However, the promise to constitutionalize indigenous justice was frustrated in March 1999, when a package of constitutional reforms, including a clause to recognize the rights of indigenous people to exercise their own forms of "customary law" (derecho consuetudinario), was rejected in a popular referendum. Fears had been stoked up by right wing elite opponents of the reforms. Motivated by fears of future indigenous land claims, they ran a highly effective media campaign against the constitutionalization of

Figure 4.1 Billboard at the entrance to Santa Cruz de Quiché, 2010. The caption reads "In Quiché we respect all women." (photo: Rachel Sieder)

collective rights for indigenous peoples, warning that Guatemala would be "Balkanized" if the amendments were passed. They alleged that the recognition of "customary law" would lead to one law for indigenous people and another for the rest, contravening the principle of equality of all citizens before the law and even leading to "reverse racism" against non-indigenous people (Warren 2003). Guatemala eventually ratified International Labor Organization Convention 169 in 1996, which states that indigenous peoples have the right to administer their own forms of justice, as long as these respect fundamental and internationally recognized human rights,[10] and that state parties to the Convention must respect the decisions reached by indigenous peoples in their specific forms of justice (in all fields of law – civil, criminal, family, labor, etc.).[11] During the last two decades indigenous social movements have consistently argued for greater official recognition of indigenous peoples' exercise of their own forms of justice as part of a strategy to secure greater autonomy. As a consequence of this pressure, and the actions of international agencies, donors and NGOs, the justice practices of Guatemala's indigenous communities have increasingly been recognized as part of the republic's political and legal order. However, the legal status of indigenous justice practices continues to be highly ambiguous. Indigenous peoples' right to exercise their own forms of justice is not explicitly protected in the constitution, nor have any secondary laws been passed stipulating jurisdictional competences of state and indigenous law (*leyes de coordinación*). This means that indigenous justice practices effectively occupy a space somewhere "threat and guarantee" (Poole 2004), partially endorsed by a state that pays lip service to the idea of multicultural government, but is potentially subject to charges of illegality when they are exercised. As a consequence indigenous authorities are often reluctant to get involved with serious crimes, fearing that they will be prosecuted for usurpation of state functions.

This process of partial and ambiguous multicultural recognition has prompted transformations in the nature of indigenous community justice itself.[12] Indigenous activists throughout the country have worked to strengthen different structures of non-state indigenous authority. Through these processes, they have reframed a huge diversity of local customs, norms and practices into a pan-Mayan construction of law (referred to as "Mayan law"), a legal order based on specific forms of communal and supra-communal authority, procedures, and ethical and moral principles rooted in ideas of collective identity based on cultural specificity and ethnic difference (Sieder 2011). The circulation of such legal and political imaginaries has affected the ways in which indigenous people frame their claims and complaints and is a factor influencing the practices of indigenous communal authorities throughout the country. In particular, efforts to inculcate particular forms of behavior by appealing to notions of collective responsibility and morality combined with demands that the government respect indigenous people's individual and collective human rights, have produced innovative forms of legality and opened new possibilities for addressing gender discrimination within community-based forms of law. For example, in Santa Cruz del Quiché some villages have worked together with local non-governmental indigenous defense organizations (*defensorías indígenas*) to draw up "*reglamentos comunitarios.*" These are written documents that aim to "codify" community norms, setting down certain requirements of villagers and their authorities, referring to all aspects of community life. For example, the *reglamento* of the village of Xatinap, in a section referring to "family, social and neighbourly norms," includes clauses stating that:

> [r]espect should be maintained within a couple to avoid problems of family breakdown ... Community authorities should provide orientation to families in order to avoid jealousies, harassment, rape and sexual abuse ... In any cases of violence (physical, psychological, sexual, economic and political) within the family, the communal indigenous authorities should sanction this in accordance with communal norms, also taking into account the national laws applying to these matters.[13]

These documents do not necessarily reflect practice on the ground. Nonetheless, such examples of the codification and reframing of custom within the broader context of efforts to strengthen indigenous autonomy and political participation at least holds out the promise that women's rights to participation, dignity, protection and physical integrity will be protected.

Addressing sexual violence within complex legal pluralities

Sexual violence against indigenous women is perpetrated by members of their families and communities and also by state officials and non-indigenous men, involving different scales of power and gendered and racialized inequalities. In theory rape is severely sanctioned within both state penal law and indigenous communal justice, yet in practice sexual violence against indigenous women is particularly ill-attended to within both the state justice system and indigenous community justice (ASIES/OACNUDH 2008). Precisely because it is such a social taboo, it is extremely hard for victims to denounce. Women who have been raped are socially stigmatized and feel enormous shame. A high value is put on virginity in indigenous communities and unmarried women known to have been raped are unlikely to be able to marry. Indeed, settlement of such cases within indigenous law may involve either the marriage of the victim and the man accused of her rape, or the payment of a significant financial sum in compensation. This can be explained in part because what constitutes consensual or non-consensual sex is a grey area: given the taboos against sex outside marriage, rape may be alleged by girls or their families, particularly if sex before marriage has resulted in pregnancy. In such cases indigenous authorities may bring pressure to bear on the boy's family to ensure that a marriage takes place. In more clear-cut cases, indigenous authorities often suggest a financial payment by the aggressor as compensation to the woman and her family. The logic behind such payments is for women to have some economic means to support themselves as the shame and stigma associated with rape make it unlikely they will be able to marry in the future. Married women who denounce rape often face rejection and even violence from their husbands and families (ECAP-UNAMG 2009). Prevailing social attitudes are also shaped by broader historical legacies and the ways in which sexual violence has been embedded in particular economic and political regimes. Before the armed conflict sexual violence was used by non-indigenous plantation administrators and owners as a tool of ethnic and class domination within the system of agro-export production (Casaús Arzú 2007). During the years of the counterinsurgency the sustained and systematic rape and sexual torture of women and girl children by military and paramilitary forces was used as part of the campaign of terror against the civilian population accused of supporting the guerrilla (REMHI 1998; CEH 2000; ECAP-UNAMG 2009; Consorcio Actoras de Cambio 2006). Quiché, which is over 90 percent Maya K'iche', was one of the areas most affected. The UN Historical Clarification Commission documented 626 massacres in the department, and confirmed that acts of genocide had been carried out by government forces against the indigenous population. According to one study, nearly 50 percent of the cases of sexual violation documented in 16 of Guatemala's 22

118 Gender Justice and Legal Pluralities

departments by the UN Historical Clarification Commission occurred in Quiché (Consorcio Actoras de Cambio 2006: 5).[14] Yet despite the truth commissions carried out following the peace settlement to document human rights violations perpetrated during the armed conflict, sexual violence was notoriously underreported and its discussion has been extremely difficult.[15] As well as suffering the physical and psychological consequences of sexual violence, women raped during the armed conflict were sometimes ostracized within their communities and condemned as "soldiers' whores" (Consorcio Actoras de Cambio 2006; ECAP-UNAMG 2009). Sexual violence against indigenous girls and women who migrate to work as domestic servants in the homes of middle and upper class *ladinos* is also common practice, again underlining the class and racial dimensions of gender violence.[16] The individual shame of women victims and the collective shame suffered by communities for failing to protect women from sexual violence have profound consequences for addressing such violations in the present.

In the following section I examine two cases: the first concerns the rape of a k'iche woman by members of the national police force that turned into a test case within the official state justice system; the second involves the attempted rape of a young indigenous girl by a member of her community, and efforts to deal with this via "Mayan" or community-based forms of law. Through discussion of these cases I aim to show how and where women seek redress for extreme examples of gender violence in a context of complex legal plurality or interlegality. I also analyze the negotiation of gender roles within these processes of seeking justice and redress, and the understandings of self and gendered personhood that are constructed through them. As the two cases discussed here illustrate, denouncing rape involves not only confronting state power, but also intimate negotiations within families and communities. It also means confronting the limitations of language itself; as Fiona Ross has observed: "[s]ome things simply cannot be articulated within the sanctioned languages and social spaces currently available to experience" (Ross 2010: 86). Both cases here point to changing discursive possibilities for denouncing sexual violence, but also underline the myriad complexities of such denunciations.

"Todos somos Juana Méndez"

In December 2004 Juana Méndez Rodríguez, an illiterate, monolingual 44-year-old k'iche' woman, the mother of 11 children from a village in the municipality of Uspantán, Quiché, was detained in connection with alleged cultivation of marihuana near her home. Initially taken into police custody (without a judicial order) and transferred to the southern city of Chimaltenango, in January 2005 she was moved back to Quiché to the police station in the northern town of Nebaj. After she arrived at the station she was handcuffed to the bars in a cell, then during the night was subjected to insults and verbal abuse and then raped by two inebriated police officers. The men subsequently forced her to bathe in an attempt to destroy any evidence of the assault. The following day, Juana was interviewed, with the aid of an interpreter, by the public defense lawyer assigned to her case, Hernán Villatoro. Villatoro had been alerted to Juana's ordeal by a homeless woman who slept outside the police station who he was acquainted with. After he managed to convince Juana that he was there to help, she broke down and, through an interpreter, told him what had happened. Villatoro lodged a complaint at the local office of the governmental human rights ombudsman (Procuraduría de Derechos Humanos, PDH) and another with the Office of Professional Responsibility of the police force, the body charged with internal police oversight. He also alerted the judge assigned to Juana's case. On 18 January, when the judge finally arrived to take her declaration, he recommended she undergo a medical examination, which was carried out in Nebaj.

On the basis of Juana's declaration, the human rights ombudsman's office opened a case file, and the Office of Professional Responsibility of the police began an internal investigation into the conduct of six police officers present in the station on that night. However, after months neither of these processes had moved forward. Juana's case was then adopted by the Guatemalan Institute of Comparative Penal Studies (ICCPG), an NGO based in Guatemala City that monitors human rights violations in the justice system.[17] The ICCPG wanted to use it as an instance of strategic litigation in an attempt to bring attention to the all-too-common practice of sexual abuse against women detainees in police custody and the country's prisons.[18] The ICCPG legally represented Juana Méndez in the internal police complaints hearing, which was finally held in May 2006, some 18 months after the initial complaint was made. During the public hearing, Juana identified two of the six policemen under investigation as the material authors of the rape. Members of the ICCPG managed to establish that significant evidence had been falsified and destroyed in the internal police investigation. It was also established that a key witness, the homeless woman who had alerted the public defender to Juana's rape, had been killed before the case went to trial.

In the end, in large measure because of the ICCPG's efforts to gather evidence and testimony, the internal police tribunal found two of the policemen guilty of torture and cruel and inhumane treatment against detainees in their care. It also ordered that disciplinary action be taken against the commanding police officer in Nebaj and the police investigator for obstructing the course of justice. Despite the severity of the crime of rape – which carries a minimum statutory jail sentence of between six and 12 years – the public prosecutor's office in Nebaj had refused to initiate criminal proceedings against the police officers, alleging there was not enough evidence to press charges. Members of the ICCPG ensured that the crucial testimony of one of the policemen was subsequently taken by the public prosecutor's office in

Santa Cruz del Quiché. The officer, Lázaro Dubón Cano, had been in charge of the prisoners on the night that Juana was raped and had in fact witnessed the assault on her by the two officers, who had threatened to kill him and his family if he said anything. His statement, together with the administrative judgment of the police complaints tribunal, ensured that criminal proceedings against the two officers, Antonio Rutilo López Matías and Nery Osberto Aldana Rodríguez, were initiated. However, both men absconded after orders for their detention were issued. Members of the governmental human rights ombudsman's office (PDH) in Nebaj received death threats when they tried to pursue the case, as did members of the local public prosecutor's office.

Following a tip-off in February 2007, the ICCPG alerted the public prosecutor's office in Nebaj as to the whereabouts of Antonio Rutilo López Matías. He was subsequently arrested. Responsibility for the criminal case was transferred to a different public prosecutor's office in Guatemala City, in large part because the prosecutor in Nebaj was unwilling or afraid to continue with the prosecution. The ICCPG worked with Juana to reconstruct the scene of the crime and the events on the night she was assaulted. They requested protective measures from the Inter-American Court of Human Rights for Lázaro Dubón, the key witness for the prosecution, and kept in close contact with him to ensure that he would give his testimony in court. They also engaged an expert forensic witness to testify to the inconsistencies in the medical reports presented, and presented two separate psychological reports that confirmed the effect on Juana Méndez of the rape and the subsequent death threats she received. In April 2008, some three years after the rape occurred, Antonio Rutilo Matías López was sentenced to 20 years in prison.[19] The second policeman, Nery Osberto Aldana Rodríguez, remains a fugitive from justice.

Despite her immense suffering, Juana was clear in her determination to pursue justice.

> Everything I said was true, I never lied. I wasn't afraid because I searched in my heart and I said "it's true, everything they did to me." I'll find the courage within me to stop this man, so that he never ever does the same thing to another woman, because I suffered a great fright (*susto*) and that harmed me.[20]

Critically, Juana was supported in her efforts to secure justice by both her husband and her children. Without their backing for her actions it is unlikely that her case would ever have gone to court. The ICCPG helped to find a k'iche' woman interpreter, Delfina, experienced in working with women survivors of domestic violence. She accompanied Juana throughout the police disciplinary hearings and the subsequent criminal trial. In her declarations, Delfina reframed Juana's rape as an act of discrimination against women.

> What I want to say to the police is that they should respect women more, because they were borne of a woman. They should respect women and not discriminate against them. The time of discrimination is over ... If they really want to work for the government then they should try and help people, not do them harm. That's what I'd say to the police: if they discriminate against a woman it's as if they were lacking respect towards their own mothers.[21]

The ICCPG also helped to provide Juana with psychosocial accompaniment. Juana Marta Tojín, a k'iche' woman working in a local civic organization in Santa Cruz del Quiché that provides psychological support for victims of the armed conflict, was able to build up a relationship with Juana over many months. This accompaniment, aimed at rebuilding her strength and health, involved working with the community, and therapies based on Mayan cosmovision and spirituality involving the refocusing of energy and the use of medicinal plants. With Juana Marta's support, Juana was able to overcome her depression, tell her children what had happened to her and get through the trial. This support also enabled the taboo subject of rape to be represented within Juana's community as a "violation of her rights":

> because you can't talk about rape, its not well looked upon, so that's how we talked about it [as a violation of rights] and we worked with [Juana] and she accepted this, she even called the people to a meeting and we worked with the [community] leaders. So it's been very useful, at first she was very scared that they'd find out, but now there is community support [for her].[22]

The ICCPG, together with other civil society organizations, was also instrumental in building a support network to accompany the legal process. The women's defender in the governmental human rights ombudsman's office in Santa Cruz del Quiché, Aída López Cordero, was a key figure in bringing together women's organizations in the region to support Juana throughout the trial. As López Cordero observed, many women suffer sexual assault, but even if they gather up the courage to make an initial complaint, very few ever continue to a criminal trial (cited in Gaviola Artigas 2008: 78; ASIES/OACNUDH 2008). The day before the trial, members of various women's groups converged on Santa Cruz del Quiché and more than a hundred women marched through the town carrying banners calling for justice in Juana's case and in all cases of sexual violence: one placard read "When one woman is raped all women are raped." K'iche' women and men from many different local organizations were present during the hearing, and Mayan

122 Gender Justice and Legal Pluralities

ceremonies were carried out in the central park of Santa Cruz, in front of the court. During the ceremonies different spiritual leaders invoked collective accompaniment for Juana, as well as referring to the history of rape and impunity that characterized the region during the armed conflict as an aggression against all indigenous people.

Juana Méndez's case is important and unusual for a number of reasons. First, because Juana herself was determined to secure justice and continued with the trial, something most victims of sexual violence do not do. Second, it was only possible to secure a successful conviction because of the support and resources provided by the ICCPG, the human rights NGO that adopted her case. Without their involvement, which secured crucial evidence, it is unlikely a conviction would ever have been secured, or even that a criminal trial would have taken place. Third, the support of Juana's husband and extended family was critical; families play a fundamental role in determining whether sexual violence is denounced or not. If the family had wished to silence the abuse, fearing the shame and social sanction it would bring, then Juana would have had either to drop her pursuit of justice or pay the extremely high cost of separating from her family and quite possibly leaving her community. Fourth, and crucially, the different forms of accompaniment Juana benefited from during her pursuit of justice allowed the rape to be framed in the language of rights and rights violations. This reframing took place within a broader context of human rights organizing, and against the memory of massive human rights violations, including rape, which had occurred during the armed conflict. The slogan used during the campaign – "todos somos Juana Méndez" (*we are all Juana Méndez*) – alluded both to the collective experience of sexual violence during the armed conflict, but also to the violence and impunity most Guatemalans continue to suffer at the hands of state officials. In this sense it underlined collective understandings of personhood shaped by racialized histories of discrimination.

The attempted rape of Marta Cecilia[23]

In September 2006, members of the indigenous defense organization Defensoría K'iche' gathered in a family house in a village some seven kilometers from Santa Cruz del Quiché. The Defensoría K'iche' is an organization of local Mayan rights activists that was set up after the end of the armed conflict to provide conciliation services and legal accompaniment to the population of Santa Cruz del Quiché.[24] It also works with indigenous community authorities to try to strengthen the effectiveness and legitimacy of "Mayan law." The Defensoría's discourses and practices are informed by an ethos of human rights and the collective rights of indigenous peoples. Issues of women's rights and violence are frequently addressed within their leadership training programs for men and women and their popular

Todos y todas somos portadores de derechos y obligaciones. Su aplicación depende de su conocimiento, de oportunidades y decisión de ejercerlos.

Figure 4.2 "We all have rights and obligations. Their application depends on knowledge of them, opportunities and the decision to exercise them." Defensoría K'iche' (2010: 44).

educational materials (see Figure 4.2), including radio spots for local community radio in K'iche' and Spanish, emphasize women's rights to live without violence.[25]

The delegation from the Defensoría had traveled to the village to attempt to mediate a delicate case. Mariana, a K'iche' woman in her late twenties, had accused Miguel, a neighbor, of having attempted to rape her nine-year-old daughter, Marta Cecilia, some three months earlier. Miguel had been accused of attempting to sexually abuse other women in the village on previous occasions when under the influence of alcohol. Following the incident involving Marta Cecilia, Mariana had tried to pursue the matter with the village authorities, but they had failed to take any effective action against him. She subsequently took the unusual step of making a formal complaint at the public prosecutor's office in Santa Cruz and took her daughter for a medical examination, which had confirmed that the attempted rape had not been consummated. The case was languishing in the formal justice system and Mariana had gone to the offices of the Defensoría K'iche' to try to seek some form of redress.

Members of Mariana's extended family were present at the mediation, as were Miguel's brother and mother. Juan Zapeta, a respected local leader and member of the Defensoría, explained the reason for their presence to Miguel.[26]

> We've come to talk to you because of what happened with the girl, with [Mariana's] daughter. She came to our office because of what happened, and it seems that since then things have gotten worse. But we've discussed it, [we know that] it's better to talk with you, to have a dialogue, to agree amongst ourselves and not make the problem any bigger than it is. There's no need to go to judges; that could bring more problems. That's why we're here.

Mariana related how she had witnessed the attack, which had allegedly happened when Miguel and the girl had gone to chase after some cows which had wandered off into a neighbor's corn plot. She accused Miguel of having led Marta Cecilia into the woods and forcing her to the ground under a tree: "[Y]ou terrified her; she's pale now, totally pale. I can only imagine what you were going to do to her. She told me."

Miguel initially denied any responsibility, but Mariana said she would only have called on Juan Zapeta for help if this was a "serious offence," telling him: "[Y]ou should be thankful that when we found out about this we didn't give you a beating, but we're not used to doing things like that."

The atmosphere in the house was one of great tension and sorrow. Deliberations about what had happened on the day of the alleged attempted rape went on well into the night. Mariana's brother-in-law appealed to Miguel, invoking notions of religious and moral obligation and the importance of respect for women's dignity.

> What you did was wrong. Think about God – what you did was a sin. Maybe we wouldn't have realized, but before God it's not that easy. Before God we all have to respect each other, we should respect people – you should respect young women, like Don Juan [Zapeta] is telling you. I implore you not to do this again.

Juan kept on questioning Miguel, asking him if it was certain he had intended to rape the young girl. Eventually Miguel, visibly upset, admitted "the truth is … it just came into my head, suddenly I thought 'my God what I'm doing is wrong.' I didn't do anything to the girl, but if I hadn't changed my mind who only knows what I would have done to her. Maybe she would have died there."

Juan insisted:

> "Is it true? Did you want to abuse her? Did you think about doing that?"
> "Yes I did."
> "There it is."
> "But I didn't harm her."

Miguel's confession was greeted with relief, especially by Juan: "It's true; this is good, isn't it? Don't you feel a great relief? I feel a great relief when he accepts his guilt. If he doesn't accept his guilt it causes a huge pain in our hearts."

All the family members were in tears by this point. Miguel's brother expressed his outrage, emphasizing the shame caused to his family by Miguel's behavior.

> How could you do this? You should control yourself. How could you try and do that to a girl? They're women. This is a matter of great shame. Can't you see how much shame you're causing our mother? She's sick; she has pains in her heart.

The delegation from the Defensoría offered Miguel and the family members present the choice of whether they wanted to resolve the problem "here, amongst us Mayas," or to continue to judicial proceedings in the state justice system. After a lengthy discussion, the family members called for Miguel to be "corrected" through the application of *x'ik'ay*. These are ritual beatings with thin branches of the quince tree. Traditionally they were applied within k'iche' families or communities by parents or elders in order to "correct" those who had committed a wrong. In recent years they have been refunctionalized by some indigenous leaders in the Santa Cruz area, who argue that they are an important part of "Mayan law" and an essential means to correct people's energies.[27] Miguel's brother called on Juan Zapeta to administer the *x'ik'ay*: "What can we do with him? We can't correct him. We've talked to him so many times."

Mariana had initially sought justice from her village authorities for the attack against her daughter, but they had failed to take any effective action against Miguel. Her recourse to the state justice authorities raised the threat that he would be punished with a trial and imprisonment, even though the likelihood of this occurring in practice was minimal. The fact that Mariana had engaged in such extra-communal "naming and shaming" was in fact a consequence of her own experience of abuse. In many senses, "everyday" or "routine" domestic violence is normalized and taken for granted: cases where men beat their wives only tend to be brought to the attention of communal or state authorities when these are severe, sustained and life-threatening. In Mariana's case the brutal campaign of physical abuse by her husband had led to repeated interventions by her family and communal authorities. These ultimately failed to halt the violence and she eventually left the marital home and returned to live with her own family. Family support is crucial in enabling indigenous women to confront domestic violence; if families maintain that women should stay with their husbands then in practice it is extremely difficult for them to leave.

Mariana and her immediate family had rejected her status as a victim and she was determined to denounce Miguel's attack against her daughter and secure some kind of sanction or reparation. In their interventions members of the Defensoría emphasized the great suffering of Mariana and her daughter and the multiple indignities they had endured. They appealed to the family to resolve matters *"amongst us Maya"* and not to pursue the matter through the state justice system. Their mediations emphasized the importance of confession, acceptance of responsibility, and reparations or correction through the application of *x'ik'ay*.

The existence of such indigenous defense organizations in Santa Cruz del Quiché means that k'iche' women can denounce sexual violence in an environment where indigenous peoples' rights and identity are defended. The human and gender rights discourses enunciated by these organizations are framed in a language of collective Maya k'iche' identity and women's dignity. The fact that respected local indigenous leaders intervene to defend women and condemn violence against them is slowly changing the parameters of socially accepted behavior. In this case the village authorities were greatly ashamed at not having done more to protect Mariana from her husband's violence. Yet they were also unable to take effective action against Miguel, perhaps fearing reprisals from state authorities or from Miguel himself if they intervened. Even the mediation by the Defensoría did not secure lasting change. Miguel was subsequently involved in another alleged rape, this time of a slightly older girl who had accepted a ride home on his motorbike. Opinion within the village was divided, revealing the complex apportioning of guilt in cases of sexual violence: some favored banishing Miguel from the village for good; others insinuated that the girl bore some share of the responsibility. Members of the Defensoría were frustrated at their inability to prevent Miguel's recidivism, but predicted that he would eventually be banished from the village, so egregious was his behavior.

Conclusions

I have suggested here that the complex forms of legal plurality and inter-legality that have developed in the postwar period in Guatemala have slowly improved the possibilities that indigenous women have to denounce sexual violence. The circulation of different discourses of human rights and gender rights has named gender violence as a wrong, even though rape and sexual violence remains an extremely difficult subject for women to discuss within their families and communities.

New state institutions and laws have been established to address issues of gender violence. However, poverty and lack of linguistic access to state justice institutions, combined with shame and fear of repercussions mean that intra-familial violence, sexual violence and violence against women in general is greatly underreported. The impunity that prevails in the official justice system means that Mayan social movements have come to play an important role in the day-to-day provision of justice. The work of these indigenous social movements to reshape, "recover" and revitalize "Mayan law" has had an impact – albeit slow and far from uniform – on the exercise of community justice. The initiatives of such indigenous social movements – and most importantly of organized indigenous women throughout the country – are slowly generating new ideas about women's rights, specifically emphasizing their rights to freedom from violence and for their dignity to be respected. These ideas are linked to emerging ideas about collective "Mayan" personhood which stress that respect and protection for women is intrinsic to indigenous identity. However, the ambiguous and limited recognition of indigenous law by the Guatemalan state means that community authorities are often unwilling to intervene in serious cases. The fact that the vast majority of indigenous communal authorities are men also inhibits more effective treatment of sexual violence.

In both of the cases examined here, pro-rights organizations opened new spaces for "naming, blaming and claiming" (Felstiner et al. 1981) and for the circulation of discourses about rights, obligations, protection, entitlement and, ultimately, gendered personhood. The IGGCP's intervention ensured that Juana's rape while in police detention was addressed by the official justice system. And the mediation by the Defensoría K'iche' provided some measure of collective sanction against Marta Cecilia's attacker within "Mayan law." Without the intervention of these organizations it is unlikely that any kind of resolution would have been secured. In both cases, notions about justice in the present were elaborated with reference to past injustices and violence – towards indigenous peoples within Guatemala's colonial and post-colonial past, towards indigenous women during the armed conflict, and towards Mariana as a victim of domestic abuse. In short, all efforts to improve indigenous women's access to justice are a product of the historical constellations of racialized and gendered governance within which they are located. Transnational rights discourses of liberal personhood have had a significant and positive impact, but so too have the more collective understandings of self at play in efforts to strengthen "Mayan" forms of authority and law.

Indigenous women in Guatemala continue to suffer unacceptably high levels of structural and physical violence. Gender discrimination is deep-seated and accepted patterns that undervalue and marginalize women are difficult to change within both state and non-state justice. Interlegal

128 Gender Justice and Legal Pluralities

configurations involving new framings of personhood, rights and dignity are potentially important elements in any attempts to secure greater gender justice. However, these continue to coexist with the violence and fragmentation of contemporary state forms that also characterize legal pluralities, and it is these that ultimately constrain their emancipatory potential.

Acknowledgements

I would like to extend my thanks to Bjørn Enge Bertelsen, María Teresa Sierra, Natalia De Marinis and Morna Macleod for their detailed comments on a previous draft of this chapter. I am also grateful to all the participants in the workshop that took place in Mozambique in February 2010 for their feedback on a preliminary version of this chapter.

Notes

1 In his analysis of legal pluralities, de Sousa Santos proposed the concept of "interlegality," emphasizing notions of fluid, hybrid legalities and the importance of human agency in negotiating, reinterpreting and deploying legal ideas such as rights (de Sousa Santos 1987, 2002; see also Merry 2006).
2 It goes without saying that physical and sexual violence against women should be analyzed within the broader social context within which they occur. Indigenous women's organizations have insisted on the need for an intersectional approach to analyzing violence against indigenous women (see FIMI 2006; Sieder and Sierra 2010).
3 In common with other highland departments, Quiché suffers from acute problems of social exclusion: 85 percent of the population is poor and some 33 percent live below the poverty line (ASIES/OACNUDH, 2008: 21, citing 2002 data from the National Institute of Statistics and 2005 data from the UN Human Development Report). Some 53 percent of indigenous women in Quiché are monolingual K'iche' speakers and 32 percent are bilingual, speaking both K'iche' and Spanish (DEMI 2007: 29–30).
4 According to the 2002 census, 4.4 million – or around 40 percent of Guatemala's then-population of 11.2 million – people were Mayan, but this is generally regarded as a low estimate. Of this 4.4 million, 81 percent belonged to four main ethno-lingustic groups: K'iche', Q'eqchi', Kaqchikel and Mam. Other ethnolinguistic Mayan groups include: Q'anjobal, Poqomchi', Achi', Ixil, Tz'utujil, Chuj, Akateko, Awakateko, Ch'orti', Jakalteko (Popti'), Poqomam, Sikapakense, Itza', Mopan, Sakapulteco, Tektiteko and Uspanteko. The non-Mayan ethnolinguistic groups are Garifuna, Xinca and the majority Spanish-speaking population (PNUD 2005: 64–5).
5 UNDP figures indicate that 50.9 percent of the population of Guatemala lives in poverty – 73 percent of all the indigenous population and 35 percent of the non-indigenous population. Some 26.4 percent of the indigenous population lives in extreme poverty, unable to satisfy basic necessities, compared to 7.3 percent of the non-indigenous population. Poverty is worse in rural areas, with 74.5 percent of the rural population living in poverty and 24.4 percent in extreme poverty, compared to 27 percent of the urban population living in poverty and five percent in extreme poverty (PNUD 2008). Guatemala ranks 131 out of 187 countries in the UN Human Development Index.

6 Guatemala has one of the highest rates of violent crime in Latin America, with around 40 murders a week in Guatemala City and a total of nearly 100 per week in the whole country. The total population in 2010 was 14.3 million (World Bank 2011).

7 More indigenous women are monolingual than indigenous men: some 50 percent of indigenous women over 50, 40 percent of indigenous women between the ages of 31 and 50, 33 percent of indigenous women between 16 and 30 years of age, and 40 percent of indigenous women under 15 are monolingual. Percentages are significantly higher for indigenous women living in rural areas (PNUD 2005).

8 The most common reason indigenous women resort to the police and other institutions of the justice system is intra-familial violence. Of 147 cases of intra-familial violence processed by the courts in Quiché in 2004, in 136 cases the victims were women, and in 119 cases indigenous; in 2005 of 226 reported cases of intra-familial violence, 149 involved indigenous women (DEMI 2007: 35–6).

9 This campaign, which ran from 2008 to 2015, called on governments, the private sector, civil society and the media to work together to prevent and eliminate violence against women and girls.

10 Article 8: "In applying national laws and regulations to the peoples concerned, due regard shall be had to their customs or customary law. These peoples shall have the right to retain their own customs and institutions, where these are not incompatible with fundamental rights defined by the national legal system and with internationally recognized human rights. Procedures shall be established, wherever necessary, to resolve conflicts which may arise in the application of this principle."

11 Article 9: "To the extent compatible with the national legal system and internationally recognized human rights, the methods customarily practiced by the peoples concerned for dealing with offences committed by their members shall be respected. The customs of these peoples in regard to penal matters shall be taken into consideration by the authorities and courts dealing with such cases." Article 10 mandates states to give preference to noncustodial forms of sanction for indigenous people.

12 For an analysis of this phenomenon in Mexico and Guatemala, see Sierra et al. forthcoming.

13 *Reglamento comunitario*, Xatinap, 2008. On file with the author.

14 According to the Historical Clarification Commission, of the 285 reported cases of sexual violations nearly 90 percent of victims were indigenous Maya, while just over 10 percent were non-indigenous mestizas (Consorcio Actoras de Cambio 2006: 16).

15 Fiona Ross's work on South Africa has questioned the appropriateness of public and "confessional" mechanisms such as truth commissions or court proceedings for dealing with issues of sexual violence. She points to the complexities of speech and silence in relation to sexual violence and questions of justice (Ross 2010).

16 Aura Cumes is currently undertaking her doctoral research at CIESAS, Mexico on domestic servitude in Guatemala; her research backs up this claim, which is also confirmed by my observations.

17 This occurred through the figure of *querellante adhesivo* specified in the penal procedures code; a kind of special advocate for the prosecution.

18 A 2005 study by the ICCPG revealed that up to 75 percent of women in preventative detention are victims of abuse and sexual violence at the hands of government officials. Although 43 percent of these women had made a complaint to a judge, only one case had been taken up by the public prosecutor's office (ICCPG 2005).

130 Gender Justice and Legal Pluralities

19 The sentence was subsequently appealed by Matías López's lawyers, and in August 2008 an appeals court in Antigua Guatemala reduced his sentence to ten years.
20 Interview with Juana Méndez, October 2008, cited in Gaviola Artigas 2008: 31 (my translation).
21 Interview with Delfina Cruz, September 2008, cited in Gaviola Artigas 2008: 72.
22 Interview with Marta Juana Tojín, September 2008, cited in Gaviola Artigas 2008: 75–6.
23 All names except those of the members of the Defensoría K'iche' have been changed.
24 The Defensoría provides accompaniment to women in cases ranging from domestic violence (by far the most common complaint) to incest and fraud, and in claiming their rightful inheritance.
25 For example, a three-minute socio-drama for radio on domestic violence, produced by the Defensoría K'iche' in 2009, on file with the author. This rights-consciousness raising work is supported by international funders, such as the European Union and Oxfam UK.
26 This section derives from a video recording of the proceedings made by members of the Defensoría K'iche', which was shared with the author, and from interviews with members of the Defensoría who were present during the proceedings.
27 I have written in more detail elsewhere about the controversy over the use of *x'ik'ay* (Sieder 2011).

References

Arias, E. D. and Goldstein, D. M. (2010) *Violent Democracies in Latin America*, Durham, NC: Duke University Press.
Asociación de Investigación y Estudios Sociales and Oficina del Alto Comisionado de las Naciones Unidas para los Derechos Humanos en Guatemala (ASIES/OACNUDH) (2008) *Acceso de los pueblos indígenas a la justicia desde un enfoque de derechos humanos: Perspectivas en el derecho indígena y en el sistema de justicia oficial*, Guatemala: ASIES/OACNUDH.
Brett, R. (2008) *Social Movements, Indigenous Politics and Democratisation in Guatemala, 1985–1996*, Amsterdam: Cedla Latin America Studies/Brill.
Casaús Arzú, M. E. (2007) *Linaje y Racismo*, 3rd edn, Guatemala: FyG Editores.
Comaroff, J. and Comaroff, J. L. (eds) (2006) *Law and Disorder in the Postcolony*, Chicago, IL: The University of Chicago Press.
Comaroff, J. L. and Comaroff, J. (2009) "Reflections on the Anthropology of Law, Governance and Sovereignty," in Benda-Beckmann, F. von, K. Benda-Beckmann and J. Eckert (eds) *Rules of Law and Laws of Ruling. On the Governance of Law*, Surrey and Burlington, VT: Ashgate, pp. 31–59.
Comisión de Esclarecimiento Histórico (CEH) (2000) *Guatemala: Memoria del Silencio. Tz'inil Na'Tab'Al*, Guatemala: Publicación de la Oficina de Servicios para Proyectos de las Naciones Unidas.
Consorcio Actoras de Cambio (2006) *Rompiendo el silencio. Justicia para las mujeres víctimas de violencia sexual durante el conflicto armado en Guatemala*, Guatemala: FyG Editores.
Defensoría K'iche' (2010) *Acceso a la Justicia comunitaria*, Guatemala: Defensoría K'iche'.

Sexual violence and gendered subjectivities in Guatemala 131

DEMI (2003) *Primer Informe: Situaciones y Derechos de las Mujeres Indígenas en Guatemala. Nabe' wuj ke ixoqib*, Guatemala: DEMI.

——(2007) *Segundo Informe: El Acceso de las Mujeres Indígenas al Sistema de Justicia Oficial de Guatemala. Ukab' wuj ke ixoqib'*, Guatemala: DEMI.

de Sousa Santos, B. (1987) "Law: A Map of Misreading. Toward a Postmodern Conception of Law," *Journal of Law and Society* 14 (3): 279–302.

——(2002) *Toward a New Legal Commonsense: Law, Globalization and Emancipation*, 2nd edn, Toronto: Butterworths.

Equipo de Estudios Comunitarios y Acción Psicosocial; Unión Nacional de Mujeres Guatemaltecas (ECAP-UNAMG) (2009) *Tejidos que lleva el alma. Memoria de mujeres mayas sobrevivientes de violación sexual durante el conflicto armado*, Guatemala: ECAP-UNAMG.

Felstiner, W. L. F., R. L. Abel and A. Sarat (1981) "The Emergence and Transformation of Disputes: Naming, Blaming, Claiming ... ," *Law and Society Review* 15: 630–49.

Foro Internacional de Mujeres Indígenas (FIMI) (2006) *Mairin Iwanka Raya: Indigenous Women Stand Against Violence*, New York, NY: FIMI, http://www.fimi-iiwf.com (accessed March 2012).

Gaviola Artigas, E. (2008) *Informe de sistematización. El caso de Doña Juana Ménez Rodríguez vrs. El Agente de la Policía Nacional Civil, Antonio Rutilo Matías López*, Guatemala: ICCPG.

Goldstein, D. M. (2004) *The Spectacular City: Violence and Performance in Urban Bolivia*, Durham, NC and London: Duke University Press.

Goodale, M. (2008) "Legalities and Illegalities," in Poole, D. (ed.) *A Companion to Latin American Anthropology*, Malden, MA and Oxford: Blackwell, pp. 214–29.

Griffiths, A. (1997) *In the Shadow of Marriage: Gender and Justice in an African Community*, Chicago, IL: The University of Chicago Press.

Hellum, A., J. Stewart, A. Sardar Ali and A. Tsanga (2007) *Human Rights, Plural Legalities and Gendered Realities: Paths are Made by Walking*, Harare: Weaver Press.

Hessbruegge, J. and C. F. Ochoa García (2011) "Mayan Law in Post-Conflict Guatemala," in Isser, D. (ed.) *Customary Justice and the Rule of Law in War-Torn Societies*, Washington, DC: United States Institute of Peace Press, pp. 77–118.

Instituto de Estudios Comparados en Ciencias Penales de Guatemala (ICCPG) (2005) *Cifras de impunidad del crimen policial contra mujeres*, Guatemala: ICCPG.

McCreery, D. (1996) *Rural Guatemala, 1740–1940*, Palo Alto, CA: Stanford University Press.

Merry, S. E. (2006) *Human Rights and Gender Violence: Translating International Law into Local Justice*, Chicago, IL: The University of Chicago Press.

MINUGUA (2002) *Los Linchamientos: Un flagelo que persiste*, Guatemala: MINUGUA.

Poole, D. (2004) "Between Threat and Guarantee: Justice and Community in the Margins of the Peruvian State," in Das, V. and D. Poole (eds) *Anthropology in the Margins of the State*, Baltimore, MD: Johns Hopkins University Press, pp. 35–65.

Procurador de los Derechos Humanos (PDH) (2009) *Informe Anual Circunstanciado: Resumen ejecutivo del Informe Anual Circunstanciado al Congreso de la República de las actividades y de la situación de los derechos humanos en Guatemala durante el 2009*, Guatemala: PDH, http://www.pdh.org.gt (accessed March 2012).

Programa de las Naciones Unidas para el Desarrollo (PNUD) (2005) *Diversidad Étnico-Cultural: La Ciudadanía en un Estado Plural. Informe Nacional de Desarrollo Humano*, Guatemala: PNUD.

——(2008) *Guatemala: ¿Una economía al servicio del desarrollo humano? Informe Nacional de Desarrollo Humano 2007/2008*, Guatemala: PNUD, http://desarrollo humano.org.gt (accessed March 2012).

Recuperación de la Memoria Histórica (REMHI) (1998) *Guatemala: Nunca Más. Informe del Proyecto Interdiocesano de Recuperación de la Memoria Histórica*, Guatemala: ODHAG.

Ross, F. C (2010) "An Acknowledged Failure: Women, Voice, Violence, and the South African Truth Commission," in Shaw, R. and L. Waldorf (eds) *Localizing Transitional Justice: Interventions and Priorities After Mass Violence*, Stanford, CA: Stanford University Press, pp. 69–91.

Sieder, R. (2011) "Construyendo autoridad y autonomía maya: la 'recuperación' del derecho indígena en la Guatemala de posguerra," in Sieder, R. and C. Y. Flores, *Autoridad, autonomía y derecho indígena en la Guatemala de posguerra*, Guatemala: F& g Editores-Casa Comal-UAEM, pp. 13–75.

Sieder, R. and M. T. Sierra (2010) *Indigenous Women's Access to Justice in Latin America*, Bergen: Chr. Michelsen Institute.

Sierra, M. T. (ed.) (2004) *Haciendo justicia. Interlegalidad, derecho y género en regiones indígenas*, Mexico: CIESAS / Miguel Angel Porrúa.

Sierra, M. T., R. A. Hernández and R. Sieder (eds) (forthcoming) *Estado, derecho(s) y violencia. Pueblos indígenas frente a la justicia en México y Guatemala*, Mexico: CIESAS/FLACSO.

Snodgrass Godoy, A. (2006) *Popular Injustice. Violence, Community and Law in Latin America*, Palo Alto, CA: Stanford University Press.

Warren, K. B. (2003) "Voting against Indigenous Rights in Guatemala: Lessons from the 1999 Referendum," in Warren, K. B. and J. E. Jackson (eds) *Indigenous Movements, Self-Representation and the State in Latin America*, Austin, TX: University of Texas Press, pp. 149–80.

World Bank (2011) *Crime and Violence in Central America: A Development Challenge*, Washington, DC: World Bank, http://siteresources.worldbank.org/INTLAC/Resources/FINAL_VOLUME_I_ENGLISH_CrimeAndViolence.pdf (accessed 3 March 2012).

Chapter 5

Between Sharia and CEDAW in Sudan: Islamist women negotiating gender equity

Liv Tønnessen

Introduction

This chapter explores how women's rights and obligations are understood and negotiated within the context of an Islamic state in Sudan. It particularly deals with the ongoing debate on the Convention on the Elimination of All Forms of Discrimination against Women (CEDAW) and Sharia (Islamic law). CEDAW was adopted by the United Nations in 1979 and is the most comprehensive international agreement on the basic human rights of women. CEDAW has been ratified by 185 countries. Sudan, together with Iran, Somalia, Nauru, Palau, Tonga and the USA, is among a small minority of countries that have not yet ratified the convention. The fundamental argument put forward by Islamists, who have ruled Sudan since 1989, for not signing the convention is based on cultural relativism: that Sudanese culture and religion provide indigenous answers to their particular problems which should be judged within the local. Islam is the solution, not a blind adoption of Western and feminist legal frames. But how do the state's Islamic gender policies affect women's political and economic participation? Is the Islamic state constraining or enabling greater gender justice?

This chapter will concentrate on the views of Islamists who were interviewed for this study during fieldwork in Khartoum state from 2006 to 2011. The Islamists feminists belong to state-supported organizations and political parties: the Sudan Women's General Union (SWGU), the International Muslim Women's Union (IMWU), the National Congress Party (the ruling Islamist political party) and the Popular Congress Party (the Islamist party in opposition).[1] The chapter puts emphasis on the socio-economic and political contexts of disputes and negotiations over women's rights and duties in Islamic law as exposed in the debate on CEDAW. For many international development agencies and Western donors Sharia is regarded as anti-women and an obstacle to women's empowerment and equality. Islamists postulate a view that promotes women's empowerment within an Islamic frame. Putting an emphasis on gender equity (*insaf*), they bargain with patriarchy and negotiate gender relations employing both legal norms originating from

134 Gender Justice and Legal Pluralities

Sharia and CEDAW. The result is that Islamist women advocate equality in rights in the public sphere, including politics and even the military. Within the family, however, male guardianship remains the rule (Tønnessen 2011a, 2011b).

Through a review of the debate, this chapter explores the entanglements or interlegalities of "Islamic" and "Western" normative legal orders or rather, interpretations of these legal orders in the state's discourse on gender relations. I argue that although Islamists' discourse deems Western tenets of feminism based on gender equality to be unessential to Sudanese society and falsely universalizing in its premises, it simultaneously draws upon them in order to demonstrate their "alternative" route to women's empowerment (Tønnessen 2011a). These negotiations are linked both to Western colonial rule in the past and Western aid donors, peacekeepers and development agencies in the present. By analyzing a range of Islamist women's positions, it becomes apparent that they reject CEDAW and gender equality on the one hand, and on the other promote issues that empower women politically and economically in Sudanese state and society. While the Islamist position is empowering for Sudanese women in many ways, it is important to have a "critical eye for the ways in which they might not be purely liberatory" (Abu-Lughod 1998: 9). It is situated within a multi-religious and class divided Sudanese context. The Islamic elite reinforces the importance of an authentic reading of Islamic *texts* rather than recognizing the socio-economic *contexts* of the grassroots as a starting point for discussing how to improve the situations of women of different religions and class backgrounds in an emerging northern Sudanese state (Tønnessen 2011a).

Sudan: a short background

Sudan has been in a state of perpetual conflict that stretches back long before independence. Throughout its existence the Sudanese state has been characterized by a series of dichotomies: of Islamic law (Islamism versus secularism), of ethnicity (Arab versus African), and of centralization (Khartoum versus the rest of the country). The last 50 years of Sudan's history have also been characterized by civil war. The war between the government and southern armed groups (1955 to 1972 and again from 1983 to 2005) has received most of the attention, but war has not been confined to the south. There have been multiple armed conflicts in the East, in Kordofan, and in Darfur. Yet, astonishingly, Khartoum, which has been the location of my fieldwork, has remained a strikingly peaceful, albeit authoritarian and oppressive, island, surrounded by the violence of peripheral regions (Tønnessen 2011b).

The colonial rulers first separated the north and the south administratively, and at independence handed over the reins of power to a small group of Arab Muslims from the riverine elite in Khartoum. This minority has in effect ruled the country since independence in 1956, under both military and civilian governments. The call for Islamization has been an important part of the decolonization process in the country. The current Islamist government in Khartoum, which has been in power since the coup d'état in 1989, continues the failure of previous governments to provide stability, unity and democracy. Nonetheless, the level of repression it has carried out, particularly in the early 1990s, is unprecedented in Sudanese history. The regime has not only been preoccupied by armed conflict in the regions, but also has taken strong measures to silence political opposition and dissidents in the center. Whereas Islam had a latent presence through sectarian political parties, throughout Sudan's post-independence history Islamists called for a comprehensive Islamization of the country's legal, political and economic system from above by force. This is unparalleled to any other attempts to introduce Sharia in Sudan. During this period, the rulers in Sudan attempted to build a Sudanese nation based on the premise that Islam, the majority religion, and Arabic, the language of the Quran, were the foundation of Sudan's unity and should define its legal, political and economic systems (Ahmad 2007; Gallab 2008; Sidahmed 1996). Furthermore, Islamization brought new levels of intervention of the state, using Islamic law to control women (Nageeb 2004; Tønnessen 2011b).

After 17 years of civil war, international efforts to support a process for peace negotiations between the government and the southern rebels finally gained new momentum in 2001. In January 2005, a peace agreement between the two warring parties was signed in Naivasha, Kenya. The Comprehensive Peace Agreement (CPA) represented a major opportunity for positive change and sustainable peace at the same time that armed conflict broke out in Darfur and other locations in the country. The CPA aimed to establish a one-state, two-system rule, in which the north imposed Sharia law while the south remained secular. The current government in the north continued its Islamist rhetoric, insisting on imposing Sharia and re-affirming the country's Arab-Islamic identity (Ahmad 2009). In January 2011, the overwhelming majority of southern Sudanese decided to secede by a popular vote and a new nation was born in Africa. Northern Sudan is expected to change its constitution again to establish Sharia law as state law following the secession of south Sudan (Tønnessen 2011b).

The international presence in the country has been huge, including peacekeepers in Darfur and international and national aid organizations elsewhere in the country. Work on issues that Western agencies deem "violence against women" has proven particularly difficult and politically sensitive (Tønnessen 2012). The secular gender equality agenda is often constructed by pro-regime actors and institutions or imposed by Westerners from outside of Sudan. Historically, however, the woman's movement in Sudan was closely linked to the growth of communism and Marxist feminism. The first group of politically organized women emerged from the Sudanese Communist Party, which had been active since the end of the Second World War in

136   Gender Justice and Legal Pluralities

the cause of Sudanese national independence (Fluehr-Lobban 1987; Hale 1996). After the 1989 Islamist coup, the new political situation made it difficult for Marxist opposition to the government to continue (Al-Bashir 2003). This created a new context in which women wanting to oppose the government turned to the resources of Islam rather than openly pursuing communism or other secular alternatives calling for the abolition of the Sharia.

Many aspects of Muslim family law (regulating marriage, divorce, maintenance, inheritance, and custody of children) developed through judicial circulars both during Turkish–Egyptian and Anglo–Egyptian rule in the country (Fluehr-Lobban 1987; Ibrahim 2008). It was not until 1991 that the Islamic state codified Muslim family law. It became an important symbol of the whole nation's Islamization. Claims and counterclaims regarding reform of Islamic laws in general and the Muslim family law specifically, have come onto the agenda of the political opposition in the country, particularly in the post-CPA period.[2] As such the Muslim family law has become a primary arena for political contestation.[3]

This chapter critically discusses the Islamist "state feminist" project and the gender ideology underpinning it. It analyzes the debate on CEDAW and Sharia in the context of a postcolonial state. It focuses further on the Islamists arguments against ratifying CEDAW and the implications this involves for Sudanese women of different socio-economic backgrounds.

Islamism and gender equity (*insaf*)

Hasan al-Turabi is an internationally renowned Islamist who advocates women's rights in Sharia. He was also the architect of the Islamist-military coup d'état in 1989. In 1973 al-Turabi published a small book entitled *Al-Mara bayna ta'alim al-din wa taqlid al-mujtama'* (*Women between the Teachings of Religion and the Customs of Society*), in which he demanded changes in the patriarchal interpretation of women's rights in Islamic jurisprudence (*fiqh*) (al-Turabi 1973). This book set the framework for the Islamist discourse on women's rights in Sudan. The basic assumption is that many men have interpreted the Islamic texts in order to broaden the authority granted to men, while reading the same texts strictly in order to impose limitations on women. Ihsan Ghabshawi, former minister of health, states that Islamic clergy were exclusively male and that that this has affected the development of Islamic jurisprudence.[4] The "blame" is placed on Muslim males, who have misinterpreted Islam. The lack of gender equity therefore does not lie with the essence of Sharia, but with deviation from the Islamic ideal in the actual practice of religion and customs in Muslim societies. In the words of an Islamist and female professor at an Islamic university in Omdurman, Sudan: "[w]omen suffer from the misunderstanding of Islam."[5] The approach consists of identifying traditions and misunderstandings of the Islamic norms rather than "Islam" itself as the sources for all Muslim women's woes. Provided they are adapted to contemporary modern society, it is argued, Islamic references can be an instrument for promoting women's rights (Tønnessen 2011a).

The Islamist women interviewed by the author between 2006 and 2011 struggled primarily for women's rights within the public sphere and not within the private sphere where family law or personal status law operates. This differentiates Islamist women from Islamic feminists in Sudan and elsewhere, who aim to eradicate inequality in rights between men and women within both the public and private spheres of law (Tønnessen 2011b). The Islamist women postulate a view of Islam that reinforces patriarchy within the family, emphasizing that "the family is the natural and fundamental unit in society."[6] Most Islamist women interviewed for this study claim to be active seekers of gender equity (*insaf*), but they consider equality within the family desirable. Suad al-Fatih al-Badawi, who is a Member of Parliament for the ruling Islamist National Congress Party (NCP), claims that "there is no equality in Islam in the Western sense, but equity. There is balance. The person nearer to Allah is worth more in Islam; that might be the man or the woman." For al-Fatih, piety (*taqwa*) matters more than equality in rights. The ultimate motivation underlying their stance is *taqwa*, not equality (Tønnessen 2011a). Hassanat Awad Satti concurs with this emphasis and claims that "Islam differentiates between someone who is strong in piety and someone who is weak in piety. Therefore women can even be better than men in piety."[7]

Islamists promote the paradigm of gender equity (*insaf*) within an Islamic frame emphasizing piety, distinguishing it from gender equality, which they consider Western and secular and thereby irrelevant to Muslim Sudanese society. The Islamist gender ideology builds strongly on the concept of *qawama* (male guardianship) where women and men have different, and complementary, roles and responsibilities because they are born biologically different. Mazair Osman, the current secretary general of International Muslim Women's Union, explains that "men and women are different, not equal, biologically speaking." As a result "women and men should have different rights and duties."[8] According to Islamists, the Muslim family should build on *qawama*. The ideal man has the role of protector and caretaker, whereas the ideal woman has the role of the nurturer and caregiver.

The Islamic principle of *nafaqa* is closely related to the idea of male guardianship in the household. *Nafaqa*, in theory, specifies that once a marriage has been consummated, the husband becomes responsible for providing his wife and children with food, clothing, and shelter, regardless of the wife's own economic resources. Failure of the husband to provide *nafaqa* may result in a jail sentence, according to the current Muslim family law that was codified in 1991.[9] According to Barbara Stowasser, men's "spending of their means" becomes the justification for other elements often perceived as discriminatory against women in family life, namely the role of the male

138   Gender Justice and Legal Pluralities

guardian (*wali*) in contracting women's marriage, the wife's duty to obey her male guardian, and the right of husbands to unilaterally dissolve the marriage (Stowasser 1998: 33). However, the Islamists do not view *qawama* as unfair or discriminatory. According to Mazair Osman, *qawama* "must be viewed within the frame of the whole of Islam."[10] Rather, she and other Islamists see it as an advantage. Suad Abu Qashawa explains in more detail:

> Similar rights refer to equality and degree of advantage refers to discrimination. These two concepts are purposely mentioned in this Quranic text (*surat al-bakarah* verse 228) so that the Muslim should not get confused or assume a contradiction between the two concepts and their connotation on gender relations [...] the degree of advantage should be understood within the thesis of *qawama*, which obliges men to support and sustain the household financially, but this does not necessarily imply that *qawama* entails sexual inequality.
>
> (Abu Qashawa in al-Bashir 2003: 210–11)

Interestingly, Islamists argue for complementarity between men and women in the family household, but this does not mean that women cannot work outside the home, participate in politics and even the military.[11] In fact, Sudanese women under Islamist rule have served as ministers, presidential advisors, Supreme Court judges, parliamentarians, civil service bureaucrats, doctors, professors and traders. Not only did a woman run as a candidate for the presidency for the first time in Sudanese history in the elections in April 2010, but she argued for equal pay for equal work.[12] Maha Freigon who is leading the foreign affairs section of the Sudan Women's General Union, says of women's participation:

> 65 per cent of the university students are women. Women are working in the public sector, in the armed forces now; also in the high ranks of the army. Women are working in the civil police force in foreign affairs as ambassadors. And now we have entered the political era with a 25 per cent quota (...). The biggest aim is to empower women at all levels. A woman has a role in life; in the community and in political decision-making.[13]

Within political spaces in particular, Islamist women demand inclusion. In 2008, Islamists together with women from oppositional parties and civil society organizations successfully lobbied for a 25 percent woman's quota for the national and state parliaments (Abbas 2010; Tønnessen 2011c). Abu Qashawa says that "it is important for women to participate in politics," because "it is part of the religion."[14] They legitimize women's participation in politics and economic life with reference to Islam. During the Prophetic era, for example, women participated actively in trading, and acquired education. When the opinions of Muslims were sought to decide on a caliph after the assassination of Umar Ibn al-Khattab, women were included in the consultation process (al-Turabi 1973). This is why "the Islamists encourage women to be equal in politics," Maha Freigoun explains.[15] Al-Turabi therefore claims that:

> [a]n Islamic democracy [is not] government by the male members of society. Women played a considerable role in public life during the life of the Prophet, and they contributed to the election of the third Caliph. Only afterwards were women denied their rightful place in public life, but this was history departing from the ideal.
>
> (al-Turabi 1983: 244)

The concept of *qawama* and gender equity stands in stark contradiction with current international gender policies. If we, for example, take the World Bank as a point of departure, this contradiction is revealed. The most recent World Development Report 2012 on gender and development not only put gender equality as a universal goal for women everywhere, but links equality to economic opportunities and income generation. Further it states that from women's economic freedom and independence follows agency and action; women question inequalities in rights (World Bank 2012). Despite the fact that Islamist women work outside the home as members of parliaments and ambassadors, they do not, however, question the *qawama* underpinning Muslim families. They see privileges within this system and refuse to be considered "oppressed" for this reason. In the words of Maha Freigoun, *qawama*:

> does not hinder a woman's activity outside the house. Non-Muslims think: since men pay, they dominate the women. In Sharia law it is not like that. In Sharia law the man and the woman sign a marriage contract to build a family together. He has rights and duties and she has rights and duties.[16]

However, patriarchy is continuously bargained with and legal norms within the Sharia are being "contested, redefined, and renegotiated" (Kandiyoti 1988: 286). The Islamists' construction of gender equity thus challenges dominant ideas of women's agency suggested by liberal-feminist approaches to gender equality. In the views of Lila Abu-Lughod and others these approaches, as exemplified by the World Bank and also scholarships on women and Islam, have been overly romanticized due to their lack of consideration of how power relations are historically transformed and produced (Abu-Lughod 1990). She points out that women's agency is not always inherently linked to opposing or subverting male domination and guardianship. Saba Mahmood underlines further that the importance of piety (*taqwa*)

140 Gender Justice and Legal Pluralities

in understanding women's agency in mosque movements in Cairo and with that she encourages us "to conceptualize agency not simply as a synonym for resistance to relations of domination, but as a capacity for action that specific relations and subordination create and enable" (Mahmood 2001: 212).[17] Sharia thus becomes a dynamic body of law that is continuously being (re) interpreted by social actors underlining the importance of understanding Islamic law not as something pre-determined, but as (re)constructed by Islamists and others as they are operating in specific historical and political contexts.

An alternative route to women's empowerment

Interviews with many Islamist women activists revealed rejection and even contempt for the concept of feminism, which they interpret as a movement to free women from all social constraints and obligations to the family and community at large, leading to sexual chaos, adultery, sex before marriage, moral corruption, homosexuality, excessive individualism and secularism (Tønnessen 2011a).[18] They understand Western feminism as a monolithic static entity that is backward and ignorant. Muslim women are perceived as better off and "more privileged than Western women."[19]

Suad al-Fatih al-Badawi spoke of Western feminists as ignorant because they deem Islam to be misogynous in respect of women's empowerment. Western feminism is presented as distorted and alien to the Islamist image of Islam and gender arrangements. Suad al-Fatih al-Badawi proclaims that "Islam would push feminism into a corner."[20] She calls for solidarity among Muslim women across Islamic societies, providing *Islamic* solutions in a contemporary global world. The current situation of women is regarded as a consequence of misinterpretation and malpractice of Islam, not the religion itself. If authentic and "true" Islam is restored, then Muslim women will achieve gender equity.

The strategies of Muslim women's empowerment employed by Islamists are a way to create an alternative to Western feminism, in order to counter what they deem "invading ideologies." In their opinion, the West is attempting to re-colonize the Muslim world "under the pretext of civilized notions and norms and the emancipation of women". They go on to say that "such ideologies target the ethics and morality of our communities by intimidating women and demoralizing them in order to cause family disintegration. Since the family is the nucleus of society then the whole society is corrupted" (International Muslim Women's Union n.d.: 3). It is important to note here that the Islamist discourse is transnational. The establishment of the International Muslim Women's Union in addition to the Sudan Women's General Union illustrates this. Muslim women from 65 countries met in Khartoum in 1996 under the auspices of the Islamist government and decided to create the International Muslim Women's Union. Later meetings of the International Muslim Women's Union have been held in Turkey, Yemen, Iran, Pakistan, Indonesia and Malaysia, but Sudanese women have continued to take the lead in the organization, particularly through the leadership of Suad al-Fatih al-Badawi.

The alternative route to women's empowerment seeks to reach beyond the boundaries of the nation-state in the struggle for equity for Muslim women in a global world. This transnational discourse calls for solidarity among women across geographic and social boundaries, providing Islamic solutions to the problems of contemporary Muslim women. The International Muslim Women's Union thus aims to create a coalition among Muslim women in order to transfer their experiences "from the local to the universal" (al-Bashir 2003: 139).

This construction of Sudanese Islamic authenticity is an important underpinning of the establishment of an Islamic state in Sudan. Al-Turabi contends that the Islamic state in Sudan "chose not to allow women's liberation to be brought about by Westernized liberal elites or communists ... It took the lead itself ... it evoked religion" (al-Turabi in Lowrie 1993: 46–7). This connects to processes of decolonialization and helps set the background for the continued effectiveness of anti-imperialist rhetoric by Islamist politicians, including the president himself, who remains vehement and persuasive in present-day Sudan. Links are made between the colonial past and international pressures against the Islamist government in the present, which are portrayed as neocolonialist (De Waal 2007). On 4 March 2009, the Pre-Trial Chamber of the International Criminal Court (ICC) issued an arrest warrant against President Omar Hassan Ahmad al-Bashir, having found reasonable grounds to hold him responsible for crimes against humanity and war crimes committed in Darfur. President Bashir immediately responded by saying that the ICC's warrant was a Western ploy to target Sudan. "We have refused to kneel to colonialism; that is why Sudan has been targeted ... . We only kneel to God," he told crowds in Khartoum.[21] The establishment of an Islamic state is seen as a means to counter the secularization processes during colonial rule in the country. In the words of al-Turabi:

> The real secularization and de-Islamization of public life in Islam came about through Western Imperialism. They physically disestablished Islam and destroyed public institutions which were left behind. They established in the place of Sharia, positive laws ... and secular institutions ... but for every fall, there is a revival.
>
> (Al-Turabi in Lowrie 1993: 15)

The Muslim woman carries a heavy burden of symbolic representation in Sudan's postcolonial state. They represent the birth of an authentic Islamic nation. Suad al-Fatih al-Badawi explained that *taqwa* (Islamic piety) matters

142 Gender Justice and Legal Pluralities

more than equality in rights. She claims that "we have *taqwa* – piety. If we understand *taqwa*, we will never have feminism in Islam" (al-Badawi in Hale 2003: 208). Wisal al-Mahdi is a lawyer and Hasan al-Turabi's wife. She attended the UN conference on women held in Beijing in 1995, but she is clear about the fact that she does not find viable solutions for Muslim women in Western feminist frameworks. Her views are similar to Suad al-Fatih al-Badawi:

> Feminism is distorted, Islam is natural ... Islam gave women their natural rights, but we do not want to put women in men's shoes. We are different, but equal ... We are content with Islam ... The mother is important; she is the nucleus of the family and the Islamic nation. Women are superior to men in Islam, especially mothers. The root of everything is women. Western-inspired women want careers, they have fewer children. But bringing up your family is a contribution to society. God's intended job for women is the family. We do not like feminists, because they allow homosexuality and this is against nature and the survival of the family. We do not want to be feminist; we want to live in a natural society.[22]

This highlights the fact that gender struggles in Sudan must be analyzed within the context of identity and representation in a postcolonial world (Ibrahim 2008). It is against this background that Islamists actively advocate against the ratification of CEDAW, particularly article 16, and claim that it "destroys family values."[23] The main objection revolves around the family as an institution: "There are texts that are not in accordance with Islam. CEDAW gives the right to homosexuals. This is prohibited in Islam because it would abolish the natural family."[24] According to Maha Freigon, "CEDAW reflects a Western ideal."[25] Claims to gender equality as stipulated in CEDAW are perceived as a foreign implant aiming to weaken Sudanese society by attacking the Muslim family. Islamists construct a link between feminism and the betrayal of authentic Islam and Sudanese culture and tradition. They pose the dignity of the pious Muslim woman against a commodified and sexually exploited Western woman. Feminism is portrayed as an invading ideology that targets the morality of Muslim communities by demoralizing women in order to cause family disintegration. Since the family is the nucleus of society then the whole society is corrupted.

However, opposition to Western feminism also remains ambivalent. While they challenge Western tenets as unessential to Islamic societies, they simultaneously draw upon them in order to demonstrate their "alternative" feminism. Abu-Lughod and others make the important point that those who claim to reject feminism *selectively* reject particular aspects or dominant codes of the Western feminist discourse: "Those who claim to reject feminist ideals of Western imports actually practice a form of selective repudiation that depends on significant occlusions" (Abu-Lughod 1998: 243–4). Ihsan Ghabshawi for example acknowledges that the economic policies at the fore front of the CEDAW convention are beneficial (for example equal pay for equal work), but that the problem with the convention lies elsewhere with its stipulations on family life, inheritance and divorce.[26] What is characteristic of the Islamists is that they stigmatize sexual independence as Western while simultaneously defending women's education and political rights and embracing the ideals of bourgeois marriage. These "are elements of the turn-of-the-century modernist projects that might well carry the label 'feminist' and whose origins are just as entangled with the West as are the sexual mores singled out in horror" (Abu-Lughod 1998: 243–4). The patriarchal and bourgeois ideal of a family with a male breadwinner is not necessarily Islamist or Islamic. According to Abu Lughod:

> The assertion of the proper role of women as wife and mother, with the assumption of a happy nuclear family [...] is now [...] couched in an Islamic religious idiom that gives it a pedigree. [...] I would argue that this vision of family and women's proper relation to husband and children is profoundly modern and its sources are entwined with the West.
> (Abu-Lughod in Willemse 2005: 161)

If we move beyond the "symbol" politics of gender in the highly polarized context of a postcolonial Islamic state facing national and international pressure, the Islamist discourse on women illustrates how "Western" and "Islamic" normative orders are intertwined with each other, constituting each other dialectically rather than being the autonomous or semi-autonomous legalities we sometimes see them as (Tønnessen 2011a). It might perhaps be described as a situation in which there is "an intersection of different legal orders" creating a context in which diverse legal spaces are "superimposed, interpenetrated, and mixed" (de Sousa Santos 1995: 473). This perspective of "interlegality" suggests that the interaction is dynamic and fluid. De Sousa Santos puts emphasis on the role of social actors and agency in this process of interpretation and negotiation of new legal hybrids. Islam, or rather (re)interpretations of Sharia, mediates these negotiation processes. Islamist women, while agreeing that women's primary role is mainly as wives and mothers, demonstrate through their activism that their Islamism can be an emancipatory discourse (Karam 1997: 243). This conforms to Anne Sofie Roald's study of the Muslim Brotherhood's reception of CEDAW in Jordan. By analyzing various political stands it became apparent that Islamists on the one hand reject CEDAW and gender equality, and on the other promote issues that in the long run might empower women in Jordanian society. There is thus a trend towards female empowerment in the organization of the Muslim Brotherhood, according to Roald (2009). In their negotiation for both agency and "relationality" to their larger social, religious, ethnic and national communities, Islamists demonstrate their capacity for action in ways that at times confound the emancipatory vision of feminist politics rooted in liberal notions of the self. Suad Joseph's concept of "relationality" provides a framework for understanding the dual emphasis on the individual and the collective. In their negotiation for both agency and "relationality" to men and their larger social, religious, ethnic and national communities, Islamist women demonstrate not only their bargaining power, but also their capacity for action in ways that at times confound the emancipatory vision of feminist politics rooted in liberal notions of the self (Mahmood 2001; Saliba and Howard 2002). For the Islamist women interviewed, this is crucial not only to their senses of self but also to their understanding of Muslims as a group in Sudan and globally. The discourse is thus simultaneously highly individualized and highly collective.

The social implications of religious doctrine

Islamist feminists in Sudan call for solidarity among women in the Islamic world so as to provide Islamic solutions for the problems of contemporary Muslim women. Their main argument for not ratifying CEDAW is their quest for an alternative to Western forms of feminism, which they claim is universalizing in its premises. It can be asked, however, if Islamist feminists provide culturally indigenous answers to the problems facing Sudanese women. Sudan is a multi-religious country stricken by war, poverty and displacement. The Islamists' claim to authenticity and cultural indigenousness is made in contrast to what they perceive as a Western hegemonic world order, but their discourse could be criticized for a lack of rooting in their own local communities. The Islamist discourse exclusively focuses on Muslim women and thereby excludes non-Muslims (Tønnessen 2008). This remains problematic even after the secession of the south in July 2011. Large numbers of southerners, mostly non-Muslims, have settled in the north, particularly in greater Khartoum. The continued emphasis on *Muslim* women and their interests thereby risks reinforcing gender as a boundary marker in the discourse of inclusion and exclusion from an emerging northern Sudanese state (Tønnessen 2011a, 2011b; Willemse 2005). It also has an important class dimension that is often overlooked. Islamist discourse amongst an educated urban middle and upper class in Sudan, and idealized notions of *qawama* and *nafaqa*, fail to take into consideration the socioeconomic situations of most Sudanese women (Tønnessen 2011a, 2011b; Willemse 2005). While there certainly should be room for locally defined concepts such as *insaf* (equity) in international development policies, we cannot uncritically embrace the Islamists' approach without thoroughly analyzing women through an intersectional lens where among other factors class is brought into the larger picture (on intersectionality, see for example Grabham et al. 2009).

The role of women in Islamism rests in part on the concepts of *qawama* (male guardianship) and *nafaqa* (maintenance) and their realization in Muslim family law. Islamists women, as noted above, describe *qawama* as advantageous for women, as did some other Islamist women. Maha Freigoun of the Sudan Women's General Union explained:

> For us Muslims, *nafaqa* is by Sharia law for the man to pay for his family, take care of his family. Non-Muslims see the *nafaqa* not within the Islamic picture, but in terms of economic dependency. I am a working woman earning my own money. But I keep my money for my own, not for any other person. I can do whatever I want with it. My father, my brother and my husband should pay for whatever I need. There is no obligation for a woman.[27]

It is hard to ignore the class dimension of this statement. The social implication is that such piety (*taqwa*) is not possible for poor women. Rural, uneducated, and poor women, whose male guardians' incomes are insufficient to support them, have no alternative but to contribute to the economic survival of their families (Tønnessen 2011a). According to Balghis Badri, "the majority of contemporary Sudanese citizens are living in rural areas where poverty is estimated to affect 85 percent of the people and women are suffering hardship in finding water, collecting fuel wood and cultivating fields under harsh conditions with simple technologies only." Despite being a country with vast natural resources, poverty is widespread in Sudan. The United Nations Development Programme's 2011 Human Development Report ranked the country 169th of 187 (UNDP 2011). Badri states further that "this means men often can no longer be the sole breadwinners to satisfy their family's needs" (Badri 2006: 4). While it may be economically feasible to implement *nafaqa* within an educated middle- and upper-class elite, centered in Khartoum, its extension to wider society is not economically feasible (Hale 2001; Willemse 2005). Due to poverty and high unemployment, *nafaqa* cases are the most frequent family court cases in Sudan. Sudanese women claim that their husbands fail to provide for them. Female-led households are becoming more common, either as a result of war and displacement or divorce or abandonment. The solution to the problem by Islamist women is not a change in the law itself, but in implementation (Tønnessen 2011a, 2011b). *Nafaqa* is seen as perfectly compatible with the national interim constitution (2005) and especially the articles on affirmative action towards women. According to Afaf Ahmed Abdel Rahman, who is currently the minister of social welfare in Khartoum state:

> [t]here is a high percentage of divorce due to *nafaqa* in Khartoum … Men are in jail for this. There are street children from broken homes because of this. But we believe in *nafaqa*. It is the man's responsibility.

> We do not have a lot of problem in the law itself. We have to apply it ...
> the law is good and does not need change. It is the man's obligation to do
> *nafaqa* according to Islam.[28]

Although my fieldwork concentrated on educated Islamists in Khartoum, in September to November 2009 I went to visit a local branch of the Sudan Women's General Union near a camp for internally displaced people in Jabal Awlia. The union offices are located about two hours' drive from the capital, but still within Khartoum state, it is a poor rural area of mud houses, providing a sharp contrast with the urban center. When I asked women at the Sudan Women's General Union's center in Jabal Awlia about the Islamist ideal of *nafaqa*, they all laughed and said "*ya reet*" (I wish). They are the ones who provide for the economic needs of themselves and their children, they said, and support by a husband is an ideal far removed from their everyday lives. All women must work, because the men do not. Electricity bills arrive in the name of the husband, but are paid with the money the wife has earned. Many women must resort to legal action to get money for the household (Tønnessen and Kjøstvedt 2010).

In Jabal Awlia, men clearly are not able to live up to their role as guardians and protectors, as the Islamist moral discourse on *qawama* dictates. The concept of *qawama* and the idealized image of "Muslim masculinity" as guardians and protectors of families are key components in the authenticity of the Islamist project, sustaining a symbolic moral order. *Qawama* then must be understood in relational terms, not only from a woman's perspective. Men who have failed to be good fathers and husbands have to bear the responsibility, not the Islamist state and its lack of economic policies targeting the poor (Tønnessen 2011b). Also, the marginalization of poor men can potentially alter gender relations in the family. The lived reality of women-headed household challenges the idea of *qawama* or male guardianship – an idea that is made conditional upon male provision of financial support. In some instances, this marginalization, as Salwa Ismail shows in her work on Cairo, leads women to occupy new positions and take on unconventional duties and to claim rights at the same time (Ismail 2006). At the same time, I got the impression that the idea of *qawama* was cherished by the women at the center in Jabal Awlie. They were not resisting it, but yearning for it and claiming rights on behalf of it. My fieldwork did not allow me to look into the everyday practice of these women, but research on the daily lives of female-led households in Palestine show that women continuously under-communicate their new economic roles (Bøe 2011). When women take on new economic responsibilities in the family, they do so "without transcending the ideological discourse and the normative imaginary of femininity and masculinity" (Muhanna in Bøe 2011: 4). This means that even though women earn the money, men still have the authority to make the major household decisions on how the money should be spent (Bøe 2011).

Women at the center were antagonistic about the fact that they did not receive any economic compensation for their work for the Sudan Women's General Union. The state-sponsored Sudan Women's General Union, which was formed in 1990, has approximately four million members working in 27,000 branches and sub-branches across rural and urban areas (Tønnessen and Kjøstvedt 2010). It is active in three principal areas: education (literacy training), economic empowerment and religious enlightenment. Thus the Sudan Women's General Union is regarded as a major instrument for Islamizing society in conformity with the "authentic" Islamist ideology. However, although both elite and grassroots women participate, the organization is based on the principle of voluntary work, which implies the assumption that women do not need to earn a living because their husbands, fathers, and brothers maintain them financially (*nafaqa*). However, most of the women who bring their children for kindergarten at the women's center in Jabal Awlia work in the informal labor market as street vendors, not because they want or chose to but because their husbands are not able to provide for them. In most rural areas, women work in the agriculture sector on land belonging to their husbands or brothers or fathers (Tønnessen and Kjøstvedt 2010) (see Figure 5.1).

Figure 5.1 Woman coffee and tea seller in the informal sector, Khartoum (photo: Liv Tønnessen)

The women at the center had voiced their concern about the lack of economic compensation to the central branch in Khartoum, but they were not heard. This had consequences for the running of the center. As women take on new economic roles in the families, they simply do not have the time to do voluntary work on top of their other responsibilities and obligations in the family. The women told me that the teacher who volunteered at the center had stopped coming, and it was difficult to hire a new teacher. As all activities are based on voluntary work, they could not offer a salary and therefore no one was interested: "To volunteer for the women located centrally in Khartoum, who get salaries as MPs or civil servants, is quite differently perceived than amongst the women at the grassroots in Jabal Awlia, who do not have the same economic means" (Tønnessen and Kjøstvedt 2010: 29).

The Islamists I spoke to were reluctant to acknowledge the harsh realities of women in Jabal Awlia. They readily asserted that it is a man's responsibility to provide financially for his wife and family and that this is a right that women are granted in Islam. However, when I asked them why Muslim men in Sudan fail to support their families even though they are obligated to do so in Islam, they either refused to acknowledge that this is a reality in Sudan or suggested that these men are bad Muslims who need to be educated to follow the "right" path. This kind of man was simply portrayed as a bad Muslim who practiced Islam in a customary as opposed to an authentic manner. Islamist women also often emphasized the need to educate women at the grassroots on their rights and legal awareness so that they can claim their rights within the family more efficiently. They thus seek solutions within the Islamic texts and current laws rather than taking into account the socio-economic conditions of ordinary women. In other words the bourgeois Islamist women in the capital seek "to solve every problem by establishing an authentic Islamic society" (Seesemann 2005: 93). This is a significant indicator of the elitist character of Islamist discourse on gender as it plays out in Khartoum.

According to Karin Willemse, "the national ruling elite had to construct boundaries to differentiate themselves from the 'non-elite' in order to safeguard its privileged position" (Willemse 2005: 169). Sondra Hale writes further:

> The essentialist views of women expounded by Islamist women ... — emphasis on family and child rearing and the importance of women in resocializing the society—are all strategies for the [Islamist] revolution carried out by a group of middle-class capitalists striving to control their own means and mode of production. In the face of international interlopers, the authentic culture campaign is class-interested and culturally nationalist in the service of those class interests.
>
> (Hale 1994: 66)

The realities of *nafaqa* in practice in Sudan make clear that one must consider class and other positionalities as well as gender. Suad Joseph puts the lesson in general terms.

> Women ... although sharing some interests and circumstances, have not been a homogeneous category or "class." Their differing identities and commitments more often have aligned them with men of their class, religion, ethnicity, tribe, or family than with other women across these social boundaries despite the multiplicity and fluidity of boundaries.
>
> (Joseph 2000: 10)

Women need to be differentiated not only from men but also from other women in relationship to their socio-economic status. Indeed, class is perhaps more salient than gender in affording or curtailing rights and responsibilities as citizens in an Islamic state in Sudan. While the Islamist gender ideology clearly is meaningful to the educated elite of women who can aspire to the ideals it promotes, other women are excluded and alienated (Al-Bashir 2003; Willemse 2007). "Those who fall short of attaining the status of an authentic Islamic woman are excluded from the benefits of the Islamist paradise on earth" (Seesemann 2005: 110). Women's everyday lives in Jabal Awlia have not been profoundly affected by Islamist state feminism. Instead they have "relied on themselves, their families, their neighbourhoods, and their communities." Those who gain most in the Islamic ideals postulated by Islamists are typically educated, employed, middle- or upper-class, urban, heterosexual women who belong to the dominant race, religion, or ethnic group. They bargain with patriarchy on behalf of all women. In so doing, they gain the power to speak for others, "while the 'others' must fight their way through with whatever 'ammunition' is at their disposal" (Shahidian 2002: 16).

Conclusions

This chapter has attempted to reframe normative debates concerned with considering whether Islamic law is bad for women and to what extent it stands in contradiction with international human rights. In contrast to earlier publications, it tracks Muslim women's rights "into the multiple social worlds in which they operate, paying particular attention to their mediations and transformations." If we step back from the usual terms of debate and follow Muslim women's rights as "they travel through various worlds and projects, circulate through debates and documents, organize women's activism, and mediate women's lives in various places," it reveals the entanglements or interlegalities of "Islamic" and "Western" normative legal orders or rather, interpretations of these legal orders in the state's position on gender (Abu-Lughod 2010: 2). This chapter shows how Islamist women deploy, resist, appropriate and construct different legal repertoires to advocate gender equity (*insaf*) that is clearly differentiated from gender equality. In analyzing the Islamists' "alternative" route to women's empowerment, it shows that the Sudanese government's rejection of CEDAW is ambivalent and intimately linked to complex historical and political trajectories. The debates on CEDAW and Islam are part of an ideological terrain where broader notions of cultural authenticity are debated. Claims are made and responded to within the specific cultural, social, economic and political context of a postcolonial state in Sudan where Islam and Sharia have served as important tools in decolonialization. An analysis of the debate therefore has to consider how these experiences are implicated in contemporary debates about gender which in the postcolonial world are often couched in the language of cultural authenticity versus colonial influence (Abu-Lughod 1998). The Islamist advocacy of Islamic rather than Western solutions for Islamic societies thus resonates with the search for third world feminisms in an attempt to find indigenous answers and local solutions to women's woes (Tønnessen 2011a).

An understanding of Islamic norms and approaches as a tool for engaging in meaningful change is important in a world where international development agencies seemingly support religious law insofar that it is in perfect alignment with international human rights. In line with the contributions in this volume, this chapter emphasizes the need to appreciate culturally (like Andean "*buen vivir*") and religiously defined concepts in development as contextually grounded expressions of women's empowerment. But there is simultaneously a need to critically investigate these approaches. Examining the Islamist construction of *insaf* (gender equity) from different socio-economic contexts, this chapter has questioned whether women's rights under *qawama*, with a particular focus on *nafaqa*, are realizable outside of the elite women's life worlds. The limited application of *nafaqa* within poverty-stricken Sudanese society suggests that both poor women and men are marginalized in the context of an Islamic state. Islam has not provided solutions for poor Sudanese women and men who do not fit the idealized model of *qawama*. It seems that the Islamists are preoccupied with authentic readings of the Islamic texts or in the words of Comaroff and Comaroff (2009) "fetishization of law"; instead of putting socio-economic conditions and practices at the heart of discussing how to improve the situation of women in the country. On the one hand the Islamist agenda thus seems to represent an empowering discourse for educated urban women, opening space for successful negotiating patriarchy. However, on the other hand, it remains a way of life beyond the reach of most Sudanese women. As such, it serves as an instrument for marginalization, domination and assertion of political hegemony in a class-divided society.

Acknowledgements

Funding for fieldwork to conduct the research for this chapter was provided by several projects as part of my PhD research (Tønnessen 2011b): *Moderation of Islamist Movements*, headed by Anne Sofie Roald; *Poverty Reduction and Gender Justice in Contexts of Legal Pluralism*, headed by John-Andrew McNeish and Rachel Sieder (both funded by the Norwegian Research Council); *Women and Peacebuilding in Sudan*, headed by Liv Tønnessen (funded by the Norwegian Ministry of Foreign Affairs); and *Women's Fight against Violence and for Justice in Northern Sudan*, headed by Liv Tønnessen (funded by the Norwegian Research Council). A special thanks to comments from participants at a workshops in Mexico and Mozambique on legal pluralism and gender justice led by Rachel Sieder and John Andrew McNeish. The findings were also presented at The Eighth Nordic Conference on Middle Eastern Studies place in Bergen, 24–26 September 2010. A special thanks goes to Hilde Kjøstvedt and Samia al-Nagar, whom jointly conducted fieldwork with the author on the projects *Women and Peacebuilding in Sudan* and *Women's Fight against Violence and for Justice in Northern Sudan*.

Notes

1 A minimalist definition of Islamism, then, can be said to be a Sharia-fication or Islamization of the state and society. Islamists are thus engaged in a common political project: the Islamization of state and society (Vikør 2005).
2 My other writings on the topic have focused on the fragmentation of women's activism in Sudan in the post-CPA period. I propose that there are two alternatives to the official Islamist position of the state: on the one hand, an "emancipated" Muslim woman, framed within a rights-based approach that assumes that Sharia law agrees with international women's human rights (Islamic feminism), and on the other, a "protected" Muslim woman, framed within a conservative, gender-segregated doctrine that refutes all non-Islamic laws (*Salafism*). See Tønnessen 2011b.
3 The core elements of the Muslim family law of 1991 (*Qanun al-'Ahwal al-Shakhsiyya lil-Muslimin*) are the following: the age of consent for marriage is puberty. According to the Law, both parties have to consent to marriage. However, the woman needs a guardian (*wali*) to validate the marriage. The bridegroom is obliged to give the bride a dowry. The Law explicitly states that the dowry is considered the property of the wife (Articles 27–28). The man is the breadwinner of the family (Article 51). A man can deny his wife the right to work outside the home, even in cases where he himself fails in his financial obligation (Article 91 to Article 95). A man is also allowed to marry up to four wives, although he has to treat all his wives justly (Article 51(d)). A husband can divorce (*talaq*) his wife outside the court for no reason whatsoever. The divorce will come into force when he utters the divorce sentence "I divorce you." The husband has the right to take the wife back if he revokes the divorce sentence within the *idda*. *Idda* is a waiting period of three months after the divorce. The wife can only obtain a divorce in court (*tatliq*: a divorce granted by a judge) on certain conditions stipulated by the Law. They are: (1) if the husband fails to fulfil his financial obligation to support her (*nafaqa*); (2) if her husband has more than one wife and she can prove that

152 Gender Justice and Legal Pluralities

her husband does not treat all his wives justly; (3) if the husband has a defect she did not know about before marriage; (4) if the husband suffers from an incurable mental illness; (5) if the husband is impotent; (6) if he behaves cruelly; (7) if he is abroad for more than one year; and (8) if the husband is sentenced to prison for more than two years. The wife can also obtain a divorce if a judge declares her to be disobedient (*nushuz*) to her husband (Article 151 to Article 203). The wife is entitled to financial maintenance (*nafaqa*) for up to six months after the divorce. The husband is the financial provider for the children even when they are under the custody of the mother. The father is financially responsible for his daughters until marriage and for his sons until they provide for themselves. The mother has custody (*hadana*) of her daughters until they are nine years old and of her sons until they are seven years old. After this, the principle "the best interests of the child" (*maslaha al-tifl*) applies in some cases. But if the woman remarries, the father will automatically get custody of the children. The inheritance laws are in accordance with the classical *shari'a*. A woman inherits half the amount of property that her brother(s) inherits. The reasoning behind the inheritance law is that the husband is the breadwinner of the family. So a woman's inheritance is then considered her own property, while a man's inheritance will be used to fulfil his financial obligations (*nafaqa*) within the family: *Qanun al-'Ahwal al-Shakhsiyya lil-Muslimin* (The Muslim family law, Khartoum, 1991). For more detailed information about the law, see Tønnessen 2011b.

4 Interview with Ihsan Ghabshawi, former secretary-general of the International General Women's Union and former minister of health, 21 January 2008.
5 Interview with Aisha Ghabshawi, member of the International General Women's Union and professor at the Islamic university in Omdurman, 19 January 2008.
6 Interview with Farida Ibrahim, the President's advisor for legal affairs, 24 January 2008.
7 Interview with Hassanat Awad Satti, assistant Professor at the international university of Africa and member of the National Congress Party and the Sudan Women's Union, 13 January 2008.
8 Interview with Suad al-Fatih al-Badawi, current Member of Parliament and Sudanese representative to the African Parliament; the former secretary general of the International Muslim Women's Union and former advisor to the President, 31 January 2008.
9 Article 51, *Qanun al-'Ahwal al-Shakhsiyya lil-Muslimin* (The Muslim family law, Khartoum, 1991). For more detailed information about the law, see Tønnessen 2011b.
10 Interview with Mazair Osman, the current secretary general of the International Muslim Women's Union, 21 January 2008.
11 Interview with Raga Hasan Khalifa, the current secretary general of the Sudan Women's General Union and a Member of Parliament for the National Congress Party, 6 February 2008 and 25 October 2009.
12 Fatima Abdel Mahmoud from the Sudanese Socialist Democratic Party ran, but only got 0.3 percent of the votes.
13 Interview with Maha Freigoun, in charge of the foreign affairs section of the Sudan Women's General Union, 23 April 2008.
14 Interview with Suad Abu Qashawa, professor at the University of Khartoum and member of the leadership of the National Congress Party, 29 January 2008.
15 Interview with Maha Freigoun, in charge of the foreign affairs section of the Sudan Women's General Union, 23 April 2008.
16 Interview with Maha Freigoun, in charge of the foreign affairs section of the Sudan Women's General Union, 29 October 2009.

17 The same quote is found in the introductory chapter of this book.
18 Secularism is here understood as an a-religious or anti-religious doctrine.
19 Interview with Ihsan Ghabshawi, former secretary-general of the International General Women's Union and former minister of health, 21 January 2008.
20 Interview with Suad al-Fatih al-Badawi, current Member of Parliament and Sudanese representative to the African Parliament; the former secretary general of the International Muslim Women's Union and former advisor to the President, 31 January 2008.
21 "Bashir calls ICC arrest warrant a 'conspiracy,'" http://www.telegraph.co.uk/news/worldnews/africaandindianocean/sudan/4942470/Sudan-President-Omar-al-Bashir-calls-ICC-arrest-warrant-a-conspiracy.html (accessed 1 April 2011).
22 Interview with Wisal al-Mahdi, al-Turabi's wife, lawyer and former secretary general of the International Muslim Women's Union, 2 May 2008.
23 Interview with Farida Ibrahim, the President's advisor for legal affairs, 24 January 2008.
24 Interview with Hassanat Awad Satti, assistant Professor at the international university of Africa and member of the National Congress Party and the Sudan Women's Union, 13 January 2008.
25 Interview with Maha Freigoun, in charge of the foreign affairs section of the Sudan Women's General Union, 29 October 2009.
26 Interview with Ihsan Ghabshawi, former secretary-general of the International General Women's Union and former minister of health, 21 January 2008.
27 Interview with Maha Freigoun, in charge of the foreign affairs section of the Sudan Women's General Union, 29 October 2009.
28 Interview with Afaf Ahmed Abdel Rahman, minister of social welfare in Khartoum state, 25 May 2011.

References

Abbas, S. (2010) "The Sudanese Women's Movements and the Mobilization for the 2008 Legislative Quota and its Aftermath," *IDS Bulletin* 41: 100–8.
Abu-Lughod, L. (1990) "The Romance of Resistance: Tracing Transformations of Power Through Bedouin Women Author(s)," *American Ethnologist* 17 (1): 41–55.
——(1998) *Remaking Women: Feminism and Modernity in the Middle East*, Princeton, NJ: Princeton University Press.
——(2010) "The Active Social Life of 'Muslim Women's Rights': A Plea for Ethnography, not Polemic, with cases from Egypt and Palestine," *Journal of Middle East Women's Studies* 6 (1): 1–45.
Ahmad, E. (2007) "Political Islam in Sudan: Islamists and the Challenge of State Power (1989–2004)" in Soares, B. and R. Otayek (eds) *Islam and Muslim Politics in Africa*, New York, NY: Palgrave Macmillan.
——(2009) "The Comprehensive Peace Agreement and the Dynamics of Post-Conflict Political Partnership in Sudan," *Africa Spectrum* 44 (3): 133–47.
al-Bashir, N. M. A. (2003) *Islamist Women's Politics and Gender Activism: A Case Study from Sudan*, unpublished PhD thesis: University of Vienna.
al-Turabi, H. (1973) *Al-Mara bayna ta'alim al-din wa taqlid al-mujtama'* [Women between the Teachings of Religion and the Customs of Society], Jeddah: Al-Dar al-Su'udiyya li al-Nashr wa al-Tawzi.
——(1983) "The Islamic State" in Esposito, J., *Voices of Resurgent Islam*, New York, NY: Oxford University Press.

154 Gender Justice and Legal Pluralities

Badri, B. (2006) "Sudanese Women Profile: Indicators and Empowerment Strategies," unpublished paper presented at "Pathways to Wellbeing and Justice: Constructing a Concept of Women's Empowerment" in Cairo, Egypt.

Bøe, J. (2011) "Women as Bread winners in the Occupied West Bank", unpublished paper presented at Birzeit University.

Comaroff, J. L. and J. Comaroff (2009) "Reflections on the Anthropology of Law, Governance and Sovereignty," in Benda-Beckmann, F. von, K. von Benda-Beckmann and J. Eckert (eds) *Rules of Law and Laws of Ruling: On the Governance of Law*, Surrey and Burlington, VT: Ashgate.

de Sousa Santos, B. (1995) *Toward a New Common Sense: Law, Science and Politics in the Paradigmatic Transition*, London: Routledge.

De Waal, A. (2007) "International Dimensions to the State and its Crisis," London: Crisis States Research Centre.

Fluehr-Lobban, C. (1987) *Islamic Law and Society in the Sudan*, London: Frank Cass.

Gallab, A. A. (2008) *The First Islamist Republic: Development and Disintegration of Islamism in the Sudan*, Aldershot: Ashgate.

Grabham, E., D. Cooper, J. Khrisnadas and D. Herman (eds) (2009) *Intersectionality and Beyond: Law, Power and the Politics of Location*, Abingdon: Routledge-Cavendish.

Hale, S. (1994) "Gender Politics and Islamization in Sudan," *Comparative Studies of South Asia, Africa and the Middle East* 14 (2): 51–66.

——(1996) *Gender Politics in Sudan: Islamism, Socialism and the State*, Boulder, CO: Westview Press.

——(2001) "The Islamic State and Gendered Citizenship in Sudan," in Joseph, S. (ed.) *Gendering Citizenship in the Middle East*, Syracuse: Syracuse University Press.

——(2003) "Sudanese Women in National Services, Militias, and the Home," in Abdella Doumato, E. and M. Pripstein Posusney (eds) *Women and Globalization in the Arab Middle East: Gender, Economy, and Society*, Boulder, CO: Lynne Rienner.

Ibrahim, A. A. (2008) *Manichean Delirium: Decolonizing the Judiciary and Islamic Renewal in the Sudan, 1898–1985*, Leiden: Brill.

International Muslim Women's Union (n.d.) "ANSAM: A Decade of Fruitful Activities and Continuous Achievements," document on file with the author.

Ismail, S. (2006) *Political Life in Cairo's New Quarters: Encountering the Everyday State*, Minneapolis, MN: University of Minnesota Press.

Joseph, S. (ed.) (2000) *Gender and Citizenship in the Middle East; Contemporary Issues in the Middle East*, Syracuse, NY: Syracuse University Press.

Kandiyoti, D. (1988) "Bargaining with Patriarchy," *Gender and Society* 2 (3): 274–90.

Karam, A. (1997) *Women, Islamism and the State: Contemporary Feminisms in Egypt*, Basingstoke: Palgrave Macmillan.

Lowrie, A. (ed.) (1993) *Islam, Democracy, the State and the West: A Round Table with Dr. Hasan Turabi, May 10, 1992*, Fla: Tampa.

Mahmood, S. (2001) "Feminist Theory, Embodiment, and the Docile Agent: Some Reflections on the Egyptian Islamic Revival," *Cultural Anthropology* 16 (2): 202–36.

Nageeb, S. A. (2004) *New Spaces and Old Frontiers: Women, Social Space, and Islamization in Sudan*, Lanham, MD: Lexington Books.

National Liberation Council of the Sudan People's Liberation Movement (SPLM) (2005) "The Interim National Constitution of the Republic of the Sudan, 2005," http://www.sudan-embassy.de/INC_of_Sudan.pdf (accessed 2 April 2007).

Roald, A. S. (2009) "Islamists in Jordan: Promoters of or Obstacles to Female Empowerment and Gender Equality?" *Religion and Human Rights: An International Journal* 4 (1): 41–63.

Saliba, T. C. A. and J. A. Howard (eds) (2002) *Gender, Politics and Islam*, Chicago, IL: The University of Chicago Press.

Seesemann, R. (2005) "Islamism and the Paradox of Secularization: The Case of Islamist Ideas on Women in the Sudan," *Sociologus* 55 (1): 89–118.

Shahidian, H. (2002) *Women in Iran: Emerging Voices in the Women's Movement*, Westport, CT and London: Greenwood Press.

Sidahmed, A. S. (1996) *Politics and Islam in Contemporary Sudan*, New York, NY: St Martin's Press.

Stowasser, B. (1998) "Gender Issues and Contemporary Quran Interpretation," in Haddad, Y. and J. Esposito (eds) *Islam, Gender, and Social Change*, Oxford: Oxford University Press.

Tønnessen, L. (2008) "Gendered Citizenship in Sudan: Competing Debates on Family Laws among Northern and Southern Elites in Khartoum," *The Journal of North African Studies* 13 (4): 455–69.

——(2011a) "Feminist Interlegalities and Gender Justice in Sudan: The Debate on CEDAW and Islam," *Religion and Human Rights: An International Journal* 6 (1): 25–39.

——(2011b) *The Many Faces of Political Islam in Sudan: Muslim Women's Activism for and against the State*, unpublished thesis, University of Bergen.

——(2011c) "Beyond Numbers? Women's 25% Parliamentary Quota in Post-Conflict Sudan," *Journal of Peace, Conflict and Development* 17: 43–62.

——(2012) "From Impunity to Prosecution? Sexual Violence in Sudan beyond Darfur," Policy Brief, Oslo: Norwegian Peacebuilding Resource Center.

Tønnessen, L. and H. Kjøstvedt (2010) *The Politics of Women's Representation in Sudan: Debating Women's Rights in Islam from the Elites to the Grassroots*, Bergen: Chr. Michelsen Institute.

United Nations Development Programme (UNDP) (2011) *Human Development Report: Sustainability and Equity: A Better Future for All*, http://hdr.undp.org/en/media/HDR_2011_EN_Complete.pdf (accessed 3 January 2012).

Vikør, K. (2005) *Between God and the Sultan: A History of Islamic Law*, London: Hurst.

Willemse, K. (2005) "On Globalization, Gender and the Nation-State: Muslim Masculinity and the Urban Middle Class Family in Islamist Sudan," in Davids, T. and F. Van Driel (eds) *The Gender Question in Globalization: Changing Perspectives and Practices*, Aldershot: Ashgate.

——(2007) *One Foot in Heaven: Narratives on Gender and Islam in Darfur, West-Sudan*, Leiden: Brill.

World Bank (2012) *World Development Report: Gender and Development*, http://siteresources.worldbank.org/INTWDR2012/Resources/7778105–1299699968583/7786210–1315936222006/Complete-Report.pdf (accessed 29 November 2011).

Chapter 6

Indigenous rights and violent state construction: the struggle of Triqui women in Oaxaca

Natalia De Marinis

Introduction

Following legal reforms recognizing limited rights to indigenous self-determination approved in Latin America during the last two decades, the demand for autonomy has become a common strategy for indigenous people seeking to defend their territory and collective rights. These demands have opened up opportunities to rethink law, justice and security, in many cases confronting the violence of state formation in marginal regions. Indigenous mobilization has also opened important spaces to rethink "custom," revealing the tension between individual and collective rights. It is in this intersection of rights that gender relations have become a central issue.

Many reports show that indigenous women face different barriers to accessing justice – both within the formal state sector and within indigenous community justice – because of their gender, ethnicity and socio-economic marginality (FIMI 2006; Sieder and Sierra 2010). The construction of discourses about women's rights within indigenous peoples' movements has been seen as a singular feature of contemporary indigenous peoples' struggles. First, because these are inscribed in the global circulation of rights discourses, including women's rights. Second, because these movements have opened possibilities for the renegotiation of gender relations and women's participation (Hernández Castillo 2010; Sieder, Chapter 4 in this volume; Speed 2008: 121). And, finally, because indigenous women's organizations confront the idea that the customs of indigenous people are somehow "static", pointing instead to the violence that they continue to suffer as a consequence of different historical processes of state formation. Even though such processes of organizing cannot on their own ensure women's access to justice, they have opened up important spaces for women to gain visibility and voice through their participation within indigenous movements.

In Mexico indigenous rights became a key issue of national political debate in the wake of the constitutional reform of 1991 that recognized Mexico as a pluricultural nation. One of the most important developments in this respect was the armed uprising of the indigenous Zapatista

Movement (EZLN) in 1994 in the south-eastern state of Chiapas. In the same year that Mexico entered the North American Free Trade Agreement (NAFTA), the Zapatistas rejected neoliberal economic policies and demanded autonomy and territorial and political rights for indigenous people. Through the peace talks between the movement and the federal government held in San Andrés Larraínzer, Chiapas, the indigenous issue gained unprecedented importance within the national political arena.[1]

In spite of the government's failure to implement the accords reached at San Andrés in 1996, the gains made by the Zapatista movement set a precedent for other indigenous organizations across the country. In Oaxaca, the state with the largest indigenous population in the country, the sympathy that the EZLN evoked in many grassroots organizations coincided with the decline of the Institutional Revolutionary Party (PRI), which had governed Oaxaca for more than 80 consecutive years. In order to confront the threat of imminent social unrest and guarantee governability, the state government determined to elaborate a new pact with the indigenous population. One of main reforms approved for such purposes was the Law of the Rights of Indigenous People and Communities of Oaxaca State, passed by the state legislature in 1998, which concluded a process of different legal reforms begun in 1995 and through which "uses and customs" (*usos y costumbres*) were defined as a way for indigenous people to exercise a degree of political and legal autonomy.

Nearly ten years after the approval of these reforms, a popular rebellion formed by different indigenous and non-indigenous organizations occupied Oaxaca City. The Popular Assembly of the People of Oaxaca (APPO) sought to overturn the hold of the PRI on power in the state and to institute a constituent assembly. As had occurred in the case of the rebellion in Chiapas, autonomy became a key issue for the unification of the demands of different organizations that made up the APPO, even though this in fact channeled many social and political demands not just those of indigenous people. This mobilization for autonomy rights questioned the legal and administrative language of recognition contained in the pact of governability represented by the law of 1998. Protesters criticized the limited idea of "uses and customs" set out in the reforms, i.e. as a way to elect municipal authorities under a "traditional system" and to exercise community-based justice in cases of minor misdemeanors, instead expanding the meaning of "autonomy" to include the broader notion of "liv[ing] with dignity" (Poole 2009: 60). Interestingly, in the case of other indigenous movements, such as in Bolivia or Colombia, or indeed the Ejército Zapatista de Liberación Nacional (EZLN) in Mexico, disputes surrounding legal pluralism are not simply about official recognition of indigenous jurisdictions. Rather they point to the mobilization of law produced by what de Sousa Santos (2002) calls "interlegality" and, with this, ideas about justice, and demands and aspirations for a dignified life that question modernist ideas of development and

158 Gender Justice and Legal Pluralities

the domination and dispossession that characterizes state construction in marginal zones.[2]

In this chapter I will focus on the violent situation in one region of Oaxaca state, that inhabited by the Triqui ethnic group.[3] Since 2009 extreme violence exercised by different armed paramilitary groups against the movement for autonomy in the region has increasingly targeted women and children. This situation led to the forced displacement of everyone who supported the local autonomy project, laying bare a violent history of caciquism, militarization and partisan intervention stretching back to the middle of the twentieth century. It was in this situation of forced displacement that Triqui women began to organize, denouncing the illegal practices of armed groups operating in their region with government support and total impunity. It was through demands that Triqui peoples' collective rights be guaranteed that women became important actors in the struggle for access to justice. Confirming the apparent absence of the state in this situation of extreme violence against a civilian population, state officials refused to guarantee people's fundamental human rights, pointing instead to the "savage" customs of the Triqui people as the reasons underlying the intra-ethnic conflict that dates back almost 50 years.

This chapter focuses on a number of questions that echo the concerns of this volume as a whole: first, under what conditions is the legal recognition of indigenous rights opening up spaces for indigenous people's access to justice, but at the same time limiting the responsibility of state in guaranteeing human and collective rights? Second, to what extent have legal and illegal practices of state construction produced an ambiguous zone of enormous violence among indigenous communities, a violence that is officially viewed as the result of "savage" indigenous "customs" in an apparent absence of the state? Third, to what extent have the circulation of rights discourses and the opening of different legal forums through the official recognition of legal pluralism increased the visibility of the violence suffered by Triqui women? And to what extent, if at all, have these developments favored organization by Triqui women to secure greater gender justice?

In order to analyze the prospects for indigenous women's access to justice and the effects of legal pluralities on these in the Triqui region of Oaxaca, I adopt a long-run historical perspective on state construction. Only by understanding the violent process of state formation in indigenous regions can we appreciate the meanings and potentialities, but also the barriers that contemporary developments pose for indigenous women's access to justice. The chapter is organized as follows: first, I analyze how the recognition of indigenous rights in Oaxaca was used to generate new strategies of governability within indigenous regions, rather than signifying a real disposition on the part of the government to guarantee indigenous rights. Second, I consider the ways in which patterns of state construction in the Triqui region have led to the conformation of armed organizations that have administered security and state recourses, converting this region into a war zone, perhaps one of the most violent regions among indigenous communities in the whole country. Third, I analyze the effects that this context of legal pluralism and mobilization for indigenous rights has had on the efforts of Triqui women to address their situation, at the same time pointing to the limits they confront in accessing justice.

Multicultural reforms in Oaxaca: the new pact for governability

Many authors have argued that the multicultural reforms in Oaxaca that began in the 1990s did not imply either a radical transformation of the relationship between the state and indigenous peoples or a change in their historical marginalization (Kraemer 2006; Leal 2006; Martínez 2004; Recondo 2007). Instead these reforms legalized historical, political and legal practises by the government (dominated by the Partido Institucional Revolucionario, PRI) that aimed to secure channels of patronage and domination in indigenous regions. The historical tolerance of practices of "semi-autonomy" was the government's means of generating governability in the most culturally diverse state of Mexico. It is worth emphasizing two aspects of the state level reforms recognizing indigenous rights. One is the legalization of the "uses and customs" (the preferred term for "traditional" systems of indigenous governance) for electing local authorities. For the first time ever this meant that communities could select their local authorities according to communitarian decision-making processes, rather than partisan competition between candidates selected for legally registered political parties. The second aspect is the legalization of indigenous justice practises in cases of minor misdemeanors. Here I explore, first, the effect of this legalization of indigenous political and justice practises in terms of indigenous peoples' access to justice; and, second, the extent to which these reforms (and the overall context of legal pluralism) opened spaces for indigenous peoples to demand greater degrees of autonomy than those circumscribed by the format of official "recognition."

A number of factors explain why Oaxaca, one of 32 states in the Mexican federal republic, has been the object of numerous analyses about the effect of multicultural reforms to recognize indigenous rights.[4] First, it is the state with the highest percentage of indigenous population in Mexico: according to official figures, the indigenous population represents 34 percent of 3,800,000 people in the state.[5] Second, Oaxaca legislated one of the first multicultural reforms after the constitutional reform of 1991 that recognized Mexico as a pluricultural nation. Third, although Oaxaca contains some of the most bio-diverse resources in the country, it shares the distinction of being amongst the lowest ranking states in the Human Development Index, together with Chiapas and Guerrero.[6] Finally, because of its geographic, historical and cultural characteristics, Oaxaca contains 20 percent of the municipalities of Mexico, which makes for a singularly complex political map, particularly given the administrative and political importance of the municipality.[7]

Following the immediate post-revolutionary period of state formation (1920–36), all governments of the state of Oaxaca until 2011 were PRI governments. State formation occurred in the absence of democratic alternation. Although the high number and small size of the 570 municipalities of the state has not allowed the PRI party to concentrate power in a direct way – compared, say, to Chiapas where the PRI formed "institutional revolutionary communities," analyzed by Juan Rus (1994) – what was established instead was a form of "indirect rule" (Recondo 2007: 46). This means that domination was exercised through local authorities within those same communities, such as bilingual teachers, something which allowed for the preservation of a certain degree of autonomy in indigenous peoples' political and social organization.

The official strategy was to tolerate this limited autonomy as part of the political modus operandi and to co-opt local officials. In this way the PRI "state-party" (González Casanova 1981) was able to ensure votes and the consolidation of a patronage pact through caciques who controlled not only the flows of economic production, but also the administration of state policies through personal loyalties. In some senses, the PRI party converted itself into an important part of the "uses and customs" of a very large number of indigenous communities in Oaxaca (Hernández Díaz 2007: 45; Recondo 2007: 81). As Recondo says: "[I]nstead of forming its own partisan activists, [the PRI] incorporated communitarian institutions, converting their assemblies into mechanisms for electing its candidates" (Recondo 2007: 213, my translation).

This pact entered into crisis following the neoliberal economic reforms that began in the late 1970s. These reforms, which included the privatization of national resources and administrative and political decentralization, implied a weakening of the central power of the state and the beginning of a political struggle that resulted in the victory of other political parties in some state elections.[8] The process of municipal decentralization promoted after 1995 that increased the amounts of money received by the municipalities was central to transforming local powers into more attractive centers of political dispute (Hernández Díaz 2007: 65).[9]

Because of its importance as a space for decision-making at local levels, the multicultural reforms that began in the 1990s privileged the municipality as the focus of "autonomy."[10] The 63 articles of the Law of the Rights of Indigenous People and Communities of Oaxaca State, approved in 1998, define what is understood by "indigenous people," "autonomy," "indigenous territory," and "local justice system." The recognition of the right to autonomy for all the indigenous groups in the state appeared to be one of the most important aspects of the law, recognizing as it did indigenous "*usos y costumbres*" (uses and customs).

However, the reforms should be understood as a response, in part, to the declining legitimacy of the PRI and the emergent threats to governability in Oaxaca (Anaya Muñoz 2004; Martínez 2004; Recondo 2007). First, the multicultural legal reforms were approved by the state legislature, rather than through a constituent assembly or peace talks (such as occurred in Colombia in 1990–1, Bolivia in 2007–9 and Guatemala in 1994–6). Given the apparent electoral decline of the PRI in municipal and state elections, it is clear that these reforms were intended as an important tool for the party to establish a new governing pact with indigenous groups. The fact that the PRI held the majority in the Oaxaca Chamber of Deputies meant that this was the only channel for indigenous people to influence the new legislation. Moreover, the legalization of electing municipal authorities via "uses and customs" (supposedly the "traditional" legal system of indigenous groups) meant that PRI candidates could now be inscribed via this mechanism instead of via the ballot box (Recondo 2007). Second, the indigenous revolt in Chiapas in 1994 generated support for indigenous organization in Oaxaca. In a context of neoliberal reforms, the threats that this situation implied in terms of governability and the access to important economic projects required immediate governmental responses (Anaya Muñoz 2006: 96).

What is clear, some 15 years later, is that the recognition of "customary law" for electoral purposes significantly affected indigenous municipalities and agencies (a subdivision of the municipality). Communities could continue to elect their authorities by "traditional" practices (such as the community assembly), but for the first time were able to inscribe the results outside the party system. However, as many authors have observed, elections by "uses and customs" did not necessarily mean non-partisan elections. By 2012, 418 out of the 570 municipalities in Oaxaca elected their authorities according to "uses and customs." However, in the first election after the 1998 reform only 89 municipalities registered themselves as "communitarian" and selected authorities without any partisan affiliation; another 320 municipalities declared they selected their authorities via "uses and customs" but chose PRI candidates, while the remainder chose representatives of other political parties (Hernández Díaz 2007: 36; Recondo 2007: 265). Although the legal reforms in Oaxaca have had very little impact on the modus operandi of local politics, they have encouraged a greater presence of other political parties, such as the PAN (Action National Party) and the PRD (Democratic Revolutionary Party) in state and national elections.[11]

In sum, it could be argued that the impact of multicultural reforms in Oaxaca has been largely symbolic. The official recognition of the cultural diversity of the state for the first time did not have direct implications for reforms to ensure more access to justice for indigenous people (Leal 2006).

An analysis of indigenous people's access to justice in Oaxaca by the Office of the United Nations High Commissioner for Human Rights (OHCHR) in Mexico signals a great distance between the internationally recognized rights of indigenous peoples and state practices. In criminal proceedings, indigenous detainees lack an interpreter in 84 percent of cases, together with an adequate defense. They are also subjected to practices of torture and the denial of their rights to exercise their own legal practices in cases concerning minor misdemeanors.[12]

A report by the Organization of American States also registered 656 indigenous territorial conflicts in Oaxaca, which have led to greater violence between communities (Luzula 2007). These cases concern the coexistence and superposition of different legal claims to land tenure,[13] but also contracts with foreign companies for mining, forestry and hydroelectric resource exploitation, which in many cases were concluded without consultation with the indigenous people that live in the regions affected.[14] The growing presence of military and police forces in these regions (ostensibly to fight organized crime) has increased the number of human rights violations such as sexual harassment and rape, as well as homicides. More importantly, in many cases the state colludes in a process of dispossession by failing to intervene to resolve conflicts or provide adequate legal redress for the victims of violations. In sum, together these phenomena signal the enormous distance between the multicultural reforms and the reality of access to justice for indigenous people in Oaxaca. As Kraemer (2006: 269–73) has observed, these reforms coexist with the total ignorance of indigenous law by the state officials, racist visions and discriminatory practices when cases involve indigenous people, ignorance among the indigenous population about their rights, and great loopholes in the interpretation of the legal reforms.

The crisis of this new pact of governability took place in a context of the state-wide mobilization of the Popular Assembly of the People of Oaxaca (APPO) in 2006, which lasted for nearly a year. Indigenous movements took part in the APPO demanding greater autonomy rights and an end to the intervention of political parties in indigenous communities. The mobilization began with state repression directed against a sit-in by teachers and it is significant that a high percentage of teachers in Oaxaca are in fact indigenous. The indigenous peoples' organizations (principally from the Triqui, Mixe and Mixtec groups) were gradually incorporated into the Assembly. According to Stephen (2010), the participation of indigenous movements in the APPO reveals the profound connection with the ongoing struggle for indigenous rights framed in the San Andrés Accords of 1996. Poole (2009) also analyses this event as a "de-territorialization" of the limited sense that "uses and customs" have in terms of official recognition. In effect, the 2006 mobilization for indigenous rights in Oaxaca laid bare the partisan domination of indigenous communities which continued despite the legal recognition of their rights as indigenous peoples. As a young Triqui boy told me

"We had no idea about this thing called indigenous rights ... in the APPO they told us about this."[15] For the first time ever many indigenous peoples heard the word "autonomy" imbued with a meaning radically different to that set out in the official framework of rights recognition.

Within the Triqui region, Triqui people's participation in the APPO constituted a new "force field" where, in a context of extreme political violence initiated by two opposing Triqui organizations, the MULT (Movement of Unification and Triqui Struggle) and UBISORT (Unity of Welfare of the Triqui Region), both supported by partisan ties to factions within the political parties, another political group emerged demanding recognition of their rights as indigenous people. Within the discourse of this third group, the recovery or "recuperation" of "Triqui tradition" is viewed as a way to establish a new means of living together as communities, envisaging tradition as distinct from the intra-communal and intra-ethnic violence that has characterized the history of the region. This third group aimed to break with partisan ties and obtain a greater degree of security without the intervention of state forces. In 2007 San Juan Copala, the political and religious center of the lowland Triqui, was declared an autonomous municipality with the support of nearly half of the total number of communities that make up the region. The first action of the autonomous municipality was to drive out the state police forces in the town and to install their own communitarian police. Another important project was the communal radio, "the voice that breaks the silence," that began broadcasting in January 2008, staffed by young Triqui women volunteers.

State construction in the Triqui region: partisan ties, caciquism and militarization

Graffiti declaring *"one hundred per cent PRI territory,"* written in the party colours of red, white and green (the same as the Mexican flag), can be seen in many indigenous municipalities around the Triqui region. The autonomy movement's main aim was to break down the historical channels of patronage and control. As a Triqui woman told me: "[B]efore 2006, we were partisan [supporting the PRI]. Well, the officials told us who to vote for. But after voting, they forgot us, they didn't know if we existed or not."[16] Partisan alignment, however, was the rule in a context in which most state resources could only be accessed through channels of patronage.

Following the revolution of the early twentieth century, state construction in Mexico implied the beginning of the "party-state" formation (Recondo, 2007: 39) or, according to González Casanova, "the party of the state."[17] There was no clear separation between the state and the mass-based PRI party. González Casanova defined the PRI as constituted by a system of different sectors manipulated by state officials and a personal and bureaucratic system of patronage (González Casanova 1981: 129). In this regard, the relationship with indigenous communities, organized through the colonial figure of the municipality, formed a basis of support for centralized power in Mexico.

One of the main figures in this arrangement was the "cacique" who operated as an intermediary between the central power of the state and local communities in rural areas.[18] Through these political and economic mediators the state ensured the co-optation of all sectors, including indigenous communities. If the PRI government was unable to eliminate the figure of the cacique, a clear obstacle for the consolidation of a democratic order, the strategy was to incorporate them to the operation of the "party-state" (Knight 2005; Nahmad 1980). Until the 1990s policies towards indigenous populations were "assimilationist;" as many authors have recognized these were a continuum of the colonial legacy, but were framed according to new conceptions of the indigenous "problem."[19] Indigenous peoples were seen as an obstacle to the consolidation of a unified nation: this was to be resolved by integrating them into the nation, principally through schooling, thereby ensuring that indigenous people would forget their customs and "traditional" forms of organization and involve themselves in the modernization of the nation.[20]

According to the scant existing historical literature, it appears that the Triqui people had a particular relationship to these policies. First, they had been used as a belligerent force in the war of independence (and through their participation obtained the category of municipality); subsequently, they were the first indigenous group in Oaxaca to take part in armed rebellions against the government and caciques in 1832 and again in 1860. Since then, the Triqui people achieved a relative independence from external politics. This partly explains their rejection of the construction of a school in the region, and of state-sponsored indigenous politics and institutions in general.[21]

One of the causes of this relative autonomy was the absence of mechanisms of territorial control such as the *finca* or plantation system that existed in others states, such as Chiapas (Rus 1994). This meant that the Triqui enjoyed a de facto form of autonomy. However, the apparent absence of government institutions does not mean that the region was an island of total autonomy, as many authors have claimed (García Alcaraz 1997; Huerta Ríos 1981). Different perspectives on state construction allow us to analyze the ways in which the history of inter-communitarian violence represented a very important dimension of state construction, in spite of its apparent absence (Joseph and Nugent 1994; Das and Poole 2004). These new perspectives allow us to see "informal" state channels, such as the domain of the caciques, as an important part of state construction in many indigenous regions, configuring a "grey and ambiguous zone" of political domain.[22] I argue here that the apparent absence of the state in the region (at least in its formal dimensions) does not imply that the state was not operating through invisible actions. As Agamben has noted, the state of exception does not enter into a tension with democracy as a clear dichotomy. Instead, the state of exception is precisely this ambiguity of the legal order. What is more, it is this that creates the nexus between the law and violence in the bio-politic sense of the state (Agamben 2007; Foucault 2006). As we will see, in the "grey zone" of state construction in the Triqui region the analytical lines between the illegal and the legal are blurred.

The apparently favorable economic position of the Triqui region in the national and international postwar coffee market had different but related effects on their internal organization. First, this produced class differentiation between families; second, and because of this, the historical conflict between families for the political and economic control of the region increased. Third, the cacique system became more accentuated in the Triqui region compared to other indigenous areas. The disputes for local power, the differences amongst them because of their relationship with these caciques, and the arms-trafficking that the caciques controlled in the region triggered the formation of a guerrilla, which was the historical origin of the first Triqui independence movement in the 1980s – the Movimiento de Unificación y Lucha Triqui (MULT). As a result of these developments, Triqui people began to be the object of state interventions from the 1950s onwards. In 1949 the category of municipality was removed, and the area was divided into a triangle of domination formed by three surrounding *mestizo* municipalities.[23]

The beginning of these "development" policies in the region involved militarization. Until 1960, when primary education along with housing plans were introduced, the image that Triqui people had of the state was a coercive one, built upon the strengthening of the military and police and through incursions into their communities. In 1956, a police station was built in San Juan Copala and in 1978 a military station (the 98th Infantry Battalion) was installed on the top of the hill. As well as the multiple abuses committed by the military, state officials intervened in the Triqui's traditional governing system (*sistema de cargos*) through a municipal agent who was imposed to carry out the administrative functions of San Juan Copala.[24] In this period a local branch of the PRI was installed in the town, and state resources began to be administrated by the same men who used the recourses for partisan purposes.

During nearly 40 years, the region became a war zone in which murders occurred of members of both organizations (MULT and UBISORT), but mainly those who claimed some measure of self-determination. To become a member of one of the political organizations ruling the towns was the only way to obtain access to resources, security and economic development for their communities. Since 1970s this armed conflict has led to the death of more than 1,000 people and the forced displacement of nearly 25 percent of

166 Gender Justice and Legal Pluralities

the population. It made Triqui people an object of suspicion and stigmatization and cemented violence as a way to exercise political and economic control, which soon found its limits of tolerance.

After the government of Oaxaca promoted multicultural legal reforms in the late 1990s, the conflict in the Triqui region broke its established codes of practice. The means of political attack were transformed as ever greater numbers of women and children were killed.[25] After the start of 2005 everybody was potentially a victim. Changes occurred in the means of violence exercised: for example, instead of blood feuds between men, the tactics deployed in the intra-ethnic conflict shifted to include opening fire on cars travelling between one community and another, or groups of armed men opening fire indiscriminately on communities from the surrounding hills.[26] This left people in a state of shock because "the women and children don't owe anything to anybody," as a man said to me during my fieldwork.

In sum, the context of legal reforms and the national and state mobilization of indigenous people, as well as the new offensive of the Triqui organizations linked to the government, provided some Triqui organizations with a propitious juncture to claim their rights as indigenous groups. In so doing they pretended to distance themselves from the political parties that many Triqui identify as the principal sources of the conflicts amongst them. Autonomy, as expressed by the population of San Juan Copala in 2007 when they declared themselves to be an "autonomous municipality," represents the peace they hoped to achieve. Along with the rejection of the police forces in the town, the radio, "the voice that breaks the silence," began to broadcast in January 2008 as one of the principle projects of the autonomous municipality. Young women spoke about autonomy rights, women's rights and peace in their own language. On 27 April 2008, three months after the communal radio was set up, it was violently silenced when two of its young presenters, Felicitas Martínez and Teresa Bautista, were killed in an armed ambush. The young people that continued in the project were no longer able to speak about autonomy because of the terror that these murders generated amongst them.

Violence against Triqui women: addressing their situation in a context of legal pluralism

As many authors have demonstrated, in a context of military political conflict feminine sexuality becomes a symbolic space for political struggle (Hernández Castillo 2006: 18; Seifert 1994: 59; Nelson 2009). Attacks on women's bodies as a symbol of the attack on men's honor transmit a message about men's incompetence to protect "their" women and to control their sexuality. This in turn signals a generalized consent that represents women as men's belongings (Seifert 1994; Hernández Castillo 2010). In the case of

Triqui women, the vulnerable situation they live in is combined with the gender inequalities they suffer in common with other indigenous women who live under strongly patriarchal systems that reinforce violence against them. What I want to underline here is that the violence towards those women who had begun to participate and denounce the situation they suffered as indigenous women, but also as indigenous *people* in the movement for autonomy, was a form of counterinsurgency practice through women's bodies that aimed to achieve political control and silence social movements.

Although the violence against Triqui women was denounced and became an object of great concern for the first time ever after 2005, the "tolerated violence" broke down long before. In some interviews,[27] old women spoke about military incursions into their communities, when many of them had to stay to look after their houses and animals while the men ran away to avoid capture. Rape and abduction of women had also become commonplace in confrontations between armed groups. Rumors about violent practices within communitarian assemblies against women accused of having sexual relations before or outside marriage, as well as forced marriages, circulate among young Triqui women today. However, I argue that the control over women's sexuality and their exposure to collective forms of shaming cannot be understood without an analysis of the purpose that extreme violence has served throughout the history of the armed conflict in the region.[28]

When I began my doctoral fieldwork in May 2010, I encountered an unprecedented situation. The Autonomous Municipality of San Juan Copala, where I had worked some years previously, had been besieged and attacked by a group of armed men. An old leader who enjoyed the support of the PRI had returned to the region with new pacts and objectives, including the elimination of the autonomy project and the recuperation of alliances with the government in order to facilitate development projects in the region. The armed siege that began in November 2009 lasted nearly ten months until the last person was able to leave the town. During constant attacks, 35 people were murdered, among them three women and a child and two human rights activists, Jiry Jakoola from Finland and the Mexican Beatriz Cariño. Dozens of women were seriously injured and raped; nearly 600 people who supported the autonomy of their town were forcibly displaced.[29] When the situation worsened, in August 2010 many women with their children installed a sit-in (a *plantón*), with the support of different organizations, in front of the state building in Oaxaca City. At the beginning, the sit-in represented a space for women to denounce what was happening to their families who were still resisting the attacks on San Juan Copala. The women began to make official complaints and involved themselves in other actions, such as the five-day hunger strike with their children, which took place in September 2010.

168   Gender Justice and Legal Pluralities

Marta, one of the women who organized the sit-in, told me how this PRI leader had established sufficient support to attack the town.

> He "won" the people by giving away bags of food and then he received materials to build houses for some people who were with him. In this way, he was gaining people's support, with only these few things. It wasn't because of his ideas. That was what he did to generate factionalism and division amongst the people of the town. He said to the people that if they wanted to stay with him, they could have resources and that the autonomous group didn't give us anything ... He wanted to "buy" us and some people of the town were deceived because of their honesty. They were afraid that the things they had received could be taken away by him so they stayed with him.[30]

The women at the sit-in denounced the fact that this armed group received arms, radios and other recourses from governmental channels. The year-long siege, murders and atmosphere of terror in the town traumatized the women, whose suffering was immense. Susana, who witnessed the first attacks, told me that she had had a dream the night before; in the dream she could not walk and was very afraid: she had to run to her house but could not. A strange force did not allow her to. She felt her legs were like stones. She woke up. It was a quiet day although some days before a young man had been murdered by a man who had been paid by the PRI leader of the armed group. Susana felt the atmosphere was tense. She was going to buy corn for her *tortillas* when she saw a group of men walking with the autonomous leaders. At that moment she began to hear shooting from the hills. She ran but, as in her dream, she felt she could not. When she reached the corner of her house she looked back and she saw Elias, an eight-year-old boy, lying in the street. She could do nothing. She took refuge in her house and when it was quiet again she saw a man with the boy in his arms. Elias was dying. A woman tried to revive him but it was too late. Some hours passed before they could take him to hospital and the boy died before arriving there.

From this day onwards the families of San Juan Copala were unable to leave their houses. Armed attacks on the municipal building, where the autonomous leaders were hiding, and on all the houses, became more frequent. They were "imprisoned," as Margarito told me, without electricity and sometimes without water because the opposing armed group cut the water supply. The women, responsible for the families' supplies, had to leave their houses to look for food (involving hours of walking through surrounding forests). Some of them were shot and a lot of them were seriously injured. As the nearest hospital was about four hours' walk from San Juan Copala, injured women often did not return to the town, leaving their families behind. As women were the most exposed, and as they were pillars of the group under attack, the direct violence against them was easier and also strategic. The violence against women was aimed at wearing down the resistance of their men.

Many of these women were displaced from Copala and went to Oaxaca City, where they began to sell handicrafts on the streets in order to sustain their families. The displaced Triqui women, together with political organizations, decided to mount a sit-in (*plantón*) in the main square of the city to demand protection and an end to the bloodshed in the Triqui region. At the beginning there were around fifteen women with their children, most of them widows or single. But this political action intensified the attacks towards their families in the town. In October nearly 50 people, including entire families, were living in the *plantón* while other displaced families went to other communities in the region still allied with the autonomy project. Even with the presence of men at the sit-in since October, many of them authorities of the autonomy municipality, women continued leading the political struggle. The support of the Triqui movement for autonomy and of the women's male relatives was critical – many women spoke about the space men "gave" them to engage in the political decisions of the movement.

For the first time in the violent history of the region, Triqui women emerged as central political actors. Reyna Martínez, a single woman of about 40 years, became the spokeswoman for the sit-in. She told me that at the beginning she did not speak, "the press came, other organizations came to see us, but we did not speak because we did not know what to say, we did not know how to speak about 'politics.' But then, we realized we had to tell what we felt, in our own words, to tell how we had lived and suffered the violence." She added they felt with the "obligation" to do something while their families were suffering the consequences of the "resistance" in the town.

> In the past we women have not had the right to speak. Simply because we were women, the men didn't let us participate. But now, with the experience we have, with all the problems that our municipality has had, we see ourselves with the obligation and with special powers to go out, to look for aid, to claim justice for our people.[31]

In spite of the women's increasingly desperate protests, they had no response from the state. Moreover, the declarations of state officials concerning to the situation of the Triqui people were marked by racism, intolerance and omissions, such as the statement made by the Attorney General of Oaxaca state when she said that "[the Triqui] are reluctant people who are stubborn with their uses and customs, bellicose and belligerent."[32] As with the Acteal massacre in Chiapas in 1997 (when paramilitary gunmen murdered 45 indigenous supporters of the Zapatista autonomy project), government spokespeople referred to the "cultural" genesis of violence and the state declared it was not responsible for guaranteeing the rights of the people (Hernández

170   Gender Justice and Legal Pluralities

Castillo 1998).[33] However, the situation of extreme violence against women and children, the murder of two human rights activists – one of them a foreign man, the absence of state response and the struggle of Triqui women meant the siege of San Juan Copala became an object of national and international concern. In response to the special protection measures (*medidas cautelares*) for the displaced families that were requested by the Inter-American Commission on Human Rights,[34] the National Commission of Human Rights in Mexico published an extensive document which called on the Oaxacan state authorities to not only investigate and solve the murders, but also to guarantee the rights of the inhabitants of San Juan Copala and to break peace accords.[35] A Committee for the Defense and Justice of the Autonomous Municipality was established to document the cases and monitor the protective measures in collaboration with the Inter-American Commission on Human Rights and the OHCHR in Mexico.

The growing participation of women and the interventions of national and international human rights organizations in the case of San Juan Copala represented a threat that had to be silenced. Installing terror, the paramilitary groups aimed to silence and break women's organizations. As many women noted, following the political organization of the displaced Triqui women, attacks against women became more frequent. Miriam, a 42-year-old widow, was physically assaulted together with her daughter and daughter-in-law by a group of men who stole the food the women were carrying for their families. The three women were able to escape, but that same afternoon their house was shot at by the same group of men. In spite of these attacks, they continued living in San Juan Copala with their 11 children. Miriam's husband had been murdered many years ago and her eldest son was in the USA, where a lot of Triqui people work as undocumented migrants. Miriam and other women who had been victims and witnesses of several attacks made official complaints to the state justice institutions in Oaxaca City. But after they made these complaints they returned, unprotected, to San Juan Copala. On 3 September 2010 they were intercepted by a group of armed men. Miriam was beaten with weapons and raped by four men. The other woman was shot in her attempt to escape and seriously injured in her left shoulder. After the rape, the men cut off Miriam's long hair – one of the most valued things for Triqui women. A few days later she went to the *plantón* in Oaxaca City to seek the protection of other women. She has not returned to her house. It was looted, as were all the houses in San Juan Copala.

Miriam could be seen in many photos taken by the press, with the headline "Two Triqui women raped and tortured by paramilitaries." In one of the photos Miriam was on a hospital stretcher, showing her injured arm. Behind her, the woman who had accompanied her was showing her shoulder and the big cut made by a *machete*. Neither woman speaks Spanish. Miriam was taken to live in the house of an activist in Oaxaca City for her own security.

Indigenous rights and violent state construction in Oaxaca   171

But she decided to return to the sit-in with the other women, and then, ignoring security recommendations, she went to live with her daughter in a rented house in the Triqui region. Miriam's sexual abuse was far from the only case in the region, but hers was the only one that was made public. The exposure of her case became very important for the Triqui struggle for autonomy. Yet Miriam did not pursue a legal complaint and soon after rumors began to circulate that she had gone mad.

Conclusions

In this chapter I have attempted to show the effects that the circulation of rights discourses has had for Triqui women within a broader political struggle for self-determination as an indigenous people. As Sierra and Sieder have argued (Sieder and Sierra 2010), although multicultural legal reforms do not ensure direct access to justice for indigenous women, the rights discourses that have begun to circulate within state and non-state spaces have become important tools to address their situation as women within community and public spheres. What is clear for the Triqui case is that through their mobilization they broke the silence surrounding the ways in which the violence has affected women. To feel for the first time that they have the right to speak and to know they are also important in the struggle for their self-determination gave Triqui women an important political role. For perhaps the first time ever they began to think of themselves as subject of rights. However, as I have shown here, the conditions of extreme violence and impunity, and the violent structures women confront in their search for justice, represent immense obstacles to guaranteeing indigenous women's access to justice.

Although the multicultural reforms recognizing legal pluralism in Oaxaca state were welcomed as one of the broadest in Mexico in terms of recognizing indigenous rights to self-determination, they are far from being a real guarantee of indigenous people's access to justice. In this chapter, I have suggested that the historical conditions of violence, poverty and impunity that characterize state construction in Oaxaca are the primary factors limiting the guarantee of the rights these reforms established. Instead, as I have argued, these reforms were part of a new "pact" of governability with indigenous communities: the legal recognition of rights has not implied a real change in the racist and discriminatory structures of the state, even though the reforms created institutions specifically intended to address the situation of indigenous people. In the Triqui region, legal and illegal state practices combined to establish an ambiguous "grey zone" of political power. My analysis points to the hidden implications in official statements that suggest that indigenous tradition is synonymous with "savage customs." What is clear is that government officials aimed to limit guarantees of collective rights while also denying their responsibility for securing fundamental human

172 Gender Justice and Legal Pluralities

rights. Multicultural reforms recognizing legal pluralism effectively legalized historical practises of semi-autonomy. However, this was a tactic to reinforce certain political practices within indigenous communities that continued to be tied to political parties through channels of state patronage.

In this sense, even though the indigenous mobilization and intervention of different human rights organizations in the Triqui conflict has provided opportunities for indigenous voice, the limited exercise of their rights and the absence of governmental will to recognize these have led to increased violence and fragmentation. The declaration of municipal autonomy was clearly a means to denounce the violent situation provoked by the historical intervention of partisan interests, local caciques and the police and army. It was also an opportunity to begin a process of "recuperation" of Triqui traditions aimed at ending the longstanding intra-ethnic armed conflict. The idea of autonomy rights for indigenous people constitutes a critique of the limited sense that these have acquired in the administrative language of legal recognition: it expands them to signify a dignified life. In the Triqui region this meant freedom from partisan ties and coercive forces: in other words, freedom from the violence and insecurity they had suffered for decades. However, the history of political violence and mounting repression ultimately meant a highly constrained and limited exercise of autonomy.

For Triqui women, the context of legal pluralism was an opportunity to uncover a hitherto invisible situation: the violence used against them and the failure to take their voices into account. Because of their recent involvement as targets in the conflict, women broke their silence for the first time and found in the autonomy struggle the possibility to participate. However, as I have suggested here, their participation is limited in different senses. First, it depends on the decision, of men and the spaces they give to women in the movement; second, the fact that the women who participate are single or widows tells us about the limits families place on the political participation of married women, even though they are not exempt from being victims of violence. Nonetheless, the participation of some women is gradually changing gender relations inside and outside their communities.

Different social organizations have focused their attention on the situation of women as "innocent victims" in the Triqui conflict, something that has undoubtedly had an impact on their participation. By naming and denouncing sexual violence and rape, they bring into the public sphere a practice that has historically been silenced and naturalized. Yet the exposure of victims of sexual violence can also involve re-victimization; such was the case of Miriam, the widow who was publically exposed as a victim and made the object of "external" protection. The focus on Miriam as an individual stands in contrast to the sense of collective subjectivity, justice and women's agency that prevails within indigenous communities. Her refusal to pursue an individual complaint within the state justice system or to be an object of protective measures signals the enormous tension that exists between individual

Indigenous rights and violent state construction in Oaxaca   173

and collective rights. It also underlines the discriminatory and violent structures indigenous women continue to confront in their struggles for justice inside and outside their communities.

Acknowledgements

This chapter was possible thanks to the support of the project *Poverty Reduction and Gender Justice in Contexts of Legal Pluralism*, which facilitated my fieldwork and two key project workshops in Mexico and Mozambique. I am grateful for the feedback and advice of project coordinators Rachel Sieder and John-Andrew McNeish, and Liv Tønnessen, Maria Teresa Sierra, Bjørn Enge Bertelsen, Ana Cecilia Arteaga Böhrt and Eyolf Jul-Larsen. My special thanks to Rachel Sieder for her support throughout the editing of this chapter.

Notes

1 Following the armed rebellion of January 1994, talks between indigenous peoples and state representatives led to the signing of the San Andrés agreements between the Ejército Zapatista de Liberación Nacional (EZLN) and the federal government. These agreements were the result of dialogue between different actors and indigenous organizations and represented a pact between the state and the indigenous movement. However, since 1996 when the agreements were concluded, the Mexican state has consistently refused to implement them (Speed 2008: 49–52; Aubry 2002: 403–30).
2 See Poole 2009; Sieder 2002; Mattiace et al. 2002; de Sousa Santos 1998; de Sousa Santos and Rodríguez Garavito 2007; Speed 2008; Sierra 2004.
3 Triqui people are an ethnic group of about 30,000 inhabitants who live in the Mixtec region in the north-east of Oaxaca State. The Triqui territory (comprising just over 500 square kilometers) is unique in the region because of its partly tropical climate. The "lower Triqui" (*Triqui baja*), whose political and religious centre is San Juan Copala, includes approximately 30 communities in which nearly 13,000 Triqui people live. It is calculated that more than 20,000 Triqui people live in different states in Mexico (INEGI).
4 See Velázquez 2000; Martínez 2004; Anaya Muñoz 2004, 2006; Recondo 2007; Hernández Diaz 2007; Leal 2006.
5 The National Institute of Statics and Census (INEGI) bases its statistics for the indigenous population in relation to language. In this regard, it only surveys people aged five and over. In 2010, 1,165,186 people in Oaxaca were reported to speak one of the 16 recognized languages. Some authors estimate that if one uses other identity indicators over half of the population in Oaxaca is indigenous (Recondo 2007: 40).
6 Oaxaca, Guerrero and Chiapas were the three states with the lowest Human Development Index of the whole country. They are situated in a middle rank between 0.69 and 0.75 (CDI-PNUD 2006: 81).
7 The municipality is the lowest political and administrative unit recognized by the Mexican Constitution. It functions as an institution that articulates civil society with the federal and state governments. Historically, this figure has its roots in the colonial period when they were created in order to gain certain autonomy vis-à-vis

174   Gender Justice and Legal Pluralities

the colonial authorities. The Constitution of 1917 established that each state was constituted by municipalities based on popular elected governments (Díaz Montes 1992).

8 The National Action Party, formed in 1939, was the only important opponent of the PRI. It won state governorships for the first time in 1989. The Democratic Revolutionary Party, founded in 1989, is considered the third political force in Mexico.

9 Through this decentralization process the municipalities began to administer more state recourses (known in Oaxaca as the *Ramo 33* and *Ramo 28*). This expanded the possibilities for paying for political services and loyalties (Recondo 2007: 287–8); see also Hernández Díaz 2007: 65).

10 In the case of the multicultural reforms of Oaxaca, reforms to the state constitution were initially promoted by the PRI governor Heladio Ramírez (1986–92) in 1990. At the end of his term of office Ramírez promoted a reform of the electoral code based on "uses and customs," which was completed in 1995. Between 1995 and 1997, the new PRI governor Didioro Carrasco continued promoting changes to the state's constitution and electoral code. Additional reforms included the penal code, the code of penal procedure, the law of education and the creation of the Law of the Rights of Indigenous People and Communities of Oaxaca State.

11 Between 1994 and 2006 the PRI vote fell from 55 percent to 34 percent and the PRD vote rose from 28 percent to 48 percent (Recondo 2007: 440–1).

12 In percentage terms, fewer indigenous people are imprisoned for minor offenses than non-indigenous people (one percent of all indigenous people serve jail terms for this category of offenses, compared to five percent of non-indigenous people). This is in part due to the fact that minor misdemeanors tend to be dealt with by local indigenous authorities, whose jurisdiction is recognized by state justice officials (ACNUDH, 2007).

13 There are three different legal forms of land tenure in Mexico. For indigenous people, colonial titles allowed indigenous communities to gain the figure of communal lands. In the agrarian revolution, another legal figure appeared for the rural people: the inalienable collective land grant of *"ejidos."* In 1992 the constitutional reform of Article 27 allowed for the private ownership and sale of ejido lands.

14 International Labour Organization Convention 169, ratified by Mexico in 1991, states that indigenous and tribal populations have the right to free, prior and informed consultation by governments in cases when legislative or administrative measures are likely to them (Article 6.1) and in cases of exploration or exploitation of sub-surface resources (Article 15.2), among others. However, in many cases consultation has either not occurred or has been affected by multiple irregularities. The "Proyecto Platino" included in the Development Plan of Oaxaca (2011–16) proposes 13 high impact development projects, including the hydroelectric dams Paso Ancho and Paso de la Reina and the highways Mitla-Tehuantepec and Barranca Larga Ventanilla. These projects were planned without any consultation with affected communities. In other existing projects, such as the Aeolic energy farms managed by Spanish firms in Tehuantepec and mining projects in Capulalpan, the absence of consultation or irregularities in the contracts have provoked mobilizations and protest by affected communities: see Aquino Centeno 2010; Castro Rodríguez 2011.

15 Interview with a young Triqui boy, San Juan Copala, September 2008.

16 Interview with a Triqui woman, Oaxaca City, December 2011.

17 For a historical analysis of the evolution of the partisan system in Mexico, see González Casanova 1981.

18 *Caciquismo* is a category that describes the political and organizational machinery of "boss politics" within different spaces, including trade unions, politics and the agrarian bureaucracy of the Mexican state. Caciques played an important role in the political system of Mexico in the twentieth century, principally at local levels, combining repression, clientelism and charismatic authority: Knight 2005; Recondo 2007.
19 See Recondo 2007: 47; Velázquez 2000: 74; Villoro 1996: 220.
20 For a discussion, seeHernández Castillo 2001; Rus 1994; Villoro 1996; for Oaxaca state, see Recondo 2007; Velázquez 2000.
21 The Triqui people's opposition to construction of the school before 1960 was registered by Jacobo Montes in 1962. He alleged that the rejection was related to the suspicion that anyone who learned Spanish would become an informant for the government (Montes 1963: 25).
22 The "grey zone" is a concept coined by Primo Levi that Javier Auyero has used to analyze the construction of the state in marginal areas in Argentina. For Auyero, the local sphere presents itself as a confusion where there are no clear dichotomies, and where the distinctions made by the literature on collective action collapse (Auyero 2007: 41). This ambiguity, present in studies of violence and the state, validates the utilization of the concept of "grey zone" to comprehend power, violence and the blurred lines that separate the state from what is not the state. Other contributions to this perspective are the "state effect" proposed by Mitchell (1999) and "the margins of the state" (Das and Poole 2004).
23 The term "*mestizo*" has different meanings and implications: it is a way to recognize the "racial mix" between white and indigenous people, but it is also a way of referring to the white/mestizo elite who governed the post-revolutionary state.
24 Parra Mora and Hernández Diáz (1994) analyze historical reports for the abuses committed by the army as well as the confiscation and resale of guns. They also document the support certain communities enjoyed in confrontations with others (García Alcaraz 1997; López Bárcenas 2009).
25 During the conflict, attacks on armed men were commonplace, especially against those who had "problems" with other men. After 1995 armed ambushes on cars led to the death of all the people who were inside the car, without gender distinction. More victims also died in cross fire (López Bárcenas 2009).
26 According to a journalistic archive, between August 2005 and November 2009 some 30 murders occurred in the region of San Juan Copala, including nine children and young people; one a female child. Five of these 30 people were women over 20 years old. Two women were also disappeared in June 2006.
27 My PhD research is tentatively entitled "Constructing security in a violent context. State construction and Leadership among Triqui people of San Juan Copala, Oaxaca." I carried out ethnographic fieldwork between May 2010 and July 2011. The thesis (to be concluded in 2013) analyzes the process of violent state formation in the Triqui region, focusing on the construction of security through specific forms of leadership and organization and the practises of reparation enacted by Triqui women. It also explores the effects of the extreme violence they suffer and the role Triqui women play in the search for justice and security in a context of legal pluralism.
28 See Cumes 2009.
29 The armed ambush of the caravan of human rights activists and journalists in April 2010, when two human rights activists were murdered, attracted international attention. During 2010 a representative of the European Parliament repeatedly requested a meeting with the government without response. After 2011,

176 Gender Justice and Legal Pluralities

when the new governor Gabino Cue assumed office in Oaxaca, a series of meetings was held to try to resolve past acts of violence that had occurred in the Triqui conflict.

30 Interview with Rogelia, a displaced woman of the Triqui Region, Oaxaca City, December 2010.

31 Interview with a displaced woman of the Triqui region, Oaxaca City, September 2010.

32 "Ulises Ruiz ignores the humanitarian brigade who goes to San Juan Copala," Proceso, 7 June 2010.

33 The Acteal Massacre was carried out in Chiapas in December 1997 by a paramilitary group, which murdered 45 indigenous people, including children and pregnant women, all of them members of the pacifist group "Las Abejas." See Hernández Castillo 1998; Castro Apreza 2004.

34 On 7 October 2010 the Interamerican Commission on Human Rights granted precautionary measures for 135 displaced people from San Juan Copala. Its resolution MS 197/10 considered the violent displacement of many people from San Juan Copala. It also recommended that the government protect these people and investigate the causes of this violence. Available at http://www.cidh.oas.org/medidas/2010.sp.htm (accessed March 2012).

35 Numerous organizations pressured the Oaxacan authorities to resolve the situation, including Amnesty International and the OHCHR.

References

Agamben, G. (2007) *Estados de Excepción*, 2nd edn, Buenos Aires: Adriana Hidalgo Editores.

Alto Comisionado de las Naciones Unidas para los Derechos Humanos (ACNUDH) (2007) *El acceso a la justicia para los indígenas en México. Estudio de caso en Oaxaca*, Mexico: ACNUDH.

Anaya Muñoz, A. (2004) "Explaining the politics of Recognition of Ethnic Diversity and Indigenous Peoples' Rights in Oaxaca, Mexico," *Bulletin of Latin American Research, Society of Latin American Studies* 23 (4): 414–33.

——(2006) *Autonomía Indígena, gobernabilidad y legitimidad en México. La legalización de los usos y costumbres electorales en Oaxaca*, Mexico: Plaza y Valdés, Universidad Iberoamericana.

Aquino Centeno, S. (2010) "Ni oro, ni plata, ni dinero: lo que queremos es cuidar nuestros veneros," paper presented at Red Latinoamericana de Antropología Jurídica Conference, Lima, Peru, August.

Aubry, A. (2002) "La autonomía en los acuerdos de San Andrés: Expresión y Ejercicio de un nuevo pacto federal," in Mattiace, S., R. Hernández and J. Rus (eds) *Tierra, libertad y autonomía: Impactos regionales del zapatismo en Chiapas*, Mexico: CIESAS-IWGIA, pp. 403–33.

Auyero, J. (2007) *La zona gris. Violencia colectiva y política partidaria en la Argentina contemporánea*, Buenos Aires: Siglo XXI.

Castro Apreza, I. (2004) "San Pedro Chenalhó: La cúspide de la violencia en tiempos de guerra," in Perez Ruíz, M. (ed) *Tejiendo historias: Tierra, género y poder en Chiapas*, Mexico: ENAH.

Castro Rodríguez, A. (2011) "Megaproyectos en Oaxaca violan derechos de los Pueblos Indígenas," paper presented at the International Simposium *El derecho reglamentario del derecho de los Pueblos Indígenas a la Consulta y el Consentimiento Previo, Libre e Informado*, Oaxaca, November, http:// www.cencos.org/ node/27962 (accessed 23 January 2012).

CDI-PNUD (2006) *Informe sobre desarrollo humano de los pueblos indígenas de México*, Mexico: CDI-PNUD.

Cumes, A. (2009) "Sufrimos verguenza: Mujeres K'iché frente a la justicia comunitaria," *Desacatos* 31: 99–114.

Das, V. and D. Poole (2004) "State and its Margins: Comparative Ethnographies," in Das, V. and D. Poole (eds) *Anthropology in the Margins of the State*, Santa Fé: SAR Press, pp. 3–33.

de Sousa Santos, B. (1998) *La Globalización del Derecho. Los nuevos caminos de la regulación y la emancipación*, Bogota: Universidad Nacional de Colombia.

——(2002) *Towards a New Legal Common Sense: Law, Globalization and Emancipation*, 2nd edn, Scotland: Butterworths.

de Sousa Santos, B. and C. Rodríguez Garavito (2007) "La política, el derecho y lo subalterno en la globalización contrahegemónica," in de Sousa Santos, B. and C. Rodríguez Garavito (eds) *El derecho y la globalización desde abajo. Hacia una legalidad cosmopolita*, Madrid: UAM y Anthropos, pp. 7–28.

Díaz Montes, F. (1992) *Los municipios: La disputa por el poder local en Oaxaca*, Oaxaca: IIS-UABJO.

Foro Internacional de Mujeres Indígenas (FIMI) (2006) *Mairin Iwanka Raya: Mujeres indígenas confrontan la violencia*, http://http://www.fimi-iiwf.org/ (accessed March 2012).

Foucault, M. (2006) *Defender la sociedad*, Mexico: FCE.

García Alcaraz, A. (1997) *Tinujei: Los triquis de Copala*, Mexico: Centro de Investigaciones y Estudios Superiores en Antropología Social.

González Casanova, P. (1981) *El Estado y los Partidos Políticos en México*, Mexico: Editorial Era.

Hernández Castillo, R. (ed.) (1998) *La otra palabra. Mujeres y violencia en Chiapas, antes y después de Acteal*, Mexico: CIESAS, Grupo de Mujeres de San Cristóbal A.C. and Centro de Investigación y Acción para la Mujer.

——(2001) *La Otra Frontera: Identidades Múltiples en el Chiapas Poscolonial*, Mexico: CIESAS-Porrúa.

——(2006) "Fratricidal War or Ethnocidal Strategy? Women's Experiences with Political Violence in Chiapas," in Sanford V. and A. Angel-Ajali (eds) *Engaged Observer: Anthropology, Advocacy and Activism*, Piscataway, NJ: Rutgers University Press, pp. 149–69.

——(2010) "Violencia de Estado y Violencia de Género: Las paradojas en torno a los derechos humanos de las Mujeres en México," *TRACE* 57: 86–98.

——(n.d.) "Entre la justicia comunitaria y el litigio internacional: El Caso de Inés Fernández ante la Corte Interamericana," paper presented at the workshop "Mujeres y Derecho en América Latina: Justicia, Seguridad y Pluralismo Legal," Cuetzalan, Puebla, November 2011.

Hernández Díaz, J. (ed.) (2007) *Ciudadanías diferenciadas en un Estado Multicultural: Los usos y costumbres en Oaxaca*, Mexico: Instituto de Investigaciones Sociológicas de la UABJO-Siglo XXI.

Huerta Ríos, C. (1981) *Organización socio-política de una minoría nacional. Los triquis de Oaxaca*, Mexico: Instituto Nacional Indigenista.

178 Gender Justice and Legal Pluralities

Joseph, G. and D. Nugent (1994) "Introduction," in Joseph, G. and D. Nugent (eds) *Everyday Forms of State Formation: Revolution and the Negotiation of Rule in Modern Mexico*, Durham, NC and London: Duke University Press, pp. 1–23.

Knight, A. (2005) "Caciquismo in the Twentieth-century Mexico," in Knight, A. and W. Pansters (eds) *Caciquismo in the Twentieth-century Mexico*, London: Institute for The Studies of the Americas, University of London, pp. 3–48.

Kraemer, G. (2006) "El derecho indígena y el sistema jurídico dominante. El caso de Oaxaca," in Cienfuegos Salgado, D. and M. Macías Vázquez (eds) *Estudios en homenaje a Marcia Muñoz de Alba Medrano Estudios de derecho público y política*, Mexico: UNAM-Insituto de Investigaciones Jurídicas, pp. 257–77.

Leal, A. (2006) "Burocracia, Justicia y Pluralismo Jurídico. Una exploración de los espacios del poder en Oaxaca," *Alteridades* 46: 39–48.

López Bárcenas, F. (2009) *San Juan Copala: Dominación Política y Resistencia Popular, De las rebeliones de Hilarión a la formación del Municipio Autónomo*, Mexico: UAM Xochimilco.

Luzula, K. (2007) *Acceso a la justicia de los pueblos indígenas de Oaxaca: Retos y Posibilidades*, Washington, DC: Secretaría General de la OEA.

Martínez, J. (2004) "El proceso de reforma constitucional en materia indígena y la posición del Estado de Oaxaca. Una aproximación socio-jurídica," in Hernández Castillo, R. A., S. Paz and T. Sierra (eds) *El Estado y los Indígenas en los tiempos del PAN: Neoindigenismo, legalidad e identidad*, Mexico: Porrúa/CIESAS, pp. 233–60.

Mattiace, S., R. Hernández Castillo and J. Rus (eds) (2002) *Tierra, libertad y autonomía: impactos regionales del zapatismo en Chiapas*, Mexico: CIESAS – IWGIA.

Mitchell, T. (1999) "Society, Economy and the State Effect," in Steinmetz, G. (ed) *State/Culture: State Formation After the Cultural Turn*, London: Cornell University Press, pp. 76–98.

Montes, J. (1963) *Conflicto en la zona triqui*, Mexico: Instituto Nacional Indigenista.

Nahmad, S. (1980) "La educación bilingüe y bi-cultural para las regiones interculturales de México," in *Indigenismo y lingüística. Documentos del foro La política del lenguaje en México*, Mexico: UNAM.

Nelson, D. (2009) *Reckoning: The Ends of War in Guatemala*, Durham, NC and London: Duke University Press.

Parra Mora, L. and J. Hernández Díaz (1994) *Violencia y Cambio Social en la Región Triqui*, Mexico: UABJO.

Poole, D. (2009) "Autonomía desterritorializada," in Martinez, C. (comp.) *Repensando los movimientos indígenas*, Quito: FLACSO Ecuador.

Recondo, D. (2007) *La política del gatopardo. Multiculturalismo y democracia en Oaxaca*, Mexico: CIESAS.

Rus, J. (1994) "The 'Comunidad Revolucionaria Institucional:' The Subversion of Native Government in Highland Chiapas, 1936–68," in Joseph, G. and D. Nugent (eds) *Everyday Forms of State Formation: Revolution and the Negotiation of Rule in Modern Mexico*, Durham, NC and London: Duke University Press, pp. 265–300.

Seifert, R. (1994) "War and Rape. A Preliminary Analysis," in Stiglmayer, A. (ed.) *Mass Rape: The War against Women in Bosnia-Herzegovina*, Lincoln: University of Nebraska Press, pp. 54–72.

Sieder, R. (2002) "Introduction," in Rachel Sieder (ed.) *Multiculturalism in Latin America; Indigenous Rights, Diversity and Democracy*, New York, NY: Palgrave Macmillan, pp. 1–24.

Sieder, R. and M. T. Sierra (2010) *Indigenous Women's Access to Justice in Latin America*, CMI working paper, http://www.cmi.no/publications/publication/?3880=indigenous-womens-access-to-justice-in-latin (accessed July 2011).

Sierra, M. T. (2004) "Hacia una interpretación comprensiva de la relación entre justicia, derecho y género: Los procesos interlegales en regiones indígenas," in Sierra, M. T. (ed.) *Haciendo Justicia: Interlegalidad, derecho y género en regiones indígenas*, Mexico: CIESAS and Porrúa, pp. 11–56.

Speed, S. (2008) *Rights in Rebellion: Indigenous Struggle and Human Rights in Chiapas*, Palo Alto, CA: Stanford University Press.

Stephen, L. (2010) "Indigenous Mixtec and Triqui Participation in the Oaxaca Social Movement: Ethnic Alliances, Conflicts, and Transborder Organizing," paper presented at the *Second Conference on Race and Indigenous Peoples in Latin America*, University of California, San Diego.

Velázquez, M. (2000) *El nombramiento: Las elecciones por usos y costumbres de Oaxaca*, Mexico: Instituto Estatal Electoral de Oaxaca.

Villoro, L. (1996) *Los grandes momentos del indigenismo en México*, Mexico: Fondo de Cultura Económica, El Colegio de México, El Colegio Nacional.

Chapter 7

Opening Pandora's Box: human rights, customary law and the "communal liberal self" in Tanzania

Natalie J. Bourdon

Introduction

While the number of anthropologists studying the effects of transnational legal processes such as human rights remains relatively small, an accounting of the recent theoretical trajectory of these studies reveals a rapid and responsive advancement in conceptualizations between normative rights regimes, the people who make them, and the individuals and communities they affect. Barely more than a decade ago, Wilson (1997: 3) reported that "discussions of the cross-cultural applicability of human rights still revolve around the universalism/relativism debate and the importance of culture" and has since called for an exploration of the "social life of rights" (Wilson 1997) that focuses on, among other things, the "performative dimensions" of human rights (Wilson 2006).

Although discussions over the relevance and applicability of human rights regimes to local cultures may still underlie recent concerns about the translation, appropriation and vernacularization of human rights (Merry 2006a), the shift to employing a grounded theory approach to human rights has yielded profitable conceptual and theoretical shifts (see Merry 2006b; Cowan 2006; Hellum and Stewart 1998). On the one hand, the recognition of legal pluralities has drawn anthropologists to recognize and investigate how sources of law originating in domains outside of the nation state are sources of legitimacy and recourse for many people (Benda-Beckmann et al. 2009). Anthropologists and other scholars have begun studying the ways in which various actors *constitute* human rights through negotiation, reappropriation, reformulation, and rejection. These actors include non-governmental organization (NGO) members (Englund 2006; Riles 2006), state entities (Viljoen and Louw 2007), indigenous peoples (Richards 2005) and transnational actors (Merry 2006a). Concurrently, these same actors also make use of local understandings of personhood and rights and weave those conceptions into their human rights advocacy.

Anthropologists using a grounded theory approach to law no longer conceive of legal pluralism[1] as a mere conceptual tool for analyzing complex social spheres of intersecting and mutually constituting legal arrangements, but recognize it as a reality in people's struggles for inclusion and access to resources and political processes. Utilizing a grounded theory approach to the law has revealed the ways and extent to which people understand and locate themselves amongst existing legal orders, actively negotiate their identity and affiliations in light of these legal regimes, and in some cases, "forum-shop" for a law or laws that will best suit their interests (Helfer 1999). Plural legal orders offer both constraints and opportunities for people who live within (or between) them and offer new opportunities for key decision makers such as lawyers, judges and legal advocates to invoke laws with which they are most familiar, and to advance positions with which they are most ideologically aligned.

Tanzania has a long history of legal pluralities. Before European colonization, different ethnic groups formulated diverse customary legal arrangements though some broad similarities can be found among them, particularly with regards to property and inheritance rights (Moore 2000). During both the German (1885–1919) and British (1919–61) colonial eras, multiple legal orders were sanctioned by governing officials including "tribal" or customary law, Islamic law and state or civil law. In the post-colonial period, plural legal orders expanded to include international human rights laws. International rights laws have proved especially attractive to women's rights advocates and human rights NGOs; however, rights advocates must also deal with the complex realities of disputes that have already been framed by (at times) competing legal constellations.

This chapter presents two broad perspectives[2] from which we may consider women's inheritance rights *as rights* in Tanzania. From one perspective, we can view how inheritance practices and rights are differently framed depending on the legal regime they fall under. From a second perspective, Tanzanian women's rights organizations acknowledge that customary inheritance practices discriminate against women and often, though not always, argue for a liberal notion of rights found in many international instruments.[3] A central tension arises in contestations over inheritance where different parties claim their "rights" to property and land; rights based in or issuing from customary, Islamic, and increasingly international law. In holding these two broad perspectives in mind, this chapter considers the "emancipatory" potential of rights enshrined in international conventions for Tanzanian women.

I will lay the groundwork by considering a number of cases that present various affiliational ties that are often invoked and that form the foundation of inheritance contestations. In order to narrow the scope of this work, all reference to and excerpts from inheritance cases are from Shinyanga, Tanzania. The Shinyanga Paralegal Center is located in the Shinyanga Region of Tanzania, which lies approximately 175km by road southeast of Mwanza, the nearest large city. The data was collected during 14 months of anthropological research between 2003 and 2005 focusing on land and inheritance law reform and legal advocacy efforts among a core group of legal and human rights NGOs in Dar es Salaam, Tanzania.[4] The chapter will present an in-depth discussion of a strategic inheritance litigation case[5] brought to the High Court by Tanzanian women's rights advocates where they sought to test the constitutionality of Tanzania's Customary Law Declaration Order (1963).[6] Discussing first the cases from Shinyanga will illustrate both the difficulties for and important role of women's legal rights advocates in framing women's rights in the courts and more broadly on the national stage. I propose that women's rights advocates employ "liberal" notions of rights but also expand and reconfigure those ideas to accommodate the reality of Tanzanian women's multiply constituted selves.

Legal pluralities and legal procedure in Tanzania

Because of the particular form that state-sanctioned legal pluralism has taken in Tanzania since independence in 1961, women's ability to obtain equal rights to inheritance has both been hindered and found opportunity for expression in the law. I employ here the approach adopted by Hellum and Stewart (1998) which advocates an anthropological conception of legal pluralism; one that advances both that there is an official legal system that recognizes more than one system of law *and* which recognizes "that there are regulatory or normative systems other than the formal law that affect and control people's lives" (Hellum and Stewart 1998: 41). As these authors argue, this is not only a matter of semantics, but rather an important conceptual point that affects our perception of legal systems as well as of the different forces that have the opportunity to reform law and women's position within it. In Tanzania, clients and lawyers alike have some degree of choice and maneuverability when it comes to invoking (or ignoring) customary law in inheritance cases. It is thus the actors involved in any particular case who bring with them the expression of other normative systems and the frameworks of gender relations that these involve and who, through their particular subject positions, constitute the legal spaces in which their cases are heard and decided. It is therefore important to adopt an actor-centered perspective in investigating legal pluralities in order to understand the various ways in which gendered power dynamics, clients' knowledge and judges' mastery of the legal systems, together with a whole set of other individual ideas and communal relationships structure and have bearing on the case at hand.

As in many other African countries, Tanzania's former British colonial administration established criteria specifying which cases would be heard under each system of law. Following their German predecessors, British colonial officials believed that every Tanzanian belonged to a specific tribe, each with distinct cultural practices as well as established customary laws

(Iliffe 1979: 323). Broadly speaking, British officials relegated petty crimes and "family disputes" to customary courts while criminal cases were heard in the civil courts. Islamic courts were to continue functioning for Tanzanian Muslims. Included in "family disputes" were cases of intestate succession and inheritance. Upon attaining independence, Tanzania's first president, Nyerere, took the choice to maintain a system of legal pluralism but went a step further and codified customary laws for Tanzania's 120 different ethnic groups in a piece of legislation called the Local Customary Law (Declaration) Order, Government Notice No. 279 (amended GN 436) of 1963 (hereafter called the Customary Law Order, CLO).[7] The CLO is the main body of customary law regulating the guardianship of children, laws of inheritance and laws of wills. With respect to inheritance, the CLO clearly states in the second schedule, paragraph one, "*Urithi hufuata upande wa ukoo wa kiume*" (Inheritance follows the male lineage). Women's human rights organizations have denounced this along with 29 other paragraphs of the CLO as discriminating against women and therefore in direct violation of the Constitution's[8] provisions for equal rights.[9]

The CLO is only one of three ways in which intestate succession is currently regulated in Tanzania. One may also follow inheritance procedures laid out in Islamic law or the Indian Succession Act (1865), which applies to Tanzania under the Judicature and Application of Laws Act (JALA) of 2002. While the Indian Succession Act is gender neutral, it is mostly applied to Europeans and only rarely applied by magistrates to African Tanzanians (Ezer 2006). While Tanzanians have choice of law, by default most inheritance cases are regulated under customary law as the JALA states that customary law regulates succession for "a person who is or was a member of a community in which rules of customary law relevant to the matter are established and accepted" (JALA para 11b). There are two primary ways in which one can effectively avoid being considered under customary law: first, if a person makes it apparent through "their manner of life or business" that their matter is to be regulated under something other than customary law; or second, if the deceased professed Islam or Christianity or left a written will specifying that his property should be administered according to Islamic law or the Indian Succession Act.[10]

The language of the CLO presumes that all property, even that acquired jointly during marriage, belongs to the husband. The CLO goes on to articulate different scenarios for inheritance, the majority of which awards property to the deceased's male children and/or heirs on the paternal side. While in practice inheritance is variably regulated, the JALA reinscribes notions of cultural unity and stasis, instructing courts to "apply the customary law prevailing within the area of its local jurisdiction" (para 11(3)). While the JALA and CLO are fairly detailed as regards inheritance procedure, there is often great confusion on the part of advocates, lawyers and judges as to which "customary law" should be applied, especially in cases of cross-ethnic and inter-faith marriages. Further exacerbating this problem, judges and lawyers who are not originally from the cultural context in which they are practicing can generate uncertainty over which customary laws to apply. Indeed, the mass movement and integration of Tanzania's ethnic groups resulting from both the villagization policies pursued in earlier decades and contemporary migration makes the polysemic nature of "customary law" in any one location even more evident.

It is within this context of plural legal orders that Tanzanian lawyers and women's rights advocates are working. While scholars and Tanzanian legal practitioners have amply demonstrated that the CLO and associated laws clearly discriminate against women (Ezer 2006; Ezer and Ross 2006; Manji 2006; Tsikata 2003; Whitehead and Tsikata 2003), both clients and women's human rights advocates and lawyers have begun to interpolate international human rights norms into all levels of judicial proceedings. Tanzanian legal and human rights NGOs in Dar es Salaam and around the country vernacularize international human rights laws in all stages of their work from educational outreach programs, in client intake at clinics, throughout client advisory sessions and primary court preparation sessions, in alternative dispute resolution sessions, and as client representatives and advocates in District Courts, the High Court and Appellate Courts.[11]

Women's legal rights NGOs

Tanzanian human rights lawyers and development practitioners in Dar es Salaam and around the country have made a concerted effort to change laws that discriminate against women and to secure legislation that protects women's rights. Over the past two decades, a cohort of women's and human rights organizations in Dar es Salaam's Feminist Activist Coalition have been successful in their efforts to ensure that Tanzania's new land law reflects women's rights to own land and property (Manji 1998; Tripp 2004). However, inheritance law, considered by women's rights NGOs to be a key part of that Bill, was left untouched, obstructing arguably the most important avenue for a majority of Tanzanian women to acquire land and property. Facing continuous obstacles from the legislature, these same human rights NGOs made the decision to tackle inheritance reform through the law by testing the constitutionality of the CLO.

Principally, the CLO excludes women from the opportunities to acquire, hold, and dispose of land in their own right as it validates existing patrilineal tenure and inheritance arrangements operative for Tanzania's ethnic groups. While Tanzania is rapidly urbanizing, over 75 percent of Tanzanians remain rural dwellers and land is an unparalleled resource for a family's health and financial wellbeing. While the new Land Law (1999)[12] provides that women may acquire and sell land individually, not guaranteeing women's right to inherit land prevents the vast majority of women from actually acquiring it. A decision was made to assemble a team of 13 women's rights advocates who would proceed with a strategic litigation case to test the constitutionality of 30 paragraphs of the CLO.

The assembled legal team conducted background research for the case, identifying a region where clients would be interviewed, and brought the case to Tanzania's High Court. The legal researchers decided on two clients from Shinyanga. In order to give a brief sketch of some current inheritance cases in the region, I present three case vignettes below that shed light on some salient issues in inheritance cases and the factors that are considered in the judgments of the cases, highlighting the complexity and key role of legal professionals in interpreting inheritance cases.[13]

The case of S.M.

S.M.'s husband N.S. passed away in 2004 having written a will that was witnessed, signed and notarized by the district commissioner on 15 August 2003. In his will, N.S. bequeathed all of this property, including a plot of land and a house with all of its belongings, to his wife S.M. The will stated that S.M. should not dispose of the house and should remain in it until she is "taken by God." N.S., survived by two children, left one bicycle to one son but otherwise left no other inheritance to his children explaining in the will that the children did not care for him while he was sick and therefore they could not remain in his house. Upon the death of her husband, S.M. filed a petition to be the administrator of the estate and the primary court granted her rights of administration, whereupon S.M.'s two sons appealed to the district court.

In the District Court of Kahama, the judge reviewed the evidence presented (the will and depositions of the appellants and respondent) and wrote in his judgment:

> This matter is a customary law, all the parties are Nyamwezi and Haya by tribe respectively. The issue is appointment of an administrator of the deceased estate and inheritance. Under GN 426/63, the second schedule para (2) of the Local Customary Law (Declaration) Order No. 4, 1963 it says (1) *Urithi hufuata upande wa ukoo wa kiume.* In this case the respondent was not [on] the paternal side of the late N.S., she was only his wife. In law, she cannot be appointed as administrator of the estate of the deceased, her husband.
>
> (Judgment, 10 April 2004)

The judge continued by arguing that "the purported will" is "a copy. In evidence, that is not admissible" and that "under customary law, only children of the deceased have the right to inherit."

186   Gender Justice and Legal Pluralities

S.M.'s submission of appeal to the High Court at Tabora stated: "The appellate court errored [sic] both in law and facts when [it] decided to deal with the matter under customary law while we alienated the Customary law and followed Roman Cathoric [sic] rites." The appeal went on to state, "[t]he appellate court had an opinion that the parties are Nyamwezi and Haya in tribe, but so long as since then we choosed [sic] to be Christians the proper law to be followed was the Law of Succession Act and not customary law." Despite this, the High Court ruled: "As the respondents are the deceased's children and are living in their house it will not be in the interest of justice to order them to vacate the house in dispute." S.M.'s appeal was dismissed.

At that time, S.M. filed an appeal to the Court of Appeal for administration of the estate at the same time that she opened an application in the District Land and Housing Tribunal in Shinyanga in order to reclaim a kiosk she claimed the children stole and sold to one G.L. The respondents claimed that the allegations were not admitted and that the suit was not properly filed by S.M. in the Land Tribunal as it had no jurisdiction over such cases. In the Appellate Court's judgment (2007), the presiding justice, citing Section 2 of the Fifth Schedule to the Magistrates' Court Act No. 2 of 1984, confirmed the primary court's decision to uphold the appointment of administration to S.M. stating that "*any person* interested in the administration of the estate of the deceased may be appointed administrator of the estate of the deceased." The judge verified that S.M. "properly applied for appointment of an administrator" and that "[t]he District Court was wrong in its decision that in law the deceased's wife cannot be appointed as administrator of the estate of the deceased, her husband." S.M.'s appeal was granted.

For S.M. it was especially important that she visited the Shinyanga Paralegal Centre (PACESHI) between going to the primary court and writing her appeal to the district court. It was here that she learned of the possibility of framing her rights claim in terms of the Law of Succession Act instead of customary law. Paralegal aid officers noted that while Muslim women are often more knowledgeable about their rights under Islamic law, Christian women and men who contracted a civil marriage often did not know that they could frame their claim in this matter, effectively avoiding (in some cases) customary law. However, paralegal officers in Shinyanga and legal aid providers in Dar es Salaam's clinics, often will work within the bounds of customary legal arrangements if they feel confident they can still win a case. S.M.'s case also highlights the ambiguity of customary law and the interpretive license that judges may take in such decisions.

The case of T.M.

T.M. is the daughter of the second wife of M.M.T., who passed away in 2001. After years of intra-familial disputes and attempts at reconciling those disputes with BAKWATA (*Baraza Kuu la Waislamu wa Tanzania*, the Supreme Council of Muslims in Tanzania), T.M. opened a formal file against the sons of M.M.T. in Shinyanga with Sheikh I.H. at BAKWATA. After hearing the testimony of all parties involved (three of the four children, the last having passed away), the sheikh decided that the house should be sold and the money divided among the children. T.M., who was at the time residing in the house, objected to its sale, noting, "Because I am the daughter, I will not have a place to live" (*Kwa sababu mimi ni mtoto wa kike sitakuwa na mahali pa kwenda kuishi*).

Further testimony revealed that M.M.T's son, A.M., had already surreptitiously sold the house without consulting his siblings. After learning that BAKWATA showed no intention of resolving this situation, T.M. stated that the parties should have followed the "procedure of BAKWATA and that the deceased lived and followed the Islamic religion" and so they should follow Islamic rules of inheritance, even though this disadvantaged her. Aggrieved with the unwillingness (or inability) of BAKWATA to remedy the situation, T.M. opened a case at the primary court in which the original court petition noted, "a person has the right to claim their rights in court if they have been dispossessed of their rights, therefore what is passing through your esteemed court requires keen attention to this issue as there is every sign of [dispossession], as they have started to take away my rights in the question of the property of the deceased." As the child of the deceased, she went on to claim that she "should be the administrator of the estate on behalf of the family so that I could fulfill the requirements demanded by the law of the rights for administration number 358 and the Statement of Islamic Law, GN 222 of 1967."

Women in PACESHI and clients at WLAC who I have spoken to over the years often remarked that they believed cases like this were subjectively decided and unfair. Muslim women in WLAC's legal aid clinics were especially prone to "forum shop" as they expressed that BAKWATA was not interested in helping women and had heard that the legal aid clinic was a place they could "get their rights." In this case, T.M. explicitly pointed to the gendered injustice she would experience as she would "no longer have a place to live" even though she would receive a portion of the sale of the house.

The case of F.A.

In July of 2008, F.A. applied to the primary court of Shinyanga to be the administrator along with her eldest daughter (aged 19) of her deceased husband's estate, stating that she was the wife of the deceased and that they were married according to Islamic law in 1988 and had four children. F.A.'s petition to the court, in part, reads:

> After the third day of the death of my late husband, the relatives of the deceased began bringing violence [into my home] because they wanted

188 Gender Justice and Legal Pluralities

the property title of the deceased, claiming that the house should be under the family of the deceased and not the wife and children of the deceased. The relatives of the deceased held a family meeting without consulting me or my children and after these meetings they came with a document which they had prepared and asked me to sign it without [my] knowing what had been written there, this caused me a lot of worries and when I wanted to press further into what had been written they took the documents and fled from us.

(Author's translation from the Swahili)

Subsequently, the brother of the deceased and his other brother filed a motion objecting to the appointment of F.A. as manager of the estate saying that the family of the deceased had met (*kikao cha wanandugu*) and already appointed their youngest brother as administrator of the estate. He went on to say that F.A. had violated the family meeting. He also accused F.A. of forging the deceased's will.

This case represents an interesting problem. While the husband had in his lifetime converted to Islam and contracted a Muslim marriage, the relatives of the deceased were not Muslim and seemingly following "customary" procedure by holding the family meeting on the deceased's side to appoint an administrator and divide the properties.[14] While choice of law seems obviously problematic in this case, as both parties have legitimate rights claims under Islamic and customary law, respectively, it also serves as a reminder that many cases will present similar problems as people's subjective positions and identities change over time. Dual consciousness is not only a problem for the colonized (Fanon 1967) but for all people in the modern world who incorporate diverse sets of ideas in their thinking and emphasize different aspects of their identities depending on the context.

Indeed, the primary court struggled with these questions. Its judgment stated:

[t]he Court is considering whether the widow should manage the estate or if the brother of the deceased should manage it? Having a copy of the marriage certificate, the court recognizes Islamic marriage is a legal marriage according to the Law of Marriage Act (1971) and that the property in question were [*sic*] bought together with the deceased in marriage.

Citing the Magistrates' Court Act No. 2 of 1984, the court stated that both the widow and a member of the deceased's natal family could be considered for appointment of administration. The court declared that all properties be divided by the children, widow and father of the deceased, appointing the deceased's father as primary and F.A. as secondary administrators of the estate respectively.

In the documentation of F.A.'s appeal to the district court, her brother-in-law's testimony states that "according to Haya culture a woman cannot be administrator of [the] deceased's estate when the younger brother is alive" and moreover the family is afraid the widow will remarry and the deceased's property will be lost. The judgment of the district court (7 September 2009) stated:

> [i]t is *unfortunate* that the appellant/widow can be an administrator of the late husband's estate but before I part with this I wish to make it clear that an administrator appointed by the court does not mean that she/he is placed in a position of a sole heir of the entire fortune of the estate of the deceased for his/her interest.
>
> (citing para 5 of Part 11 of the Magistrates' Court Act, 2002; emphasis added)

As the family meeting took place without inviting the children of the deceased, the judge found probable cause that the family did not have the best interests of the deceased's children at heart. He therefore appointed the first born of the deceased to be the first administrator of the estate and the appellant to "remain as she was."

WLAC's legal aid clinic in Dar es Salaam and its paralegal clinics around the country receive thousands of cases like this every year, with the number of women who are willing to seek legal advice and learn about their legal rights continuing to rise. Marriage and inheritance cases continue to constitute by far the majority of the cases WLAC and its paralegal units receive each year. Having identified, criticized and publicized the gender injustices that inhere in customary law for over two decades, women's rights lawyers in Dar es Salaam decided to challenge the constitutionality of the CLO.

Elizabeth Stephens and Salome Charles vs. Another (2006) – human rights lawyers' perspectives

A majority of the lawyers and advocates in Dar es Salaam's human rights NGOs hold complex views about plural legal orders in Tanzania. In their law reform advocacy work they often rely on international human rights conventions such as the CEDAW as they seek to promote a conception of women's rights independent of their family ties or other socially embedded affiliations. However, as I have discussed elsewhere (Bourdon 2009) in their daily work with clients and in alternative dispute resolution processes, lawyers invoke cultural, moral and religious norms to guide cases to a favorable outcome for women. While some human rights lawyers in the FemAct Coalition wish to see one unified legal system in Tanzania, many others recognize the importance of customary law in providing protection to groups against government and multinational corporations' infringements on land rights.[15] Furthermore, in legal argumentation in primary and district courts, lawyers often invoke affiliational ties as the basis for granting women property rights.

While all litigation cases are inherently "strategic" in one sense, strategic or "test" litigation cases were envisioned by the lawyers in this case as an expedient avenue to legal reform. One lawyer explained how women's rights advocates were left with little choice but to proceed with inheritance litigation:

> [w]e need to know why more things are not happening. We have had a strategic plan for years – we expect to find the law of inheritance has been changed. That was our plan. We have done a lot of lobbying, a lot of networking, workshops [and] seminars, but still the government turned a blind eye on things. We changed our approach. We even drafted a bill. The government has not paid attention. So we thought if we appeal to *their* court, we decided strategic litigation should be identified as a process for purpose, we thought using the court would be good.

Initiating a strategic litigation case in the High Court, would, I was told, "cut across all districts" and "affect a majority of people very quickly." One of the lead lawyers on the case explained, "if it is successful in the court, it will bear a lesson to the community. If it's from the court, people will obey, but if it's not from the court, people will not obey." As I will demonstrate here, this perception of the law's power to change practice is a markedly different conception of the relationship between law and behavior from that advanced by the High Court judge in this case.[16]

Lawyers discussed the selection criteria they used to identify litigants to test the constitutionality of the CLO in terms of the legal technicalities and who would best "fit" the case. Legally, they had to identify regions of the country where the CLO was applied. While the CLO is broadly applied to the entire country geographically speaking, it is only applied to patrilineal societies and not along the coast, which are mostly matrilineal. Further, they wanted widows who had probate matters, who had their property taken from them, and who had already proceeded through the lower courts. While the Women's Legal Aid Center has established paralegal units in every region of the country, the team of lawyers chose Shinyanga, which is commonly described in Dar es Salaam as "the deep interior" and is also often invoked as a place where culture is "strongest;" traditional beliefs and customs are practiced and the region is known to be a locus of witchcraft.

Beyond the legal technicalities, lawyers spoke of the importance of both locating clients living in a "patriarchal culture" as well as their "readiness'" to be part of the case. Choosing Elizabeth Stephens and Salome Charles was based on their being prepared to go to court, clearly identifying Sukuma customary law as being the source of their suffering, and having already begun to "learn about their rights." Lawyers emphasized that clients should not expect compensation but should be willing to participate for the benefit of future generations of girls and women. After having interviewed numerous women at PACESHI, Stephen and Charles were chosen for the strategic litigation. Both of the women's husbands had passed away and each of their properties was, following Sukuma customary laws of inheritance, claimed and confiscated by their brothers-in-law. Both women are Christian, have children, contracted a civil marriage and had lived in the matrimonial house with their husbands.

The clients' "readiness" as outlined above is evidenced in their affidavits, both of which were written by the lawyers but clearly state in the first person: "I lost my rights over my husband's estate because of the customary laws of inheritance of the Sukuma do not allow the widows and/or daughters to inherit estates of their beloved deceased husbands/fathers."[17] The next paragraph could be construed as "evidence" that clients are cognizant of plural legal orders in Tanzania and have already begun to "learn about their rights":

> That the existence and application of the customary law of inheritance in this part of Tanzania, which restricts my ability to inherit the estate from my husband and deprives my young child of her family home, is discriminatory and violates the fundamental human rights guaranteed in the Constitution of the United Republic of Tanzania, 1977 and International Agreements.[18]

The affidavit goes on to enumerate how this customary practice violates the relevant articles of the following laws: the Administration of Estates, the Judicature and Application of Laws Ordinance, the Probate Administration Act, the Tanzanian Constitution, the CEDAW, the International Convention on Economic, Social and Cultural Rights, the African Charter, and the Convention on the Rights of the Child by removing widows from the matrimonial home and not providing widows and daughters with adequate means forcing women to rely on male relatives for their wellbeing.

In the majority of my discussions about women's rights through research in Tanzania's FemAct, NGOs lawyers, advocates and NGO professionals argued primarily for women's rights based on principles of nondiscrimination. However, within those discussions and in their daily work in client advising sessions and in their court submissions, lawyers emphasized that to deprive women of their rights was to also deprive children of their rights. Stressing these affiliational ties reflected both the reality that women were caregivers, but also bolstered their arguments for women's rights in a context that values women as mothers. On client intake forms in the legal aid clinics, there is a question asking how many people the case affects and legal advocates explained that the answers were often used to the benefit of women.

192   Gender Justice and Legal Pluralities

At the time I met Stephens and Charles they had spent in total over five years with their inheritance claims in legal proceedings, starting in the primary courts, advancing to the High Court of Tanzania and in June 2010 the claims were still under consideration by the Court of Appeals. When I spoke to them about their cases and specifically about who is and should be responsible for protecting their livelihoods, inheritance and rights, they responded that lawyers and judges should do so. Neither client, in all of their years working with lawyers and paralegal officers, knew if the Tanzanian constitution protected their rights or had ever been to a rights outreach or education seminar. They did feel though that international human rights laws were the best laws to protect Tanzanian women's rights, but could not name which of those laws did so. On the other hand, each was able to explain to me in detail Sukuma customary procedures for dividing inheritance, although there was a small disagreement over the exact allowance the youngest male child should receive. While ideas of human rights are certainly making their way into the fabric of Tanzanian society, the proximity, accessibility and impact of these laws is often out of reach for most people. As one of the clients commented, "it is so high up there."

Submission to the High Court

In the original submission to the High Court, lawyers argued that the 30 paragraphs of the CLO are unconstitutional because they discriminate against women on the basis of gender and violate human rights principles of non-discrimination, equality and equal protection. Outlining the discriminatory paragraphs of the CLO, they argued that the options for women to conduct their way of life are limited, they are forced to be perpetual dependents of their children and are practically forced to marry a clan member in order to remain in the matrimonial home and if she marries outside the clan she risks being removed from the home (*Elizabeth Stephens and Salome Charles vs. Another*, 2006 submission para. 4). In each case, the same does not apply to males. The submission moves on to invoke five international conventions, the Universal Declaration of Human Rights, and the Declaration on the Elimination of All Forms of Intolerance and of Discrimination Based on Religion or Belief and argued that the principles of customary law of inheritance are in direct conflict with these international agreements.

In conversations with lawyers, however, most advocated protecting those aspects of the CLO that were not named in the submission, as they protected "valuable cultural practices" and protected clan land from state land grabbing. Others supported one lawyer who explained:

> [s]ome cultural practices may still make sense. If children remain and take care of their parents in old age, then they will care for their mother

or father regardless and properties will remain in the family. But most of the time these days children are leaving, or may want to sell that house for profit and then the mother is out on the street. It really is about a change in culture. There's no respect anymore.

Analyzing how personhood is constructed by women's rights advocates in and among plural legal orders requires that we attend to the broader political and economic environment in which people live. With a history of state intervention in landholdings and livelihoods and with continuing and often pernicious effects of state-led "redevelopment" efforts and foreign investment (Baha 2011; Hakiardhi and LHRC 2009; Mutarubukwa 2011; Sitta 2011) a women's rights agenda that seeks both group rights protections as well as individual rights agendas becomes understandable. Women's individual inheritance rights are viewed by Tanzania's human rights NGOs as being of primary importance not only to women's individual wellbeing and livelihood, but also for the wellbeing of children, communities and national development. I will now turn to the strategic litigation case in which these hopes for women's rights hung in the balance but were ultimately denied.

Elizabeth Stephens and Salome Charles vs. Another (2006) – the perspective of the Court and Honorable Justice Mihayo

On 8 September 2006, the High Court of Tanzania upheld the CLO and rejected the plaintiffs' appeals. The court was convinced that the lawyers for the plaintiffs had not followed correct judicial procedure and further argued that the plaintiffs should have worked with the lower courts to resolve their case and could have succeeded in doing so because "courts have always been sympathetic to members of the deceased's family who have been denied their rights." The court argued that the plaintiffs had not exhausted all available remedies before petitioning the High Court and that they needed to pursue their rights through the legal machinery under the civil law or through civil action.

In Justice Mihayo's decision, he recognized the constellation of plural legal orders and commented on how best to resolve or reform law (Citing Misc Civil Cause No 10. of 2005). He stated, "[u]ntil the contrary is proved, legislation is presumed to be constitutional," further arguing, "[b]ut we should always bear in mind that not every infringement of basic rights should be declared unconstitutional" and that (citing the Court of Appeal in *Attorney General vs. W.K. Butambala* [1993] TLR 46) "invoking the constitution should be reserved for appropriate and really momentous occasions. Things which can easily be taken up by administrat[ive] initiative are best pursued in that manner." Further commenting on the role of the constitution, Mihayo proposes "to preserve the sacrosanct nature of the constitution

194 Gender Justice and Legal Pluralities

and to bring to court only matters of great importance and leave the rest to be dealt with by other authorities."

The Court did, however, recognize that many customary laws discriminate against women and considered whether it was in their best interests to admit the appeal presented. In considering this, the court proposed that while customary practices may discriminate they "evolve and change with time, a process that does not end, nor can it be ended." Recognizing the fluidity and evolution of customs the Court argued that in its opinion:

> [i]t is impossible to effect customary change by judicial pronouncements. A legal decision must be able to take immediate effect, unless overturned by a higher court. For customs and customary law, it would be dangerous and may create chaos if courts were to make judicial pronouncements on their Constitutionality. This will be opening the Pandora's Box, with all seemingly discriminatory customs from our 120 tribes plus following the same path.

The court then counseled the women to return to the Shinyanga District Council where they could submit a recommendation for the modification of the customary law for consideration to the District Administration. The Court argued that this process would be advantageous to them because it would "start from the grass roots where any custom is felt and a decision will be acceptable and [able to be implemented] by the majority."

The legal team for the plaintiffs reiterated time and again that they were certain that the subjective history and interests of the three High Court judges were most definitely at play in the Court's decision as all three justices came from the Lake Region, all three were WaSukuma and Justice Mihayo himself was born and raised in Shinyanga. Lawyers argued that the judges had a vested interest in maintaining the patriarchal customary inheritance law. In both the Court's decision and in conversation with me Justice Mihayo's reasoning hinged on two arguments: first that "only matters of great importance" should proceed to the High Court without making their way through the lower courts and, second, that judicial pronouncements should be able to take effect immediately.

Pressing Mihayo about what would qualify as "matters of great importance," he responded saying that one can bring a case to the High Court "when there's no other remedy at all" or that a case should be heard before the Court because it will affect the majority of Tanzanian women, not only women from one location or one that only affects certain societies. He explained how he views his legal judgments saying, "I like my decisions to have a natural effect. The decision must have an impact. You can't have a decision that fizzles in the air. Rather than make a judicial pronouncement that will affect those two women; no, it will not affect the majority." Mihayo went on to assert that he was not personally comfortable with customary law and that he supported women being treated equally to men. However, at times he laid the onus of responsibility on women saying, "Women need to change their mindsets, but I don't know how they can do this" and that "those ladies" (referring to the lawyers) "have a point, but we would create a situation where we would be opening a Pandora's Box with all sorts of cases [coming] to court."

While Mihayo insisted that the Stephens, Charles and other women with inheritance complaints should have petitioned the District Councils in order to have customary laws changed, when asked if he knew of any cases where people have lobbied and changed customary law in their regions in this way, he responded "No, I haven't seen it. Because the local councils don't read the law, they don't know it. Second, where women are concerned, people are just oblivious as to what is happening, there is chauvinism really, people with most complaints are women and women are not strong enough. I wish the NGOs would have taken them to the local councils where they could talk about land."

Conclusions

Lawyers and human rights advocates may be both ideologically and prag-matically uncertain about privileging human rights laws in cases that come before them in their legal clinics, taking into account the specifics of the case as well as their knowledge of justices in their local courts. Where Shinyanga paralegal officers and lawyers in Dar es Salaam knew district court judges who had been "sensitized" to human rights laws or were "sympathetic" to women's rights, they would often include human rights laws in their sub-missions. However, the use of human rights language is often circumscribed to spaces where those discourses are more acceptable – in legal reform efforts, national advocacy work and in conversations with donors. In fact the local and national legal context constrains lawyers' use of human rights laws to some extent, as local and national laws and legal procedure must be exhausted before appealing to international law.

While human rights education often takes place in legal aid clinics and in outreach and education seminars around the country, lawyers continue to work between international human rights norms and the frameworks of rights enshrined in both customary and Islamic law. On the whole, Tanzanian women's rights lawyers would like to see women's individual rights protected, but not at the expense of group rights. In the case presented above, the High Court expressed worry about focusing on women's individual rights and the potential ramifications for the local and national legal systems. It is certainly the case that Tanzania's legal machinery could be made more robust, but the way these changes are promoted should not be at the expense of gendered justice. As one lawyer remarked, "Regarding Mihayo's statement about the Pandora's Box – we'll sort out whatever comes out of the Pandora's Box."

196 Gender Justice and Legal Pluralities

Notes

1 In this chapter, I use the phrase "legal pluralism" to reflect a conceptual analytical term employed by legal scholars to come to terms with situations where the state legal system recognizes more than one system of law and where anthropologists use the term to describe how different systems of law can be regarded as a "semi-autonomous" social field (Hellum and Stewart 1998: 31, 70). Throughout the chapter, I employ the phrases "legal pluralities" and "plural legal orders" to reflect the fluidity with which different bodies of law often intersect and come to bear on any individual's case.

2 This framing in itself is problematic and it is not my intention to reify conceptions of rights as falling within two static, opposing domains of the "customary" and a "legally normative" conception of rights employed by women's rights advocates. On the contrary, I will demonstrate here the uncertainty and fluidity of both the lower courts' consideration of the cases before them as well as the ways in which rights' advocates often infuse aspects of normative gender relations when they consider "liberal" ideas of women's rights that rely on the notion of a free, autonomous individual. However, I will maintain these two broad "perspectives" from which to view inheritance rights in order to demonstrate how they have in fact come to inform one another.

3 By speaking of the "liberal" notions of rights reflected in international declarations and conventions, I am referring broadly to the liberal assumption that the individual is the bearer of these rights. Tanzanian women's legal rights NGOs often employ the Universal Declaration of Human Rights (UDHR), the Convention to End All Forms of Discrimination Against Women (CEDAW), the African Charter on Human and People's Rights, the International Covenant on Civil and Political Rights (ICCPR), and the International Covenant on Economic, Social and Cultural Rights (ICESCR). In their work, Tanzanian women's legal rights NGOs most heavily rely on the CEDAW, which chiefly promotes the rights of individuals.

4 The NGOs included in the study were all members of the umbrella Feminist Activist (FemAct) Organization and were: The Tanzanian Association of Women Lawyers (TAWLA), The Women's Legal Aid Centre (WLAC), Tanzania Gender Networking Program (TGNP), The Tanzania Media Women's Association (TAMWA), The Legal and Human Rights Center (LHRC), HAKIARDHI (The Land Rights Institute), Women in Law and Development in Africa (WilDAF), and Women's Advancement Trust (WAT).

5 This case is representative of a broader subcontinental movement to challenge the constitutionality of customary laws, especially in relation to gender justice. For a few examples, see *Bhe and Others Khayelitsha Magistrate and Others* (South Africa, 2004), *Elizabeth Gumede vs. President of the Republic of South Africa and Others* (South Africa, 2008), *Mifumi(U) Ltd. and 12 Others Attorney General, Kenneth Kakuru* (Uganda, 2007), *Ayugi vs. Ayugi and Others* (Tanzania, 2002).

6 This chapter is the result of research carried out during the summer months of 2010 and 2011 when I interviewed the lawyers, paralegal officers, clients, and High Court Judge involved in *Elizabeth Stephens and Salome Charles vs. Another* (2006). I conducted research for two months at the Shinyanga Paralegal Centre (PACESHI) where the clients in the strategic litigation case began their journey. At PACESHI, I sat in on dispute resolution cases and client-advising sessions and analyzed 24 inheritance case files. I employ both a "case study" as well as a "multiple-case study" approach in this research (Hellum and Stewart 1998: 142).

7 Customary law is codified in two Government Notices: GN 279 and GN 436, which apply only to Tanzanian patrilineal communities and apply to the following

districts: Handeni, Kahama, Kondoa, Lushoto, Musoma, Ngara, Nzega, Pangani (Local Customary Law (Declaration) Order 2); Dodoma, Iramba, Mpwapwa, Manyoni, Shinynga, Singida, Ufipa (Local Customary Law (Declaration) (No. 2) Order 2); Kasulu, Kibondo, Kigoma (Local Customary Law (Declaration) (No. 3) Order 2); Kilimanjaro, Maswa, Meru, Songea (Local Customary Law (Declaration) (No. 5) Order 3); and Biharamulo, Mpanda, North Mara, Tabora, and Ulanga (Local Customary Law (Declaration) (No. 7) Order 2). Judicature and Application of Laws Act. SUBSIDIARY LEGIS. [CAP 358, R.E. 2002] (Ezer 2006: ft. 26).

8 Tanzania's Constitution was signed in 1977 and was amended in 1998, shortly after the government adopted multiparty democracy in 1992.

9 The Constitution of The United Republic of Tanzania (Cap. 2) 12(1), 13(1, 2, 4, 5).

10 Probate and Administration Estate's Act [CAP 352, R.E. 2002] 88(1) (a), 88(2).

11 In Tanzania, lawyers and advocates cannot represent clients in primary courts, only in the higher courts. Individuals can choose to elect relatives or members of their household to speak on their behalf, Magistrates' Courts Act [No. 2, R.E. 1984] 33(1). Tanzania defines an advocate in the Advocates Act [CAP 341, R.E.2002] 8(1)(i)(ii)(iii).

12 The United Republic of Tanzania Land Act, 1999.

13 As these cases are potentially ongoing, as there could be subsequent appeals to higher courts, I am using acronyms to protect the identity of the clients and others in the cases.

14 As Ezer notes (Ezer 2006: 610), there is an assumption here, and also in the language of customary law, that the property of the deceased is in fact *his* property and not the wife's or property held jointly between the husband and wife.

15 The multiple perspectives on land reform found within FemAct NGOs have been mirrored on the national stage. For different perspectives on the protection of customary tenure within the Land Act, see National Land Forum 1997; Shivji 1998; Tsikata 2003.

16 Fareeda Banda makes the point that legal reordering will not automatically lead to social reordering; however, the fact that human rights instruments are being used to "tackle women's inferiority, tells us something about the changing perceptions of gender roles on the continent" (Banda 2004: 116).

17 Interview, 24 June 2010.

18 Throughout the remainder of the chapter, all cited material comes from the case file *Elizabeth Stevens and Salome Charles vs. Another*, 2006.

References

Baha, B. (2011) *The Politics of Investment in Large Scale Agricultural Ventures: Case of Mpanda, Rukwa Tanzania*, Hakiardhi.

Banda, F. (2004) "The End of 'Culture'? African Women and Human Rights," *Making Law in Africa: Transnationalism, Persons and Rights*, Edinburgh: Centre of African Studies, The University of Edinburgh.

Benda-Beckmann, F. von, K. Benda-Beckmann and A. Griffiths (eds) (2009) *The Power of Law in a Transnational World: Anthropological Inquiries*, New York, NY and Oxford: Berghahn Books.

Bourdon, N. J. (2009) "Mediated Norms and Legal Encounters: Localizing Women's Human Rights and Feminism in Dar es Salaam, Tanzania," PhD thesis, Michigan State University.

Chanock, M. (1998) *Law, Custom and Social Order: The Colonial Experience in Malawi and Zambia*, Portsmouth: Heinemann.

198 Gender Justice and Legal Pluralities

Cowan, J. (2006) "Culture and Rights after 'Culture and Rights'," *American Anthropologist* 108 (1): 9–24.

Englund, H. (2006) *Prisoners of Freedom: Human Rights and the African Poor*, Berkeley, CA: The University of California Press.

Ezer, T. (2006) "Inheritance Law in Tanzania: The Impoverishment of Widows and Daughters," *The Georgetown Journal of Gender and the Law* (8): 599–662.

Fanon, F. (1967) *Black Skin, White Masks*, New York, NY: Grove Press.

Hakiardhi and Legal and Human Rights Centre (CHRC) (2009) *Fact Finding Mission Report on the Prevailing Dispute at Namwawala Village in Kilombero District, Morogoro Region*, Hakiardhi and the Legal and Human Rights Centre.

Helfer, L. (1999) "Forum Shopping for Human Rights," University of Pennsylvania Law Review 148 (2): 285–400.

Hellum, A. and J. Stewart (eds) (1998) *Pursuing Grounded Theory in Law: South-North Experiences in Developing Women's Law*, Oslo: Mond Books.

Iliffe, J. (1979) *A Modern History of Tanganyika*, Cambridge: Cambridge University Press.

Manji, A. (1998) "Gender and the Politics of Land Reform Process in Tanzania," *The Journal of Modern African Studies* 36: 645–67.

——(2006) *The Politics of Land Reform in Africa: From Communal Tenure to Free Markets*, London: Zed Books.

Merry, S. E. (2006a) *Human Rights and Gender Violence: Translating International Law Into Local Justice*, Chicago, IL: The University of Chicago Press.

——(2006b) "Transnational Human Rights and Local Activism: Mapping the Middle," *American Anthropologist* 108 (1): 38–51.

Moore, S. F. (2000) *Law as Process: An Anthropological Approach*, 2nd edn, Oxford: James Currey Publishers.

Mutarubukwa, A. (2011) "New Land Scramble Worries Small Farmers," *The Citizen*, http://thecitizen.co.tz/magazines/31-business-week/16725-new-land-scramble-worries-small-farmers.html (accessed March 2012).

National Land Forum (1997) *Azimio La Uhai: Declaration of NGOs and Interested Persons on Land Issued by the National Land Forum*, A Coalition of NGOs and Interested Persons, Dar es Salaam.

Richards, P. (2005) "The Politics of Gender, Human Rights and Being Indigenous in Chile," *Gender and Society* 19 (2): 199–220.

Riles, A. (2006) "Anthropology, Human Rights, and Legal Knowledge: Culture in the Iron Cage," *American Anthropologist* 108 (1): 52–65.

Shivji, I. (1998) *Not Yet Democracy: Reforming Land Tenure in Tanzania*, IIED, Hakiardhi, and the Faculty of Law, University of Tanzania.

Sitta, S. (2011) *Fact Finding Mission on Land Grabbing for GMO in Mpanda*, Hakiardhi.

Tripp, A. M. (2004) "Women's Movements, Customary Law, and Land Rights in Africa: The Case of Uganda," *African Studies Quarterly* 7 (4), http://web.africa.ufl.edu/asq/v7/v7i4a1.htm (accessed March 2012).

Tsikata, D. (2003) "Securing Women's Interests within Land Tenure Reforms: Recent Debates in Tanzania," *Journal of Agrarian Change* 3 (1 and 2): 149–83.

Viljoen, F. and L. Louw (eds) (2007) "State Compliance with the Recommendations of the African Commission on Human and Peoples' Rights, 1994–2004," *The American Journal of International Law* 101 (1): 1–34.

Whitehead, A. and D. Tsikata (2003) "Policy Discourses on Women's Land Rights in Sub-Saharan Africa: The Implications of the Re-turn to the Customary," *Journal of Agrarian Change* 3 (1 and 2): 67–112.

Wilson, R. A. (ed) (1997) *Human Rights, Culture and Context: Anthropological Perspectives*, London: Pluto Press.

——(2006) "'Anthropology and Human Rights in a New Key:' The Social Life of Human Rights," *American Anthropologist* 108 (1): 77–83.

Chapter 8

An Accumulated Rage: legal pluralism and gender justice in Bolivia

John-Andrew McNeish and Ana Cecilia Arteaga Böhrt

Introduction

Bolivia has passed through a series of dramatic political, economic and legal changes over the last decade. In the course of the social upheaval and reforms of this period, Bolivia was recast as the world's first "plurinational" state. As a result, by the end of the first decade of the twenty-first century plurality had ostensibly become a central political dynamic in Bolivia and constituted an integral part of ongoing efforts to re-establish the state in a way that addresses the realities of the majority indigenous population and its persisting conditions of exclusion and poverty. This effort to transform the social democratic basis of the country has in large part been founded on the historic struggles and growth of indigenous movements in the country during the 1980s and 1990s, and of the particular relationship and dialectic that exists in Bolivia between class and identity. In the new national constitution (Asamblea Constituyente/Congreso Nacional 2009) it is the meeting of these forces that has determined the centrality of plurality, the expansion of citizenship rights including those of women and the radical enshrinement of indigenous peoples' rights. This not only includes the recognition of international conventions and cultural rights such as language, but of women and men in the definition and practice of indigenous autonomy, political leadership structures and customary law. As a result of the constitutional sanctioning of these elements, a transformation of ideas about justice and a revalorization of indigenous leadership and law are now taking place.

Recognizing the little studied and controversial nature of changes that link civil and political rights with the cultural, this chapter aims to consider the practical significance for gender justice of the recent constitutional recognition of legal pluralism in Bolivia. As such, the chapter seeks to follow at the local level some of the nascent impacts of legal changes that determine "plurinational" parity between indigenous and state law on gender relations. Our research, carried out by invitation in the little-studied, but now renowned,[1] lowland Isobore Secure National Park and Indigenous Territory (*Territorio Indígena Parque Nacional Isiboro Secure*, TIPNIS),[2] demonstrates the social significance of these national legislative changes and reveals the continuing spaces of *misreading* (de Sousa Santos 1987) that exist between local and national ideas of indigenous and gender justice. The chapter highlights the need to avoid easy assumptions of clear-cut boundaries and temporal divisions, and stresses instead the processes by which gender and sexual relationships between men and women are being *thought through, if not fought through*, in the light of changing social and political pressures brought about by constitutional and legal reform. As such, the chapter adopts a critical realist approach (Bhaskar 1998, 1993) in which groups and individuals participate, but also meet structural limitations, in the construction of their own social nature. We highlight the important formal advances taking place in terms of gender justice in Bolivia, but also the need to temper political claims of democratic revolution and success with recognition of the persistence of political contradictions and conflicting interpretations of rights within and at the margins of local communities. Moreover, we emphasize the possibilities that exist for misunderstanding and violent retribution – something we refer to as "an accumulated rage" – in a period of rapid legal change.

We therefore attempt to demonstrate the linkages that exist between constitutional and legal reform at the national level and local understandings and situated practices of gender justice. As well as outlining the immediate history and content of reforms, the chapter draws on particular examples in order to characterize the inter-linkages and difficulties of communication between national reform and local legal and gender practices. The chapter is divided into two sections, with the first largely focused on the controversies surrounding a case of customary punishment. Although not disconnected from the first, in the second section emphasis is given to an awakening conception of gender justice and to the specific case of female local leaders (*corregidoras*) testing the limits of local social norms. Both of these cases exemplify the complex manner in which recent reforms for gender justice are "vernacularized" at the local level (Merry 2006). As such they demonstrate, in line with the intentions of this volume, both the challenges (misreadings and the necessities of bargaining) and possibilities for expanding human dignity (self-determination and gender justice) that result because of the power dynamics within legally plural constellations of governance.

A new plurality

Following his election in 2005, President Evo Morales sought to follow up on his party's election promises of returning the sovereignty and benefits of Bolivian natural resources to its people. One of the key mechanisms used as a tool for this delivery was the formation of a democratic constitutional assembly representing the country's diverse social make-up, and the passage in January 2009 of a new national constitution. In its first pages the constitution claims to leave behind the colonial, republican and neoliberal states and assumes the "historic right to collectively construct a singular social state based on communitarian plurinationalism, which integrates and articulates the proposition of advancing towards a democratic, productive State that assists and inspires a peace committed to integrated development and the free determination of all peoples." In the following pages of the constitution the expressions of initial idealism are given legal basis through 411 articles reforming the commitments of the earlier 1998 constitution.

Of particular note are the articles in the 2009 constitution explicitly aimed at strengthening the legal recognition and position of indigenous peoples within the Bolivian state. For example, Article 180 recognizes that while forming a part of a unitary national judicial system, indigenous leaders have legal jurisdiction over their own population and at an equal level to other organs in the country's judicial hierarchy. This is supported by Article 191 which states that "indigenous nations and peoples exercise their own judicial functions and competence via their own authorities and the application of their principles, cultural values, norms and procedures." Further efforts to reform the existing conditions of the indigenous and wider marginalized peasant communities are made through the inclusion of several articles stating intentions of redistributing government revenues and redrawing the political map of the nation through the recognition of political and cultural autonomies (regional, departmental, municipal and indigenous).

Since the approval of the new constitution, indigenous justice has become a de facto recognized extension of the state legal system. In 2005 the Vice-ministry of Communitarian Justice was established and legal pluralism was raised as an important element in the discussions of the constitutional assembly. The 2010 Law of Judicial Delimitation (*Ley de Deslinde Juridiccional* No. 073) approved by the national constitutional court (NCPE) also legislated for a new equality to be created between indigenous jurisdiction and state jurisdiction from a perspective of parity, complementarity and articulation between legal norms. In this way transference has been made from a singular judicial system to a "formal plural and equal judicial" system, where acknowledgement is made of the co-existence of multiple legal systems and norms within the country, and where indigenous peoples have legitimate normative capacities, procedures and powers of judicial sanction. As a result of these legal processes, Bolivia is now constitutionally envisaged as a "Democratic State and Pluri-national entity," in which human rights and inter-culturality are made complementary terms of reference.

The new constitution also makes several specific mentions of the equal rights of women and men in terms of political participation and development possibilities. In fact, 33 individual articles relate to the rights of women. Amongst them, Article 11 states the equivalence of conditions between the sexes and Article 15 states the right to not suffer violence. Other articles set out guarantees for the protection of physical, psychological and sexual health. In Article 401 the constitution further states that it is the state's role "to promote policies aimed at eliminating all forms of discrimination against women in the access, inheritance and ownership of land." A guarantee is also made of equal pay for equal work between men and women. The constitution furthermore makes a ban on discriminating on the basis of sexual orientation.

Following the adoption of the new constitution several practical efforts have been made to incorporate gender equality in the Plurinational Electoral Body Law, Electoral System Law, Judicial Body Law, Plurinational Constitutional Court and Autonomy Framework laws.[3] Specific regulations have also been designed to ensure full respect for gender equality in these institutions. For instance, the Electoral Body Law enforces gender equality in electoral courts and calls for sanctions in the case of infringements. Likewise, the Judicial Power adopted norms to ensure respect for different cultures and gender equality in the Supreme and Agro-Environment Courts, calling for men and women alternately to be primary office holders. The Electoral System Law mandates equality in both the number of male and female candidates and in and their placement on candidate lists; political harassment is considered an electoral crime. Meanwhile, the Constitutional Court incorporated measures for equality in the pre-selection of its 28 candidates. Lastly, the Autonomy Framework Law calls for gender equality in the autonomous governments. The law also regards gender equality to be an essential consideration in public budgeting and planning.

Competing rights discourse and actions

While the new constitution and reforms were largely celebrated by those living in marginalized communities in the highlands and lowlands, the effort to adjust the legal and political basis in favor of previously marginalized social sectors caused a series of social tensions and divisions to become increasingly evident in the country. Despite the inclusive wording of the constitution's text, opponents claimed that the new document only represented the interests of indigenous peoples and discriminated against mixed (*mestizo*) and white (European) populations.[4] Critics opposed Morales' attempt to create a communal justice system and a complex web of regional and indigenous autonomies. They also baulked at a requirement that all public officials speak at least two languages – Spanish and one of 36 indigenous tongues.[5] Another significant sticking point was the incorporation of indigenous communal justice into the judicial system on an equal footing with the national judicial system. In stating that communal justice is decided collectively, critics have argued that the constitution disrespects individual rights and in instances where communal justice includes physical punishment will furthermore break accepted conventions on human rights.[6]

204 Gender Justice and Legal Pluralities

In an attempt to highlight their rejection of the constitution, a push for lowland departmental autonomy was made by lowland economic elites in 2008. In this process new claims and statutes of autonomy were drawn up by elite-based civic committees in the provincial capitals (Webber 2011). These documents aimed to rally local opinion against the autonomy provisions of the new constitution and to act as the basis of "popular" local referendum in order to establish legal and democratic proof of their platform. Elements of the autonomy campaign of the lowland *"media luna"* departments were also responsible for a series of violent confrontations, including the public humiliation of indigenous supporters of the government in Sucre,[7] the violent clashes in Pando that left eleven people dead,[8] and the eventual arrest of the regional governor. Eventually links between separatist leaders in the lowland cities and a foiled terrorist attack led by a Hungarian–Bolivian mercenary[9] led to a rapid decline in support for the autonomy campaign.

Despite the failure of the autonomy campaign, rumors and media commentary of a steady breakdown in the rule of law continued to be fuelled by an escalation of violent vigilantism and property seizures in rural and peri-urban areas of the country. Over the last decade the numbers of public beatings and lynchings of suspected criminals has risen significantly and has made a daily appearance in the national newspapers and television news. A growing number of street corners in the city of El Alto and the poor satellite neighborhoods of Bolivia's main cities and towns now sport straw dummies hanging from lamp-posts and walls as warning signs of punishment to any would-be criminals (Risør 2010). Goldstein has argued that these acts represent "spectacles that serve as devices to restructure patterns of inclusion, a technique by which the marginalised insist on their own incorporation within national structures and systems from which they have been excluded" (Goldstein 2004: 19). Such insistence also appears to be underlined by a recent series of land invasions and forced takeovers of mining installations that have taken place in the rural highlands of the country. More broadly in media and public discussion, these acts have been utilized as evidence of instability and growing lack of justice and governmental control in the "plurinational state" following the new constitution. They are also a testament to the new constitution's role in uncovering the existence of competing ideas of human rights in the country, where there are those that coincide with international treaties and conventions and others that differ entirely in their interpretation of obligations. Despite the progressive intentions of constitutional reform, local interpretations of certain social roles have been bent out of shape and others remain denied (Calla et al. 2009).

Our research in the TIPNIS and specifically the two cases included below further demonstrate the ambiguities and complex of interests at play following constitutional and legal reform. Both examples also clearly demonstrate the manner in which national reform has not only affected relationships between social groups, but has had an impact on understandings of justice and specifically gender relations within local communities. However, in contrast to the often racist-motivated accusations of recent national media coverage, these examples also demonstrate clearly that while reform has resulted in violence and competing narratives of justice this is not taking place in a vacuum of social order, or the absence of institutions for rule of law. Indeed, both of these examples demonstrate that legal institutions and legal norms are deeply embedded in the fabric and histories of social organization in the communities we visited. They also demonstrate that rather than static entities, these norms and institutions are being required by recent reform to pass through a new period of adjustment that is both painful and necessary.

A very public punishment

On 8 May 2009, Marcial Fabricano, a *mojeño* indigenous leader widely known in Bolivia for his work in CIDOB, the main lowland indigenous organization, was whipped some 32 times using a *chicote* (rope whip) by eight local leaders during a visit to the TIPNIS area as punishment for a series of locally defined crimes.[10] With Fabricano's entrance into hospital and the numerous pictures of his lacerated back displayed in the national media, the event sparked a national debate about the value and dangers of indigenous justice, or customary law, and of its relationship to national law. While some communication channels characterized the event as attempted assassination and vigilantism, others have criticized the event as the political abuse by supporters of the government of the new constitution and recent approval of the Law of Judicial Demarcation (which establishes domains of autonomy for indigenous customary law). In *El Deber*, one of the national newspapers with headquarters in Santa Cruz, an interview was carried out on the issue with Víctor Hugo Velasco (vice-president of the Independent Confederation of Indigenous Aboriginal Nations) and José Urañavi (a representative of the Guarayo people). Both of these leaders had formed a commission that would travel to the Organization of American States and the United Nations to condemn the punishment of Fabricano as an aggressive act carried out by "representatives of the governing party and terrorists paid to carry out these abuses." Similarly, in the comments made by the indigenous ex-vice-president, Víctor Hugo Cárdenas, effort was made to lay responsibility for the act at the feet of the ruling government administration.

> This reflects that in the official membership there is an attitude of complete disrespect for the law, and of a lack of knowledge about human rights. The public whipping or physical punishment no longer coincides with the practices and ideas of human rights. Bolivia has signed international pacts and treaties condemning physical punishment and it is a

shame that people related to the government have carried out this assault against Fabricano.

(Víctor Hugo Cárdenas, *El Diario*, 12 May 2009)

These comments by Cárdenas follow his own experience in March 2009, when his home was burnt down and his family was expelled from his home community.[11] In a letter to *El Diario*, Cárdenas commented that this had occurred not as an act of punishment, but rather of vengeance and reprisal for his work opposing the government in the campaign against the new constitution. As a result of his own experiences, he commented that the new constitution represents "racism in reverse." In the same press report there were testimonies denouncing what had happened with Marcial Fabricano made by other indigenous leaders who opposed the government, such as Juan Choque, Román Loayza[12] and Crispín Gaspar.[13]

Giving his own interpretation of events, Fabricano commented that what had occurred could be directly attributed to the constitutionalization of indigenous justice in which the new text was "the constituted violence and the destruction of indigenous peoples by division."[14] From his point of view, the indigenous leaders who punished him were militants of the government who during the act claimed that they "were putting into practice the community justice institutionalized in the new constitution." In line with other denunciations of the act, in another interview (PAT, 12 May 2009) Fabricano also signalled that the punishment could be attributed to political conflict: "It is a situation of political manipulation by the government who is trying to remove those of us who show dissent or have differences."

In an effort to counter these critical statements and denouncements, a number of government officials and indigenous organizations argued that what occurred with Marcial Fabricano was a genuine and defendable demonstration of indigenous justice. For example Adolfo Chavez, the Executive Secretary of the Indigenous Peoples of the Oriente (CIDOB), commented that:

[a]s we see it Mr Fabricano had to submit to communitarian justice, having escaped twice before. They had to carry out community justice because it is not the first time that Mr Fabricano is guilty; indeed they have done this to other leaders.

(Adolfo Chavez, *El Diario*, 12 May 2009)

The vice-president of CIDOB, Pedro Nuni, called on the public to resist "demonizing this kind of punishment or let it disappear because they are norms that will not be abandoned, less so now that the constitution is functioning" (*El Mundo*, 14 May 2009). The Vice-minister of Land, Alejandro Almarez, signaled in a press conference that what had happened with Fabricano was communitarian justice and had been caused as a result of his own guilt (*La Razon*, 12 May 2009). Other organizations and indigenous movements in the country were less definite in their support or denunciation of the event. The Executive Secretary of the main indigenous movement in the highlands, the *Confederación Sindical Única de Trabajadores Campesinos* (CSUTCB), Isaac Ávalos, admitted in a news article that the case needed to be better investigated.

> It was not communitarian justice, this is not justified. If there is a crime committed, we have the courts and for this there are the norms of the country … We need to investigate, those local leaders responsible for the crime should be arrested, not all, because not all are guilty.
> (Isaac Ávalos, *La Prensa*, 13 May 2009)

Customary justice

Whilst considerable debate and contrasting positions were expressed in the national media, at the level of the sub-central (the local administrative unit) and the communities within the TIPNIS area there has been no doubt as to the meaning of Marcial Fabricano's punishment. In interviews carried out with local people Fabricano's punishment was widely understood as the application of indigenous justice accepted under the new constitution. According to statements by members of the community, Fabricano's punishment fits with the rules and norms of their understanding of customary law and was carried out correctly in that it was the result of a decision by the *cabildo* (the body of local leadership) and in the course of a meeting of all the local community leaders (*corregidores*). The form of punishment (whipping and banishment), whilst severe, also complied with local standards of how to deal with a member of the local indigenous community who was responsible for multiple crimes against the community.

Amongst both the Yuracaré and Mojeño ethnic groups, several forms of sanctions are commonly applied as part of customary law, including physical (whipping), monetary (fines), communal work and expulsion from the community. There furthermore exist three types of whips (*chicote*) that local judges and healers judges (*titulares*) understand as differentiated forms of restoring order: thick (with eight strands), normal (six strands) and thin (three strands). Of these it is the thin whip that causes the most damage because of the way it cuts into the skin. The number of strokes with the whips depends on the type of whip used. In order to quantify this number easily, local people refer to the unit of "*arroba*," equivalent to 12 strokes.

According to witnesses present at the event, Marcial Fabricano was given three arrobas with a doubled thick whip. The community leaders had intended to punish him with the thin whip, but someone had forgotten to bring it with them. Two men held his arms and pushed him forward to the front of what was a public meeting. Eight people from the community then took it in turns to slowly administer these strokes. The punishment took a total of two hours, during which Fabricano lost consciousness and fell to the floor. During the administering of the punishment Fabricano was reminded in detail of his crimes against the community and asked to repent for these misdemeanors. When he regained consciousness following the whipping, Fabricano was sat in a chair with his hands bound and given the opportunity to talk. Although there are different accounts of how he responded, there is some agreement that he smiled at the crowd and refused to apologize. He was eventually led away and placed in a vehicle to be removed from the community. Before leaving he was warned that on return to the TIPNIS he would be punished far more severely. Whilst the chicote is the most common form of punishment, banishment is considered by locals to be the most severe.

In a letter dated 15 September 2009, the TIPNIS Sub-central requested the participation of state institutions in an impartial investigation of Fabricano's punishment and called on the solidarity of indigenous organizations in the country "to defend and vindicate our rights to integrated development in accordance with our political and socio-cultural conceptions, and in plain recognition of our natural authority with regards to self-determination." According to a communication issued by the TIPNIS authorities and distributed by the website[15] of the Centre for Judicial Study and Social Communication (CEJIS):

> [t]he sanction exercised against Marcial Fabricano was the result of a accumulation of crimes which had attacked the TIPNIS in particular and the indigenous movement in general, with actions that stretch from the illegal traffic of natural resources to the organization of parallel political structures, and acts of vandalism such as intervention, the destruction and burning of the centres of different and legitimate indigenous organisations.
>
> (CEJIS, 15 May 2009)

In addition to this statement, our field research in the TIPNIS area revealed that in commenting on this case most people referred little to the political connections and alliances held by Fabricano, and a lot more to what they perceived of as his betrayal of the community. His involvement in the illegal sale of timber and the organization of competing leadership structures are the main elements in this betrayal. According to the leaders of the TIPNIS his punishment "was the result of many debts to the community, of an accumulated rage."[16]

The TIPNIS in national transformation

The long list of misdemeanors makes it clear that the punishment of Fabricano was not carried out without grounds or as a result of a lack of rule of law.

However, local people and leaders' insistence that this event reflected the norms of indigenous justice hides as much as it reveals. The conceptualization and practice of indigenous justice in the TIPNIS is far from a static and unchanging expression of indigenous tradition and morality. Indigenous justice and authority in the TIPNIS have undergone a gradual process of transformation parallel to, and in direct connection with, the legal and political changes taking place at the national level. Although geographically remote and an area where communications remain difficult, the TIPNIS has been far from isolated from recent upheavals in Bolivia. Through their participation in regional national social movements they have played a key role in restructuring the vision and politics, for both indigenous peoples and the participation of women. Key moments in this social movement history include their organization of the march for territory and dignity in 1990, the march for the creation of the new Agrarian Reform Law (INRA, 1715) in 1996, multiple protests during *Octubre Negro* (Black October),[17] and the TIPNIS march in opposition to the building of a road through their territory in 2011/2012. Each of these moments in Bolivian history helped to define the course taken by the country over the last two decades.[18]

According to local informants, customary law had been previously attacked and eroded by the creation and encroachment of *haciendas* (cattle-ranches) and small-scale farmers into the TIPNIS area, and their introduction of new patronage structures. Non-indigenous people living within the area of the TIPNIS are distinguished by the terms of *terceros* (third parties) o *carayanas*, and most frequently refer to the owners of *hacienda* estates that overlap the TIPNIS boundaries and are dedicated to large-scale cattle farming. Before the 1990s, *carayana* families were the owners of enormous estates granted them by the state and acquired through illegal,[19] often violent, occupation. They often took advantage of the political power their families had developed in the democratic and dictatorial national governments. As a result of the huge extensions of their land-holdings it was necessary to contract indigenous workers. This developed into a patronage relationship that transformed indigenous organization structures and practices. In the 1990s small-scale farmers (*colonos*) with origins in the Aymara and Quechuan speaking-peoples in the highlands of the country had made their way into the TIPNIS with the construction of a new road for petroleum exploration and in search of new land settled around the existing communities of San Antonio de Moleto (Yuracaré). The leaders of the TIPNIS sub-central remember this period as one of invasion with constant confrontations between indigenous and *colono* families. The most recent period of violence between indigenous and *colono* communities took place in September 2009 near the village of San Miguelito. Construction of a new road, following agreements between Bolivia and Brazil to build a bi-oceanic corridor through the Amazon, provided physical access for 500 *colono* farmers to enter the TIPNIS area and establish coca plantations. This new

210 Gender Justice and Legal Pluralities

establishment was militantly opposed by the local community and both the national police and representatives of INRA were petitioned to enter and remove the *colonos*.[20] These events also provided the background for the TIPNIS march in 2011.

Responding to these perceived threats to territory and society, there was an internal effort in the TIPNIS to recover and re-establish both the procedures of customary law and with it local leadership and social organization. For example, use of the *chicote* has significantly expanded over the last ten years. The whip has replaced the earlier common practice of "*zunchar*," in which the skin and muscle of the limbs were pierced with a thin bone needle. The *chicote* has been adopted from the highlands of the country – possibly as a result of contact with *terceros* – as local people see the public spectacle of its use as more "exemplary" (*ejemplificador*) than other forms of sanction. In the Mojeño villages they also refer to the use of the *chicote* as "*cabildear*" (to make public). In serious cases, such as homicide, they put salt in the wounds produced by the thin whip and force those punished to carry out exercises until they publically recognize their crime. The public nature of the *chicote* is then a fundamental part of the current form of punishment.

Historically, the communities of the TIPNIS chose their leaders on the basis of age. Before the 1990s the principal leaders were between 70 and 80 years old. This mature age reflected the role of the leaders at the time, in the absence of schools, as transmitters of customs, norms, beliefs and knowledge. In the course of the last ten years this has changed such that other parameters are also seen of increasing importance, including level of education, literacy, experience of public office, leadership, oratory and language skills (*saber hablar bien*). Previous to the 1990s the positioning of leaders was largely dependent on their selection by the departmental government and alliances with the national political parties. Local leaders are now chosen by the community without any basis in party affiliation and through elections carried out in public meetings (*cabildos comunales*). The position of *corregidor* remains indefinite, or until the local community decides that a change must be made. Each year a meeting (*cabildo*) is held in order to evaluate the administration of the *corregidor*. Where there are signs of mis-management or conflict the local community can call an extraordinary meeting to remove the leader.

According to the Yuracaré, the Mojeños have a better system of authorities than their own. Over the last decade they have as a result attempted to appropriate some of the elements from this system to add to their own. As a result of having been almost entirely nomadic, the Yuracaré have been more used to adapting their organizational structures to new conditions. According to people interviewed, the Mojeño system is admired for its ability to achieve tighter social control and cohesion. Whilst adapting differently, what they admired in Mojeño society was their order and agreement on ideas of justice. The process of reorganization and appropriation of elements from the Mojeño is talked about as being a way to "wake up the people".

An awakening gender justice?

As well as sparking a re-evaluation of local leadership and organization, the participation of the TIPNIS population in national processes of political and legal transformation has also inspired an awakening interest in revising gender relations and of ideas of justice related to sexual relations both beyond and within the home. A cautionary note is, however, necessary in judging the outcome of these changes. On the one hand, female participation in the TIPNIS protest-movement and reforms have encouraged a strengthening of women's rights and inspired efforts to test gender boundaries in the TIPNIS. On the other, we see that at the local level the renewal of customary law sanctioned by national law is used by local male leadership and community membership as a mechanism to block, rather than encourage, progressive changes in gender relations. It appears then that tensions and contradictions accompany reform and changing gender relations.

According to local people, female participation in the sub-central and social movements leading up to constitutional reform helped to restructure the gender relations in the TIPNIS. As a result, the participation of women was recognized as an essential part of the wider recognition of indigenous peoples at the national level, and produced a significant reappraisal by local men of the power structures and physical and psychological violence. The women understood that initially they were asked to join the marches to only act as "shields:" it was thought that the police would be softer in their response to women placed in the front line of these marches. Despite these initial perceptions and assigned roles, the women used the space afforded by the men as a strategy to widen their political influence. The march for territory and dignity is highlighted in particular by female informants as the event that marked the first moment of their leadership and struggle to capture spaces that had until then been entirely masculine. Gender equality now entered into their negotiations with national government. Harsh comment had been made by the Central Office of Indigenous Women of the Beni (CMIB) of the failure of the Jaime Paz Zamora government (1989–93) to take on board the imbalance of rights between genders in its efforts to rewrite the national constitution. In response to this failure, CMIB pushed through the elaboration of an amendment demanding protection against violence in public and private life, access to medical services and especially those to do with prenatal and natal care, defense of the right of women to decide on the number of children they would have, access to information and non-discriminatory education, the right to participate in public office and equality of conditions, the right to an equal salary and labor rights.

212   Gender Justice and Legal Pluralities

Female militancy in the TIPNIS has continued until the present. In the 2011 TIPNIS march, women were again at the front of the protest and played a key role in pushing the government to consider their demands. Having grown weary of listening to the government minister's refusals to negotiate the route of the road through the TIPNIS territory, the women accompanying the march encircled him and forced him to frog-march with them for 20 km until they encountered the police blockade at Yucumo. The event was exaggeratedly reported in the national media as the kidnap of a key government minister, and may have been one of the reasons for the violent police action against the protesters that occurred the following day. The women themselves, however, stated clearly that this act had not been a kidnap, but rather a necessary demonstration to the government minister of the difficulties and dangers that they and their children were facing on the march.

Women's increased political agency is of course directly related to a series of changes that have been taking place in everyday gender relations in the TIPNIS. Male recognition of the importance of women's political agency, constitutional and wider reforms, and women's increased awareness of rights have led to significant shifts in the social positions and control women have exercised over their own lives during the last ten years. As a result of changing rights, norms and economic possibilities in the TIPNIS, women have been granted increasing importance in decision making on the domestic economy. Women are now accustomed to travelling out of the TIPNIS area in order to sell locally produced chocolate in the nearby cities of Trinidad and Cochabamba. Women have also gained increasing access to education and the economic possibilities and innovations that have come with increased knowledge. Men have adapted to seasonal work in the cities, whilst trying to complete their expected tasks at home. Over the last few years the number of male seasonal workers has increased and many adolescents and youths have moved to work in Trinidad on a permanent basis.

As a result of this changing panorama of work, habitation and economics, patterns of social relations and sexuality have also been transformed. Children in the TIPNIS traditionally started as infants helping their parents with daily chores. It was not until their eighth birthday that children divided in these chores according to gender. Mechanisms for socialization have been transforming slowly, however, and given the new conditions of parental labor, children are expected to contribute in similar ways. It is now common to see both boys and girls being given responsibility for the kitchen and looking after the other siblings whilst the parents are at work. According to the comments of local people in the 1980s only a third of the children were able to reach third grade in primary school. Those wanting to study further had to leave for Trinidad, and this was mostly limited to boys. This has now changed somewhat. There are now two boarding schools in the TIPNIS which are open to both boys and girls. Most of the children are now

Legal pluralism and gender justice in Bolivia 213

graduating from primary school and many more are now taking up new possibilities to study further in the city and at the public universities.

Marriage patterns have also changed in the TIPNIS. Amongst the Yuracaré and Mojeño, marriage continues to be considered an important rite of passage into adulthood. It is only following marriage that individuals are considered mature enough to take on public office. There is now an increasing flexibility in some of the norms of marriage. Study of the local kinship structures of the main village clans demonstrates a growing pragmatism in encouraging exogenous marriages (for example Yuracaré with Mojeño or Chimane, and vice versa). Also in contrast with past practice, is the general understanding that women no longer have to leave in order to live in the community of their husband; it is now common for men to move to the village of the women. It is important to highlight that in local society marriage is not considered a religious or civil process, but rather a communal agreement between two families that their children should form a union. However, again with outside and religious influence, the initial decision to get married is increasingly left to the individual. Major transformations appear to also be taking place in the sexual and reproductive rights of communities in the TIPNIS. Twenty years ago women were unable to decide, both physically and socially, on the number of children they wanted. Currently, women have been given the choice of using different forms of contraception distributed by the local health posts, a practice now generally accepted by the men in the TIPNIS despite custom or religious affiliation.

The two *corregidoras*

Significant changes are taking place in the political position of women in TIPNIS society and in the balance of domestic roles. However, we should also acknowledge that whilst some effects of these changes are positive, changing gender roles have also produced a series of tensions and contradictions that in some cases have left individuals open to physical threats. A striking example of this is the case of the two female *corregidoras* we encountered in the Yuracaré community of Galilea.

In all of the history of the TIPNIS only four women have held the highest leadership position in the community, that of *corregidor*, a position that not only provides the community direction in decision making, but that is central in the receipt of accusations and application of customary justice. In Galilea we met two women, who for the purposes of this chapter we call Ana and Gabriella,[21] who had not only held this position, but having completed their duties and periods as *corregidoras* had decided to form a single family unit as two women living together with their children. Both of these women had particular histories that explain this decision, and that also demonstrate both the direct and indirect influence of wider changes in rights discourses and constitutional reform on their lives and decisions. However, the reactions of

214 Gender Justice and Legal Pluralities

some of the men and women of the community also show the difficulties of their efforts to determine their own lives and futures.

Ana belongs to the founding clan of the community of Galilea, and is one of the daughters of the founder of the community. In remembering the key moments of her life that led her to question the patriarchal system of her community and the gender roles ascribed to women she spoke at length of the local culture of "*machismo*" (sexism) and violence exercised by her father against her mother, and by her mother against her person. At the age of 12, Ana decided enough was enough and confronted her father. The response of her father was to threaten to sell her to another man, and for her mother to beat her repeatedly for having tried to intervene in her affairs. Recalling the event she told us:

> [t]he last time my mother brought a stick grabbed me I responded "you are never going to hit me with a stick again, worse give me to a man. Whip me for another cause, do not threaten to give me to a man. If you do not want me I will leave. We can grip the stick between us and it will break and if I have convinced you not to hit me, I will make sure that you are also not beaten."
>
> (Ana, Galilea, May 2010)

Apart from the relation with her parents, another important aspect of her early life was her brothers. They taught Ana to hunt and fish and with time she realized that she was able to carry out all of the roles related to men and could live a life independent from them. When evangelical missionaries arrived when she was 14 she made the independent decision to first convert and to then leave the village to study nursing. On a hospital boat in years to come she travelled throughout the entire territory and learned both self-reliance and to lose her fear of men.

> Now I could do everything alone, including travel with patients in a canoe alone to Trinidad. My brothers and experience taught me not to be afraid when in front of a man and this enlightened me to the fact that a man is no better than a women. Everything depends on what we chose, the exercise of our rights, if we are not to be useless and if we are dedicated to being equal.
>
> (Ana, Galilea, May 2010)

Ana went on to study and work in nursing in Cochabamba before returning to her community in her twenties. She told us that her decision to return to Galilea was inspired by the sight of seeing her parents on television during the march for territory and dignity in 1990. This event reminded her of the difficult realities in her community and inspired her to return in an effort to live and change these conditions. Having returned to the TIPNIS she took part in the First Meeting of the *corregidores* in 1992. Thanks to her education and outspoken nature she was elected the Health Secretary of the sub-central at this event, a position she served for four years. It was with the completion of this office that she was then elected *corregidora* on returning to Galilea. Her occupation of this central position in the community required her to fight to be respected.

> I often confronted sexism, but left this in its place. I had the knowledge that a woman does not have to buy her way or be left behind, because all women have the same rights and the same strength as men, and if we do not want to feel less than men we do not need to. I always had this knowledge within me and when I met the first man who talked down to me I said "you control yourself, or I will control you, if you want me to respect you, we need to respect each other and between us it can be as though we are all brothers."
>
> (Ana, Galilea, May 2010)

In the course of carrying out this role in the village, Ana considered her participation in the resolution of a number of cases of violence against children as fundamental. The reinvigoration of customary law and its backing by constitutional reform was seen in these cases as a positive development. In one case she was asked "as a woman" by the sub-central of the TIPNIS to take part in the adjudication of a case of an eight-year-old girl who had been raped. The *corregidores* present decided that the young man responsible for the act should be whipped 12 times and obliged to pay a fine of 1000 bolivianos. Each of the *corregidores* was asked to take part in the provision of punishment, with Ana being asked to carry out the last two strokes of the whip. Ana stated that "yes, I whipped him and with all my might, because in truth it is painful to see a child treated in this way, she had suffered."

Gabriela was not so open about her past, but told us about her experience as the *corregidora* of the community, a post she filled directly after Ana completing her term returned to nursing and the management of the health post in the village. In contrast to Ana, Gabriela had great difficulty dealing with the opposition she experienced during the period she was *corregidora*. Indeed, a number of conflicts during this period developed to the point that she was threatened and beaten on regular occasions. Such was the aggression against her that she travelled to Trinidad, the regional capital, to lodge a legal complaint against the people responsible in Galilea. Following only one year Gabriela faced a vote of no confidence in a public meeting which forced her to step-down from her post. Reflecting on these events, Gabriela told us:

> I suffered a lot and I continue suffering. The men said ugly things about me and sometimes hurt me ... Before I was an authority everyone

respected me, but when I became an authority they said bad things about me. Now they continue to hurt me. One of the women came and pushed me to the ground, her niece also came and punched me. I felt so sick that I had to leave for Trinidad to see the doctor and to register a legal complaint. After they continued to pester me and take me by the throat. It must be because I am alone with my children.

(Gabriela, Galilea, May 2010)

Nobody's property?

The unconventional decision of these two women to live together created a great deal of tense debate amongst the rest of their community. Whilst some village members stated that the women had every right – recognizing the new constitution – to form a family unit, jokes and accusations about them were frequently made in both public meetings and in our interviews. A number of the male population claimed that the women had to be lesbians. Highlight was made by these men of the fact that the two women adopted separate "male" and "female" roles in their household, where one of the women talks and acts like a man. Some of the men stated that they hated this "male" woman's (Ana) presence in the village because she drinks and tries to sleep with their daughters when there is a fiesta. She is also reputed to have been expelled from another community, where she had previously lived with an ex-husband, on the grounds of being found guilty of "obscene acts." In talking about lesbianism the men used terms and stereotypes, referring to "the dry vice," in which sex takes place without male ejaculation. According to those that condemned the behavior of the two *corregidoras*, the only reason they said that they had not "thrown them in the river" was their previous demonstration of duty to the community and their linkages to the founding family of the village.

It is important to note that the women were commonly referred to in the community as representing two mono-parental families. This stood in contrast to the largely patrilocal ideal of Yuracaré families, where the father is characterized as the "head of the household." This ideal persists despite the reality of a growing pragmatism that encourages contraception and both matrilocal and exogenous marriages. It was interestingly also in contrast to the ascription of other single mothers who were not seen as mono-parental, but were rather referred to as dependents of their families of birth. The idea of female dependency on men remains an overriding social convention in Yuracaré society, to the point where in most families if the man does not have success in the hunt for bush meat the family will either have to sacrifice a domestic animal or gain its nutrition from rice alone.

This idea of dependency is instilled from an early age, with children being taught that it is in the female nature to be weak, fat, lazy, motherly, tearful and always in need of a man to assist them in their duties. We were told by the women of Galilea that without men "we would probably not survive, we would die of hunger." Women who do not adopt this form of life are considered to be a "type of man." It is also important to note that despite recent trends the majority of women we spoke to over 40 years of age had eight children or more, and most young women marry and have their first child when they are 15 or 16. We were told that "the more children a man has, the more man he is." On the other hand, children are also taught that boys are strong and capable of surviving on their own. Men are expected to learn to be brave, to tolerate pain and discomfort in the forest, and to look after themselves when away from the home. They are seen as part of nature, and considered to be closer to the "wild," because of their closeness to the forest in the hunt. Previous rites of passage for men, such as the scarification of their cheeks and limbs, were aimed at underlining these normative traits. Men are expected to take part in constant physical exertion. When returning from the hunt they are expected by other men to not only take part in the work of clearing fields, but also physical sports such as football. It is also of note, reflecting again on the case of Fabricano, that amongst young local men there has also developed a notion of masculinity attached to being able to tolerate punishment with the *chicote*. They argue that it is macho (masculine) to tolerate (*aguantar*) the pain. By crying on television during the media coverage of his punishment, Fabricano had failed to live up to the ideal of a Yuracaré warrior.

As dependents of their male counterparts, women are also largely marginalized in day-to-day decision making. In contrast to their desire to participate in regional politics and social movements, at the local level women's participation in *cabildo* politics is limited and frequent reference is made by men to their lack of desirable qualities in these spaces. Women are told that "you do not become an authority just by walking" or working at home. The men commonly deride women's ability to express themselves or defend themselves orally and physically. They talk of themselves as having more experience of the world, of having education, and being able to speak with confidence in public fora. In *cabildo* meetings the men continue to sit at the front of the assembly, while the women occupy the seats at the back where they can look after their children and dash out to carry out other domestic chores. In the meetings we witnessed in which men and women were present, there was only one occasion when a woman was given the right to speak in plenary. This is very different to the level of the sub-central where both men and women are actively encouraged to share their opinions and participate in decision making. It is also of note that women are making headway in relation to taking over other important roles such as in parents' groups, record keeping and health promotion. As indicated above, the few women that have made it to the position of *corregidora* have in all cases managed to do so on the basis of clan affiliation and political experience at the regional level.

Expressions of female dependency and subordination remain furthermore visible in the practice of justice and punishment. Separation is made in the local community between differing grades of legal misdemeanors (serious, medium and light). It is both notable that whereas domestic violence is considered amongst the most serious of grievances dealt with by local customary law, it is adultery that is ranked by local people as the most serious of all. It is also sobering that the persistence of high levels of domestic violence in the TIPNIS communities goes largely unpunished. This issue was frequently picked up in interviews with the women where they were asked what they liked, or disliked about local men. To this question Rosaria answered:

> I would like to be a man for a while, to fight with others and punch well, to know that it hurts.
>
> (Galilea, May 2010)

Various women also signaled that they did not really care too much about the violence, because as they said it did not inflict any serious damage. A number of them also admitted that they were also violent with their husbands in the process of defense (*yes, we also hit back*). Domestic violence is considered something private between a married couple. As a result women are not accustomed to denouncing the act to local authorities. Women are also scared that if they attempt to do so the family of their husband will take long-lasting reprisals against them. There appears to be no interest on the part of the local authorities, or local community in general, to intervene on this issue (the community does not say anything, they watch and remain silent). This is despite the fact that, as noted above, adultery and sexual violence outside the home (including rape) are the most common cases for sanction listed in local records. In these cases both women and men have received punishment, but it is men who are most commonly and most heavily punished.

In the TIPNIS communities we visited, domestic violence is often attributed to the contact with the *tercero* cattle farmers. Despite this blame on external influence, it is also clear that the expanded consumption of alcohol has also had an impact in encouraging domestic violence. In responding to the question "What do men do?" in all the focus groups we carried out the response after an account of labor activities was that men use a lot of time to consume alcohol. We were also told that in many instances domestic violence was ignored by community authorities, because the male authorities themselves were responsible for the violence committed in a state of drunken stupor.

In response to the dominant expectations of dependency and subordination they experienced in local society the two *corregidoras* were highly critical. Frustrated by the general acceptance of these features Gabriela commented that:

[w]omen feel incapable of sowing their own fields, of hunting for monkey, they depend entirely on men saying that if it were not for their husband they would be nobody ... When I was a young girl I knew how to do everything, but by getting married I was no longer able to go anywhere, and had to be at home, everything clean and watered. Now I am on my own I am at peace.

(Gabriela, Galilea, May 2010)

Ana also followed this with a clear reference to recent constitutional changes and with a challenge to those around her.

Everything is changing so you have to understand that as women we are nobody's property, they (men) continue to see us as property and therein lies the problem.

(Ana, Galilea, May 2010)

Conclusions

Recognizing their controversial nature and the few details still available about their implementation, in this chapter we have highlighted some of the ways in which recent progressive reforms for indigenous and gender rights are being "vernacularized" at the local level in Bolivia. As is evident from the history of local engagement with indigenous rights, customary law and questions of gender justice detailed above, any clear-cut marking of a before and after constitutional reform would be misleading. However, significant shifts have evidently been taking place very recently in local thought about rights and justice – we argue that this has been spurred on by the adoption of the new constitution in the country. Constitutional reform has encouraged a series of transformations in local understandings and claims for rights and justice. Whilst far from new concepts (Goodale 2009), indigenous and gender rights have more so than ever become key reference points in local social development. It is also evident, however, that in the process of being thought through not only are new liberties and progressive social changes being posed, but considerable disagreement is also occurring as to the basis, operation and limits of this new legal context. We see here not only the superimposition or inter-penetration of different legal spaces, but as de Sousa Santos proposes, a non-synchronism that results "in uneven and unstable mixings of legal codes" (de Sousa Santos 1987: 297).

As the case of Marciel Fabricano makes clear, the parity of customary law with state law remains highly controversial. As well as positive inclusion of the indigenous majority in the political life of the country, an unforeseen result of the democratic imperative to recognize the country's plurality and reform the national constitutional has been a spate of summary justice and land invasions. Local communities' interpretation of constitutional parity

220 Gender Justice and Legal Pluralities

and the apparent sanction given to the use of customary physical punishment in communities such as those in the TIPNIS has brought out the least progressive tendencies of ethnic sociality in Bolivia: often taking the character of ethnic conservatism and violence. The Law of Judicial Limitation had been aimed at avoiding these tendencies, but as a result of political hesitancy and fragmentation they have been allowed to flourish without significant reprimand.

This chapter also illustrates clearly that issues of legal pluralism are tightly connected with issues of gender in the Bolivian context. It is evident here that given the ethnic complexity of Bolivia, legal and constitutional reforms for indigenous and gender rights are intertwined. Indeed, local interpretations of reform naturally bring together custom and gender in a singular frame of reflection and response. As with expression of conflicting legal norms, the relationship between custom and gender requires nuance and awareness of the interactions of men and women within and outwith their local context. The case of Marcial Fabricano, for example, expresses the subtlety of local ideas of both custom and masculinity. Moreover, we see the manner in which men and women are actively engaged in interpreting and testing the limits of rights norms through a constant referral and effort to redefine custom and the sociality to which it refers. Reference can not only be made here to the agency expressed by women in social movements and local politics, but also their efforts to take over key functions in the local community and to question limitations on their sexuality and contributions to the local economy. The case of the two *corregidoras*, whilst perhaps an extreme exception, illustrates nonetheless the more generalized but perhaps less aggressive manner in which Yuracaré and TIPNIS women are using the moments of recent political and legal reform to rethink themselves, to question dominant social norms and to construct for themselves and others around them new notions of both gender justice. However, as highlighted above, such decisions come at a cost, and there are often encounters with both personal and structural resistance.

At the level of the community, as well as the nation, changing ideas about rights and justice have counter-intuitively re-invigorated structures, practices and norms that whilst important for the identity and survival of the community also express a restraining conservatism in their current form. Whilst able to refer to and use recent legal and constitutional reforms that expand customary law and gender rights in their own defense, the *corregidoras* and other women find themselves having to make trade-offs in trying to maneuver between the differing social norms each express (a complex of historically overlaid ideas of liberalism and custom). Moreover, as well as personal difficulties of trying to reconcile differing legal norms, women also confront both individuals and political-legal structures that continue to deny their rights to maneuver. Customary law and political practice continue to insist on the dependency of women and, despite recent overtures to progressive change, continue to punish and marginalize those who choose to differ. They also frequently turn a blind eye to men's infringements of prevailing rules. Accepting both the possibilities and limitations of individual agency and social structure here a critical realism (Bhaskar 1998) appears then to be a relevant theoretical frame for capturing social interaction. Capturing this critical realism, "patriarchal bargaining" (Tønnesen, Chapter 5 in this volume) may also be as important a concept for explaining the possibilities and limitations of gender justice in this context as it is for explaining gender relations in others. Here it is an accumulated rage founded on both ethnic and gender exclusion that drives women and men to risk considering strategies that change the "rules of the game" and work towards a more just formation of social order.

Notes

1 http://www.bbc.co.uk/news/world-latin-america-15138784 (accessed March 2012).
2 Lowland Department of Beni.
3 http://www.idea.int/americas/bolivia/bolivian_equality_laws.cfm (accessed March 2012).
4 These accusations have also been given some international support. See Human Rights Foundation Report, "Communal Justice in Bolivia," http://www.human rightsfoundation.org/reports.html (accessed March 2012).
5 As Victor Hugo Cardenas, who served as the country's first Indian vice president in the 1990s, states, "This constitution proposes the creation of two Bolivias: one for indigenous people and another for non-indigenous people, with separate and parallel judicial systems and languages." He went on to claim that in this new constitutional reality "only the indigenous people are first-class citizens." See http://dalje.com/en-world/bolivia-split-over-new-multicultural-constitution/118849 (accessed March 2012).
6 http://www.la-razon.com/versiones/20090516_006729/nota_246_812916.htm (accessed May 2009). Also http://www.lostiempos.com/diario/actualidad/nacional/20090916/lideres-crucenos-denunciaran-en-ginebra-a-morales-por-violacion-de_36726_60889.html (accessed March 2012).
7 http://boliviarising.blogspot.com/2008/05/colonial-backlash-reflections-on-recent.html (accessed March 2012).
8 http://www.boliviainfoforum.org.uk/news-detail.asp?id=63 (accessed March 2012).
9 http://www.nytimes.com/2009/04/28/world/americas/28bolivia.html?pagewanted=all (accessed March 2012).
10 In 1990 Marcial Fabricano was part of the negotiation of the sale of timber in the Multi-ethnic Indigenous Territory (TIM) for a value of US$2 million. In 1992 he approved a project for the construction of an Administrative Centre in the TIPNIS for a sum of US$1 million financed by IBIS in Denmark, of which according to local people US$3,000 was used for the personal purchase of machinery and boats. In 1994, as president of the TIPNIS sub-central, he became the owner of a piece of land in the city of Trinidad and built a house for himself with materials and money left over from the construction of the Management Centre (*Centro de Gestión*) in the TIPNIS. In 1997, Fabricano was a candidate for the vice-presidency of the Movimiento Bolivia Libre (MBL) political party. In the same year he organized an Elders' Council, a structure without any formal basis in the statutes of indigenous organization, with the aim of supplanting the

sub-central. He proclaimed himself as the principal advisor to this institution. This position allowed him to direct the contracting of the further sale of timber with CIMAGRO to a sum of US$300,000. No account was made of the transfer and use of this money. However, according to the testimonies of the Elders' Council, record was kept of the payment to Fabricano of US$500 per week for his advisory work. Eight months after the formation of this institution, the indigenous tribunal organized an investigation into the work he had carried out and disbanded the Council. In 2003, Fabricano divided the sub-central creating the parallel sub-central of Sécure and expelling the park guards from the Asunta and Oromomo area. According to local people this was done so that he could continue undetected with the illegal sale of timber from this area to the Fátima milling company. In 2004, the sub-central under the leadership of Adrian managed a project to a sum of US$150,000 for the Reforestation of 75,000 mahogany and cedar trees with the Inter-American Development Bank. The technician in charge of the project was kidnapped by people that locals say were directed by Fabricano, causing delays and damage to the outcome of the project. Between 2001 and 2003 the sub-central of Securé, headed by Fabricano, is reputed to have stolen cattle. A formal court case was started to try to clear up the issue, but failed "thanks to the political favor of the national government of the time." Fabricano was the national Vice-minister of Indigenous Issues at this time. In 2007 a meeting of the Indigenous Leaders of San Francisco de Moxos was held to return the area of the Securé to the control of the sub-central of the TIPNIS. In 2008 the Central Office of Indigenous Peoples (CPIB) and the Central Office of Indigenous Women of the Beni (CMIB) occupied the office of the Sub-central of Securé. A revision of the accounts resulted in claims against Fabricano accusing him of creating fictional projects during his period as the Director of Indigenous Affairs for the Department of the Beni. Finally, on 7 September 2008 a review of Fabricano's involvement in successive local conflicts and dubious financial dealings resulted in a formal resolution to prosecute by the sub-central. The resolution (01/08) accuses Fabricano of being a traitor to the indigenous cause, as "persona non grata" and decrees the most serious of local sanctions: punishment by whipping and expulsion from the local community and TIPNIS area.

11 Sank'a Jawira in the Highland department of Omasuyus.

12 Now a critic, he was previously a representative of the Movement for Socialism (MAS).

13 An indigenous leader who was expelled from the Chapare region, reputedly for his support for the lowland autonomy cause.

14 El Deber, 11 May 2009.

15 http://www.cejis.org/ (accessed March 2012).

16 "Eran muchas cuentas con el pueblo, era una rabia acumulada."

17 In October 2003 a series of nationwide protests were organized against the government's plans to introduce income tax on public wages and to liberalize the sale of oil and gas to Chile. The protests reached a peak with a series of violent clashes between the police and protesters in El Alto and Cochabamba and flight of the President to safety and exile in the USA. These events are also referred to in the country as the "Gas War."

18 In other words, the recognition of indigenous peoples and their rights, further land reform, nationalization of hydrocarbon resources in the country, constitutional change, overhaul of state instances of representation and highlight of government contradictions in relation to extraction and development.

19 Despite their persistence in Amazonia, *latifundia* have been outlawed in Bolivia since the Agrarian Reform Act of 1953.

20 In the confrontations between the parties, one policeman was killed and three indigenous people severely injured. See *La Razon*, 29 September 2009.
21 In the interest of anonymity the names of these two women have been changed in this chapter.

References

Asamblea Constituyente/Congreso Nacional (2009) *Constitución Política del Estado*, Bolivia: Sucre.
Bhaskar, R. (1993) *Dialectic: The Pulse of Freedom*, London: Verso.
——(1998) *The Possibility of Naturalism: A Philosophical Critique of the Contemporary Human Sciences*, 3rd edn, London: Routledge.
Calla, P., T. Arteaga and A. Arteaga (2009) *Ejercicio de los derechos humanos en el ámbito rural, por parte de los pueblos indígenas, originarios y campesinos*, Bolivia: Defensor del Pueblo.
de Sousa Santos, B. (1987) "Law: a map of misreading: Toward a postmodern conception of law," *Journal of Law and Society* 14: 279–302.
Goldstein, D. (2004) *The Spectacular City: Violence and Performance in Urban Bolivia*, Durham, NC and London: Duke University Press.
Goodale, M. (2009) *Dilemmas of Modernity: Bolivian Encounters with Law and Liberalism*, Palo Alto, CA: Stanford University Press.
Merry, S. A. (2006) *Human Rights and Gender Violence: Translating International Law into Local Justice*, Chicago, IL: University of Chicago Press.
Risør, H. (2010) "Twenty Hanging Dolls and a Lynching: Defacing Dangerousness and Enacting Citizenship in El Alto, Bolivia," *Public Culture* 22 (3): 466–85.
Webber, J. R (2011) *From Rebellion to Reform in Bolivia: Class Struggle, Indigenous Liberation and the Politics of Evo Morales*, Chicago, IL: Haymarket Books.

Index

References to figures are shown in *italics*.
References to notes consist of the page number followed by the letter "n" followed by the number of the note

9/11 attacks, impact on constitutional guarantees 10

Abu-Lughod, Lila 139, 142–43
Abu Qashawa, Suad 138
Action National Party (PAN, Mexico) 161, 174n8
additive legal pluralism 58, 74–75
ADR (alternative dispute resolution) 11, 44–45, 63, 64, 184, 189
adultery: Bolivia 218; Mozambique 92; Rhodesia 35; Sudan 140
AfPRW (African Protocol on the Rights of Women) 31, 37, 45
Africa: and CEDAW 31, 36–37, 41, 43, 45–46, 82; colonial dual legal system 5, 6, 34–36; customary law 5–6, 32, 34–35, 38–39; customary law, ascertainment of (self-statement) 13; customary law and gender equality 31–32; land reforms 24n15; legal pluralities and cross-regional issues 3–7; legal pluralities and gender inequality 31–34; liberalism, role of 6–7, 38, 39, 100, 144, 181–82; lynchings 3; post-colonial international/regional human rights system 31, 36–38; post-colonial legal systems and gender struggles 38–40; property rights for women 23n3, 37; rights to economic resources 15; women's rights 34–36, 37
African Charter of Rights and Welfare of the Child 37

African Charter on Human and Peoples' Rights 31, 36–37, 191
African National Congress (ANC, South Africa) 40
African Protocol on the Rights of Women (AfPRW) 31, 37, 45
African scholarship, women's rights and gender justice 31–32
"African values" 34, 38, 48, 49
Agamben, Giorgio 103n1, 165
al-Bashir, Omar Hassan Ahmad 141
al-Fatih al-Badawi, Suad 137, 140, 141–42
al-Mahdi, Wisal 142
Almarez, Alejandro 206
alternative dispute resolution (ADR) 11, 44–45, 63, 64, 184, 189
al-Turabi, Hasan 136, 139, 141, 142
ANC (African National Congress, South Africa) 40
Andean "*buen vivir*" 20, 76n12, 150
Anselm Odinkalu, C. 5
apartheid 6, 36, 40, 88
APPO (Popular Assembly of the People of Oaxaca, Mexico) 157, 162–63
Árbenz Guzmán, Jacobo 112
Arevalo, Juan José 112
Arteaga Böhrt, Ana Cecilia 4
ascertainment of community law (self-statement) 13
Asia: right to petition 36; *see also* Southeast Asia
Auyero, Javier 175n22
Ávalos, Isaac 207

Badri, Balghis 145
Bakhtin, M. M. 99–100
Ban, Ki-moon 114
Banda, Fareeda 197n16
Bashir *see* al-Bashir, Omar Hassan Ahmad
Belem do Pará Convention (Inter-American Convention to Prevent, Sanction and Eradicate Violence against Women, 1994) 113–14
Benda-Beckmann, Franz von 9, 82
Benda-Beckmann, K. von 82
Bolivia: 2009 Constitution: legal pluralism 5, 161, 200–203, 219–20; 2009 Constitution: opposition to 203–5; CIDOB (Indigenous Peoples of the Oriente) 205, 206; CMIB (Indigenous Women of the Beni) 211; contraception 213, 216; CSUTCB (Confederación Sindical Única de Trabajadores Campesinos) 207; domestic violence 214, 218; indigenous justice and the whipping of Marcial Fabricano 205–8, 217, 219, 220; interlegality 157–58; lynchings 204; *machismo* 214, 215–17; marriage 213, 216; rape 215, 218; TIPNIS (Isobore Secure National Park and Indigenous Territory) 200–201, 207–13; TIPNIS women community leaders (*corregidoras*) 213–16, 218–19, 220; TIPNIS women's condition 216–19; violence against women 215–16; women and community justice systems 57; women's rights 202–3, 211–13, 220–21
Bond, Johanna 82
Bourdon, Natalie J. 6, 44–45, 49
British colonial legal system 5, 23n5, 83–84, 181, 182–83; *see also* colonial dual legal systems
"*buen vivir*" 20, 76n12, 150

cacicuism 158, 160, 163–64, 165, 172
Cairo, Egypt: women's mosque movements 18–19, 139–40; women's new economic roles 146
CAMI Maseualcalli (Indigenous Women's Center, Mexico) 63, 64–67, 65, 74
Canada, indigenous women and community justice systems 57
"capabilities" approach 18
Cárdenas, Victor Hugo 205–6, 221n5
Cariño, Beatriz 167
CEDAW (United Nations Convention on the Elimination of all forms of Discrimination against Women, 1979) 1, 17; Africa 31, 36–37, 41, 43, 45–46, 82; Guatemala 113; Jordan 143; Sudan 133–34, 142–44, 150; Tanzania 189, 191
CERJ (Comunidades Etnicas Runujel Junam, Guatemala) 113
Chanock, Martin 35
Charles, Salome 189–95
Charlesworth, Hillary 32
Chavez, Adolfo 206
Chávez, Claudia 76n15
children: African Charter of Rights and Welfare of the Child 37; children's rights and legal pluralities 15; Convention on the Rights of the Child (CRC) 36; and gender (Bolivia) 212–13; inheritance rights (Zimbabwe) 47; rape case (Guatemala) 122–26; violence against (Bolivia) 214, 215
Chinkin, Christine 32
CIDOB (Indigenous Peoples of the Oriente, Bolivia) 205, 206
"claimed/created space" 51n16
CLO (Local Customary Law Declaration Order, Tanzania, 1963) 182, 183–85, 189, 190, 192–93
CMIB (Indigenous Women of the Beni, Bolivia) 211
Colombia: *guardia indigena* 68; indigenous law and multicultural reforms 5, 161; indigenous movements and interlegality 157–58
colonial dual legal systems: Africa 5, 6, 34–36; Guatemala 111–12; Latin America 4; Mozambique 83–84; *see also* British colonial legal system
Comaroff, Jean 10–11, 82, 150
Comaroff, John 10–11, 82, 150
Commission on Legal Empowerment of the Poor (2008) 12, 32, 44
communal property associations (CPAs, South Africa) 41–42
community courts/CCs (Mozambique) 82–83, 88–103

226 Index

community justice systems 3, 57; *see also* customary law; indigenous law
community law, ascertainment of (self-statement) 13
community police/*policia comunitaria* (Guerrero, Mexico) 24n14, 58, 60, 67–75
Comunidades Etnicas Runujel Junam (CERJ, Guatemala) 113
CONAPREVI (Coordination for the Prevention and Eradication of Intra-familiar Violence and Violence against Women, Guatemala) 114
CONAVIGUA (National Coordination of Guatemalan Widows) 113
Confederación Sindical Única de Trabajadores Campesinos (CSUTCB, Bolivia) 207
contraception, Bolivia 213, 216
Convention on Consent and minimum Age for Marriage (draft, 1961) 36
Convention on the Elimination of all forms of Discrimination against Women *see* CEDAW (United Nations Convention on the Elimination of all forms of Discrimination against Women, 1979)
Convention on the Rights of the Child (CRC) 36
Coordination for the Prevention and Eradication of Intra-familiar Violence and Violence against Women (CONAPREVI, Guatemala) 114
corporal punishment *see* whipping; *x'ik'ay* (ritual beatings)
cosmovision 62, 74, 121–22
Cotterrell, Roger 7
"court-centric" approaches 14
Covenant on Social, Economic and Cultural Rights (ICSECR, 1966) 36
CPAs (communal property associations, South Africa) 41–42
CRAC (Regional Coordinator of Community/Indigenous Authorities, Guerrero, Mexico) 68–73, 69
CRC (Convention on the Rights of the Child) 36
CSUTCB (Confederación Sindical Única de Trabajadores Campesinos, Bolivia) 207

cultural relativism 19, 36, 133, 180; *see also* universalism
culture-centric analysis, and gender justice 16, 18–19
Cumes, Aura 129n16
customary law: Africa 5–6, 23n3, 31–32, 34–35, 38–39; cross-regional issues 3–4; and development 11, 12; and gender justice 6; Latin America 4–5; and post-conflict situations 11–12, 14, 113; Rwanda (post-genocide reconciliation) 11; self-statement (ascertainment) 13; sub-Saharan Africa 15; Tanzania 5–6; 23n5, 50n3; Tanzania (CLO, Local Customary Law Declaration Order) 182, 183–85, 189, 190, 192–93; Tanzania (inheritance rights) 181–84, 185–86, 189, 190–91, 194–95; Zimbabwe (inheritance rights) 46–47, 49–50; *see also* colonial dual legal systems; community courts/CCs (Mozambique); indigenous law; informal justice sector; inheritance rights; Islam; land rights; legal pluralism/pluralities; Muslim family law; property rights; Sharia; vernacularization
customary law (Africa) 34–35, 38–39

Defensoría de la Mujer Indígena (DEMI, Guatemala) 110, 114
Defensoría K'iche' (Guatemala) 122–26, *123*, 127
deforestation 12
De Marinis, Natalia 4
DEMI (Defensoría de la Mujer Indígena, Guatemala) 110, 114
Democratic Revolutionary Party (PRD, Mexico) 161, 174n8
Derman, Bill 40
de Sousa Santos, Boaventura *see* Sousa Santos, Boaventura de
development: Gender in Development (GAD) 19–20; and legal pluralities 1, 2, 11–16; rights-based approaches 1, 3, 9, 31–32, 33; and security 10; World Bank World Development Reports 12, 139
discrimination against women: definition 17; *see also* CEDAW (United Nations Convention on the

Elimination of all forms of Discrimination against Women, 1979)
dispute resolution *see* ADR (alternative dispute resolution)
domestic servitude, and sexual violence (Guatemala) 118
domestic violence: Bolivia 214, 218; Guatemala 120–21, 125–26; Mexico 60–61, 63, 64, 66, 67, 69; Mozambique 89, 91, 93–94; *see also* rape; violence against women
dual legal systems *see* colonial dual legal systems

economic rights: Africa 36, 39; and neoliberalism 6, 9
Ecuador: incorporation of indigenous law 5; indigenous women and community justice systems 57
Egypt (Cairo): women's mosque movements 18–19, 139–40; women's new economic roles 146
"*el buen trato*" ("good treatment") 62
Englund, Harri 51n17
environmental governance, Polycentric Model of Natural Resource Management 12
Escobar, A. 14
Ezer, T. 197n14

Fabricano, Marcial 205–8, 217, 219, 220, 221n10
FCPF (Forest Carbon Partnership Facility), World Bank 12
Feldman, A. F. 99
FemAct (Feminist Activist, Tanzania) 184, 189, 191
"femicide" 111
feminism: and African human rights lawyers 45; and "African values" 38; and gender justice 16, 17, 18, 19; and Islamism (Sudan) 133–34, 136, 137, 139–44, 149–50, 152n3; liberal feminism 64, 139; and Marxism (Sudan) 135–36; and Mexican legal pluralities 64, 70; *see also* gender justice; NGOs (non-governmental organizations); women's rights
Feminist Activist (FemAct, Tanzania) 184, 189, 191
Ferguson, J. 14
"fetishization of law" 10, 150

FIMI (Foro Internacional de Mujeres Indígenas/International Forum of Indigenous Women) 61
flogging *see* whipping; *x'ik'ay* (ritual beatings)
forced labor: Guatemala 112; Mozambique 84, 85
forced rendition 10
Forest Carbon Partnership Facility (FCPF), World Bank 12
Foro Internacional de Mujeres Indígenas (International Forum of Indigenous Women, FIMI) 61
forum shopping 2, 10, 13–14, 109, 181, 187; *see also* idiom shopping
Foucault, Michel 14
Fourth World Conference on Women (Beijing, 1995) 37
Frazier, Nancy 22
Freigoun, Maha 138, 139, 142, 145
Frelimo (Liberation Front of Mozambique) 38, 84–86, 87, 91–92, 101
Freyre, Gilberto 84
Fundación Red de Sobrevivientes de la Violencia (Network for Survivors of Violence, Guatemala) 114

Gaventa, J. 51n16
Gender in Development (GAD) 19–20
gender justice: culture-centric approach 16, 18–19; and customary law 6; definition and issues 16–17; and feminism 16, 17, 18, 19; gender equity (*insaf*) vs. equality (Islam) 137, 139, 150; and legal pluralities 1–3, 11–12, 16–23, 38–39, 56–58; and liberalism 16, 17, 18; "minimum capabilities" approach 18; need to engage men 19–20, 21, 22; need to integrate different approaches 20–22; universalist approach 17–18; vernacularization of 57–58, 75, 201, 219; *see also* feminism; NGOs (non-governmental organizations); women's rights
gender mainstreaming 16, 19–20
gender violence *see* violence against women
Ghabshawi, Ihsan 136, 143
globalization: of human/gender rights discourse 43, 74; of human/women's

228 Index

rights organizations 37; impact on women's rights 32–33; legal implications of 7–8, 9, 10; *see also* neoliberalism
global security, post-9/11 legal "grey zones" 10
Goldstein, D. M. 204
González Casanova, P. 163–64
Goodale, M. 24n9
governance: and legal pluralities 10–11; *see also* environmental governance
"governmentality" 14
"graduated sovereignty" 9
Griffiths, A. 82
Griffiths, John 50n3
Guatemala: Agreement on Socioeconomic Aspects and the Agrarian Situation (1996) 113; Agreement on the Identity and Rights of Indigenous Peoples (1995) 113, 114, 161; Belem do Pará Convention, ratification of 113–14; CEDAW, ratification of 113; CERJ (Comunidades Etnicas Runujel Junam) 113; CONAPREVI (Coordination for the Prevention and Eradication of Intra-familiar Violence and Violence against Women) 114; CONAVIGUA (National Coordination of Guatemalan Widows) 113; Defensoría K'iche' 122–26, *123*, 127; DEMI (Defensoría de la Mujer Indígena) 110, 114; domestic violence 120–21, 125–26; forced labor 112; ICCPG (Guatemalan Institute of Comparative Penal Studies) 119–22, 127; indigenous law 5, 111–13, 114–16; indigenous women and community justice systems 57; inequality and violence 110–13; International Labor Organization Convention (no. 169), ratification of 115; lynchings 112; Mayan cosmovision/social movements 76n13, 113, 116, 121–22, 127; "Mayan law" 122, 125, 127; Network for Survivors of Violence (Fundación Red de Sobrevivientes de la Violencia) 114; poverty statistics (UNDP) 128n5; rape cases (Indigenous women) 110, 117–27; rights-based approaches 113–14, 122,

126–27; sexual violence (indigenous women) 109–10, 111, 117–18, 126–28; UN Historical Clarification Commission 117–18; UN "Sign up to put an end to violence against women" campaign 114, *115*; URNG (Unidad Revolucionaria Nacional Guatemalteca) 110, 114; *x'ik'ay* (ritual beatings) 125, 126
Guatemalan Institute of Comparative Penal Studies (ICCPG) 119–22, 127

Hale, Sondra 148
Hellum, Anne 1, 6, 20, 109, 182
Henrysson, E. 23n3
Hernández, R. Aida 56
Hernández Castillo, A. 21
Hernández Díaz, J. 175n24
Hoekema, André 76n6
homosexuality: and Islamism (Sudan) 140, 142; lesbianism (Bolivia) 216
Honwana, Alcinda M. 86
Human Development Index: Guatemala 128n5; Oaxaca, Mexico 159
human rights: African Charter on Human and Peoples' Rights 31, 36–37, 191; cross-cultural applicability of 180; Human Rights Based Approach to Development (HRBA) 39; impact of human rights language 51n17; Inter-American Commission on Human Rights 170; Inter-American Court of Human Rights 56, 120; International Council on Human Rights Policy (ICHRP) 12, 23; international/regional/transnational dimension of 9, 10, 31, 34–38, 74; and legal pluralism/pluralities 8, 11, 12, 23; and neoliberalism 6–7; Office of the United Nations High Commissioner for Human Rights (OHCHR) 162; and physical punishment 205–6; and self-statement (ascertainment of customary law) 13; Universal Declaration of Human Rights 36; vernacularization of 3, 24n9, 180, 184; World Conferences on Human Rights (Vienna and Beijing) 37; *see also* gender justice; inheritance rights; land rights; NGOs (non-governmental organizations); property rights;

Index 229

rights-based approaches; United
Nations; women's rights
Human Rights Based Approach to
Development (HRBA) 39; *see also*
rights-based approaches

ICC (International Criminal Court) 141
ICCPG (Guatemalan Institute of
Comparative Penal Studies)
119–22, 127
ICCPR (International Covenant on
Civil and Political Rights, 1966) 36
ICHRP (International Council on
Human Rights Policy) 12, 23
ICSECR (International Covenant on
Social, Economic and Cultural
Rights, 1966) 36
idiom shopping 83, 100; *see also* forum
shopping
Ikdahl, Ingunn 43–44, 49
IMWU (International Muslim Women's
Union) 133, 137, 140–41
Indian Succession Act (1865) 183
indigenous law: Bolivia 5, 202, 203,
205–8, 210–11, 215; Colombia 5,
157–58, 161; and discrimination
against women 16; Ecuador 5, 57;
Guatemala 5, 111–13, 114–16;
incorporation of 5; Mexico 24n14,
56–60, 62–63, 64, 66–75; Oaxaca,
Mexico 157, 160–61, 162–63, 171;
see also colonial dual legal systems;
customary law; informal justice
sector; land rights; legal pluralism/
pluralities; vernacularization;
whipping; *x'ik'ay* (ritual beatings)
Indigenous Peoples of the Oriente
(CIDOB, Bolivia) 205, 206
Indigenous Women of the Beni (CMIB,
Bolivia) 211
Indigenous Women's Center (CAMI
Maseualcalli, Mexico) 63, 64–67, 65, 74
informal justice sector 32, 44; *see also*
customary law; indigenous law
inheritance rights: Tanzania 39, 181–84;
Tanzania (court cases) 185–95;
Zimbabwe 46–47, 49–50
Institutional Revolutionary Party (PRI,
Mexico) 157, 159, 160–61, 163–64,
165, 168
Inter-American Commission on Human
Rights 170

Inter-American Convention to Prevent,
Sanction and Eradicate Violence
against Women (Belem do Pará
Convention, 1994) 113–14
Inter-American Court of Human
Rights 56, 120
interlegality: Bolivia 219; concept 8;
Guatemala 109–10, 118, 126, 127–28;
Latin America 157–58; Mexico 67;
Sudan 134, 143, 149–50
International Council on Human
Rights Policy (ICHRP) 12, 23
International Covenant on Civil and
Political Rights (ICCPR, 1966) 36
International Covenant on Social,
Economic and Cultural Rights, 1966
(ICSECR) 36
International Criminal Court (ICC) 141
international development *see*
development
International Finance Cooperation
(Performance Standard 7) 12
International Forum of Indigenous
Women (Foro Internacional de
Mujeres Indígenas, FIMI) 61
International Labor Organization
Convention (no. 169) 115, 174n14
international law: and legal pluralities
9; post-9/11 "grey zones" 10; *see also*
human rights; United Nations
International Muslim Women's Union
(IMWU) 133, 137, 140–41
intersectionality 21, 61, 75, 128n2, 144,
156
Islam: Islamic law (Tanzania) 50n3,
181, 183, 186–88; and
multiculturalism (Western Europe) 9;
women's mosque movements (Cairo,
Egypt) 18–19, 139–40; *see also*
Muslim family law; Sharia
Islamism: definition 151n1; and
homosexuality 140, 142; *insaf* (gender
equity) vs. equality 133–34, 136–40,
144, 150; Islamist feminism 133, 136,
152n3; Islamist feminism and social
class 144–50; Islamist vs. Western
feminism 140–44; *nafaqa*
(maintenance) 137, 144–46, 147,
148–49, 150; *qawama* (male
guardianship) 137–39, 144, 145, 146,
150; *see also* Sudan
Ismail, Salwa 146

230 Index

Jabal Awlia community, Sudan 146–49
Jakoola, Jiry 167
JALA (Judicature and Application of
Laws Act, Tanzania) 183, 191
Joireman, S. F. 23n3
Jordan, Muslim Brotherhood and
CEDAW 143
Joseph, Suad 144, 149
Judicature and Application of Laws Act
(JALA, Tanzania) 183, 191
judicialization of politics 10

Kandiyoti, D. 18
Kenya: colonial legal system 23n5;
women and land/property rigths 23n3
Kraemer, G. 162

land rights: international organizations
and land reforms (Africa) 24n15;
land restitution (South Africa) 40–42,
48, 50; land tenure and legal
pluralities (Oaxaca, Mexico) 162;
need for unitary regime 23n3; see also
inheritance rights; property rights
Latin America: colonial dual legal
system 4; customary law 4–5;
indigenous women and community
justice systems 57; indigenous
women's struggle for gender justice
56, 61–62; legal pluralities and
cross-regional issues 3–7; liberalism,
role of 4, 6, 62, 127, 220;
multicultural constitutionalism
58–59; vernacularization of gender
rights 75; vigilantism 16, 112; see also
indigenous law; Organization of
American States
law: different forms of 7; "fetishization
of law" 10, 150; international law 9,
10; judicialization of politics 10;
project law 7, 90, 97; socioeconomic
and politic context 14–15; soft law 7,
12; transnational norms and
procedures 1, 7, 8, 9, 10; see also
colonial dual legal systems;
customary law; human rights;
indigenous law; inheritance rights;
land rights; legal pluralism/
pluralities; property rights; women's
rights
legal aid: Tanzania 43, 45, 48, 186–87,
189, 191; Zimbabwe 46, 47

legal pluralism/pluralities: additive legal
pluralism 58, 74–75; analytical
approaches 7–11; anthropological
conception of 182; cross-regional
considerations 3–7; and development
practices 1, 2, 11–16; and economic/
political inclusion 180–81; and
gender justice 1–3, 11–12, 16–23,
38–39, 56–58; and human rights 8,
11, 12, 23; Mozambican "state legal
pluralism" 82–83; and property rights
42–45, 49; scholarship on 103n1,
103n2; and violence against women
126–27; "weak" and "strong" forms
31–32, 50n3; Zimbabwean case
38–39, 45–47, 49–50; see also colonial
dual legal systems; customary law;
indigenous law
lesbianism: Bolivia 216; see also
homosexuality
Levi, Primo 175n22
liberal feminism 64, 139; see also
feminism
liberalism: and gender justice 16, 17, 18;
role of in Africa 6–7, 38, 89, 100,
144, 181–82; role of in Latin America
4, 6, 62, 127, 220; see also
neoliberalism
Local Customary Law Declaration
Order (CLO, Tanzania, 1963) 182,
183–85, 189, 190, 192–93
Lukes, S. 33
lusotropicalism 84
lynchings: Africa 3; Bolivia 204;
Guatemala 112; Mozambique 91,
99, 102

Machel, Samora 85–86, 88, 94
machismo (Bolivia) 214, 215–17; see
also patriarchal power
McNeish, John-Andrew 4, 33
Magaya v Magaya (1999, Zimbabwe) 39
Mahmood, Saba 18–19, 139–40
Malawi: impact of colonial legal system
35; impact of human rights language
51n17; tribalism vs. national unity 6
Mamdani, M. 5
Mandela, Nelson 40
Mann, K. 84
marriage: Convention on Consent and
minimum Age for Marriage (draft,
1961) 36; forced marriage 35, 167;

and Islamic law 137–38; and Islamism 143; and rape 117; TIPNIS, Bolivia 213, 216; *see also* inheritance rights; Muslim family law
Marxism 16, 17, 135–36; *see also* socialism
Mauritania, women's rights to economic resources 37
Mayan cosmovision/social movements 76n13, 113, 116, 121–22, 127
"Mayan law" 122, 125, 127
Meeph'a women, (Guerrero, Mexico) 56–57, 58, 67
Mejía, Susana 76n15
memory, politics of 83
men: and gender justice 19–20, 21, 22; *see also* patriarchal power
Merry, S. E. 24n9, 100
mestiza women (Guerrero, Mexico) 58, 64, 67
Mexico: CAMI Maseualcalli (Indigenous Women's Center) 63, 64–67, *65*, 74; Chiapas 159, 160, 164; Chiapas indigenous revolt (Zapatistas) 60, 156–57, 161, 169; Constitution, amendments to 58–59, 156, 159; CRAC (Regional Coordinator of Community/ Indigenous Authorities), Guerrero 68–73, *69*; domestic violence 60–61, 63, 64, 66, 67, 69; indigenous rights, recognition of 58–60, 74–75; indigenous women rights and access to justice 60–62; indigenous women rights and legal pluralism 56–58; *justicias de mediación* (alternative dispute resolution) 63, 64; Meeph'a women (Guerrero) 56–57, 58, 67; *mestiza* women (Guerrero) 58, 64, 67; Nahua women (Cuetzalan, Puebla) 58, 62–67, 73–74; Na'savi women (Guerrero) 58, 61, 67, 70; National Commission of Human Rights 170; Office of the United Nations High Commissioner for Human Rights (OHCHR) 162, 170; pluriculturalism 156–57; rape 56, 63, 68, 69; San Andrés accords (1996) 157, 162; violence against women 60–62, 64, *65*, 66–67, 72–73; Zapatista movement 60, 156–57, 161, 169;

Zapatista women 60, 76n2, 77n30; *see also* Oaxaca, Mexico
Michaels, R. 8
Mihayo, Honorable Justice 193–95
"minimum capabilities" approach 18
Molyneux, M. 19
Montes, Jacobo 175n21
Morales, Evo 201, 203
Movement of Unification and Triqui Struggle (MULT, Mexico) 163, 165
Mozambique: 1990 Constitution 89; colonial dual legal system 83–84; community courts (CCs) and legal pluralism 82–83, 88–91, 101–3; community courts (CCs): jurisdiction and examples of cases 91–96, *92*; community courts (CCs): perceptions of gender and speech genres 96–101; domestic violence 89, 91, 93–94; forced labor 84, 85; Frelimo (Liberation Front of Mozambique) 38, 84–86, 87, 91–92, 101; independence and civil war 84–85; lynchings 91, 99, 102; OMM (Mozambique's Women Organization) 86, 91, 101; Operation Production (OP) 86–87, 98, 102; popular courts (post-independence law) 85–88, 101–2; post-war reconciliation and customary law 11; public flogging 84, 88, 98; rape 91; Renamo (Mozambican National Resistance) 85, 91, 101; "state legal pluralism" 82–83; traditional healers (*curandeiros*) 86–87, 88–89; tribalism vs. national unity 6; witchcraft (*uroi*) 88–89, 92, 95–97, 99; Women and Law in Southern Africa-Mozambique (WLSA-M) 90, 97, 101, 102; women judges 86, 91; women's rights 90, 98, 101–2
MULT (Movement of Unification and Triqui Struggle, Mexico) 163, 165
multicultural constitutionalism 9–10, 58–59
multicultural justice 56, 59–60, 75, 159–63, 166, 171
Murgoci, Agnes 104n11
Muris v Murisa (1991, Zimbabwe) 46
Muslim Brotherhood, and CEDAW (Jordan) 143

232 Index

Muslim family law 136, 137, 145; *see also* International Muslim Women's Union (IMWU); Islam; Islamism; Sharia; Sudan
Mutukwa, G. M. N. 82

nafaqa (maintenance) 137, 144–46, 147, 148–49, 150
NAFTA (North American Free Trade Agreement) 157
Nahua women (Cuetzalan, Puebla, Mexico) 58, 62–67, 73–74
Namibia, self-statement (ascertainment of community law) 13
Na'savi women (Guerrero, Mexico) 58, 61, 67, 70
National Congress Party (Sudan) 133, 137
National Coordination of Guatemalan Widows (CONAVIGUA, Guatemala) 113
Natural Resources Management, Polycentric Model of 12
neoliberalism: and ethnic/human rights 6–7, 8, 9, 11, 17; Mexico 58, 59, 75; Oaxaca, Mexico 160; South Africa 40, 48; *see also* globalization; liberalism
Network for Survivors of Violence (Fundación Red de Sobrevivientes de la Violencia, Guatemala) 114
NGOs (non-governmental organizations): alternative dispute resolution/ADR (Tanzania) 44–45; and gender justice 23; "hegemonic discourse" of 14; and hidden structures of power 48, 50; impact of neoliberalism on 9; inheritance/women's rights (Zimbabwe) 46–47, 49–50; land reforms, rights-based approach to 24n15; land restitution (South Africa) 41, 42, 48; "project law" 7, 90, 97; rape (Guatemala) 119–22; women's rights (Africa) 34, 37; women's rights (Mexico) 62, 70; women's rights (Mozambique) 90, 97; women's rights (Tanzania) 44–46, 48–50, 182, 184–85, 187, 189–93
Nkuzi (land rights NGO, South Africa) 41, 42, 48
"norm-driven" approaches 14
North American Free Trade Agreement (NAFTA) 157
Nuni, Pedro 206

Nussbaum, Martha 18
Nyerere, Julius 183

Oaxaca, Mexico: autonomy and indigenous law 157; caciquism 158, 160, 163–64, 165, 172; indigenous justice and women's rights 62, 156; Institutional Revolutionary Party (PRI) 157, 159, 160–61, 163–64, 165, 168; Law of the Rights of Indigenous People and Communities of Oaxaca State (1998) 157, 160–61; MULT (Movement of Unification and Triqui Struggle) 163, 165; multicultural reforms 159–63, 171–72; PAN (Action National Party) 161, 174n8; Popular Assembly of the People of Oaxaca (APPO) 157, 162–63; PRD (Democratic Revolutionary Party) 161, 174n8; rape 162, 167, 170–71, 172; San Juan Copala siege (2009–10) 167–71; state construction in Triqui region 163–66, 171; Triqui people 158, 162–63; UBISORT (Unity of Welfare of the Triqui Region) 163, 165; violence against Triqui women 166–71, 172–73; *see also* Mexico
Office of the United Nations High Commissioner for Human Rights (OHCHR), Mexico 162, 170
Ong, Aiwha 9
Organização da Mulher Moçambicana/ Mozambique's Women Organization (OMM) 86, 91, 101
Organization of African Unity 36–37
Organization of American States 162, 205
Osman, Mazair 137, 138
Ostrom, Ellinor 12

Palestinians, women's new economic roles 146
PAN (Action National Party, Mexico) 161, 174n8
pan-Mayan movements 113, 116; *see also* Mayan cosmovision/social movements; "Mayan law"
Parra Mora, L. 175n24
patriarchal power: "bargaining with" 18, 21, 150, 221; Bolivia 214, 215–17; Latin America 16, 61; Mexico 60, 61; Mozambique 101–2; Oaxaca, Mexico 167; South Africa 41; Sudan 133–34,

136–37, 139, 143, 149; Tanzania 190, 194; Zimbabwe 50; *see also* men
Paz Zamora, Jaime 211
Performance Standard 7 (International Finance Cooperation) 12
Peru: indigenous women and community justice systems 57; *rondas campesinas* 68
Phillips, Anne 18
physical punishment *see* whipping; *x'ik'ay* (ritual beatings)
plural legal systems *see* legal pluralism/pluralities
police brutality, rape case (Guatemala) 118–22, 127
policia comunitaria/community police (Guerrero, Mexico) 24n14, 58, 60, 67–75
political rights: International Covenant on Civil and Political Rights (ICCPR, 1966) 36; Islamism and women's political rights 143; *see also* human rights; judicialization of politics
"politics of memory" 83
Polycentric Model of Natural Resource Management 12
Poole, D. 162
Popular Assembly of the People of Oaxaca (APPO, Mexico) 157, 162–63
Popular Congress Party (Sudan) 133
Portuguese colonial legal system 83–84, 87, 89
positivism 7, 8, 17
post-conflict situations, and customary law 11–12, 14, 113
Poverty Reduction Strategy Paper (PRSP, World Bank) 89
power, types of 33
PRD (Democratic Revolutionary Party, Mexico) 161, 174n8
PRI (Institutional Revolutionary Party, Mexico) 157, 159, 160–61, 163–64, 165, 168
project law 7, 90, 97
property rights: Africa 23n3, 37; Tanzania 42–45, 49, 190; *see also* inheritance rights; land rights
punishment *see* whipping; *x'ik'ay* (ritual beatings)

qawama (male guardianship) 137–39, 144, 145, 146, 150

R2P (Right to Protect Principle) 10
Rahman, Afaf Ahmed Abdel 145–46
rape: Bolivia 215, 218; Guatemala 110, 117–27; Mexico 56, 63, 68, 69; Mozambique 91; Oaxaca, Mexico 162, 167, 170–71, 172; *see also* domestic violence; violence against women
Razavi, S. 19
Recondo, D. 160
relativism, cultural 19, 36, 133, 180
religious law 4, 7, 9, 11, 32; *see also* Islam; Sharia; spiritual sanctions
Renamo (Mozambican National Resistance) 85, 91, 101
rendition, forced 10
Rhodesia: adultery 35; support for Renamo (Mozambique) 85; *see also* Zimbabwe
rights-based approaches 1, 3, 9, 14; Africa 24n15; and gender justice 16, 18; Guatemala 110, 113–14, 122, 126–27; Human Rights Based Approach to Development (HRBA) 39; Mozambique 98, 100; South Africa 40, 48; Southern/Eastern Africa 31, 32, 33, 39–40; *see also* human rights
right to petition 36
Right to Protect Principle (R2P) 10
Roald, Anne Sofie 143
Roberts, R. 84
Ross, Fiona 118, 129n15
Rus, Juan 160
Rwanda, post-genocide reconciliation and customary law 11
Rwezaura, Barth 35–36

Sachs, A. 87–88
San Andrés accords (Mexico, 1996) 157, 162
San Juan Copala siege (2009–10, Mexico) 167–71
Satti, Hassanat Awad 137
security, and development 10
self-determination, right to 36, 165, 171, 201, 208
"self-help justice" 112
self-statement (ascertainment of community law) 13
Sen, Amartya 18
sexism *see machismo* (Bolivia); patriarchal power

234 Index

sexual violence *see* domestic violence; rape; violence against women

Sharia: dominant groups' instrument of governance 3–4; Sudan 135, 136, 139–40, 145, 150; Sudan: Sharia vs. CEDAW 133–34, 142–44; *see also* Islam; Islamism; Muslim family law; Sudan

Shivji Commission (Tanzania) 43

Sieder, Rachel 4, 33, *65*, *115*, 171

Sierra, María Teresa 4, 24n14, *69*, 171

"Sign up to put an end to violence against women" UN campaign 114, *115*

slavery, Mozambique 84, 85

social-democratic politics, poverty vs. inequality 18

socialism: and gender justice 16, 17; Mozambique 38, 83–89, 98, 100, 101–2; Tanzania 5–6, 39; Zimbabwe 39; *see also* Marxism

soft law 7, 12

Sousa Santos, Boaventura de: interlegality 8, 128n1, 143, 157–58, 219; Mozambique 82, 104n7

South Africa: 1996 Constitution 6, 39, 40, 41; African National Congress (ANC) 40; colonial legal system, impact of 35; communal property associations (CPAs) 41–42; land restitution 40–42, 48, 50; Nkuzi (land rights NGO) 41, 42, 48; Restitution of Land Rights Act 40, 41; support for Renamo (Mozambique) 85; tribalism vs. national unity 6; truth commissions and sexual violence 129n15

Southeast Asia: "graduated sovereignty" 9; *see also* Asia

Southern Sudan: self-statement (ascertainment of community law) 13; *see also* Sudan

speech genres, and community court proceedings (Mozambique) 99–100

Speed, Shannon 77n30

Spiertz, H. L. J. 100

spiritual sanctions 47, 50

Stephen, L. 162

Stephens, Elizabeth 189–95

Stewart, J. 182

Stowasser, Barbara 137–38

sub-Saharan Africa: customary law and rights to economic resources 15; international/regional human rights

instruments 31, 38; women's rights to economic resources 37; *see also* Africa

Sudan: background (history and politics) 134–36; and CEDAW 133–34, 142–44, 150; Constitution (2005) 145; Human Development Report (UNDP, 2011) 145; *insaf* (gender equity) vs. equality 133–34, 136–40, 144, 150; Islamist feminism 133, 136, 152n3; Islamist feminism and social class 144–50; Islamist vs. Western feminism 140–44; Islamization 135, 136; Jabal Awlia community 146–49; Muslim family law 136, 137, 145; *nafaqa* (maintenance) 137, 144–46, 147, 148–49, 150; National Congress Party 133, 137; Popular Congress Party 133; *qawama* (male guardianship) 137–39, 144, 145, 146, 150; self-statement (ascertainment of community law) 13; Sharia 135, 136, 139–40, 143, 145, 150; Sudan Women's General Union (SWGU) 133, 138, 140, 145, 146–48; women's economic roles 147–48, *147*; women's political roles 138–39, 143; *see also* International Muslim Women's Union (IMWU); Southern Sudan

SWGU (Sudan Women's General Union) 133, 138, 140, 145, 146–48

Tanzania: 1977 (1998) Constitution 39, 183, 191, 192, 193–94; alternative dispute resolution (ADR) 44–45; and CEDAW 189, 191; CLO (Local Customary Law Declaration Order, 1963) 182, 183–85, 189, 190, 192–93; colonial legal system, impact of 35; customary law 5–6, 23n5, 50n3; Feminist Activist (FemAct) 184, 189, 191; Indian Succession Act (1865) 183; inheritance and women's rights 39, 181–84; inheritance and women's rights: court cases 185–89; inheritance and women's rights: *Elizabeth Stephens and Salome Charles vs. Another* (2006) 189–95; Islamic law 50n3, 181, 183, 186–88; JALA (Judicature and Application of Laws Act) 183, 191; legal aid 43, 45, 48, 186–87, 189, 191;

Index   235

property and women's rights 42–45, 49; Shivji Commission 43; Tanzanian Women's Lawyers' Association (TAWLA) 44–45; tribalism vs. national unity 6; WLAC (Women's Legal Aid Center) 44–45, 187, 189, 190; women's rights NGOs 44–46, 48–49, 182, 184–85, 187, 189–93
Tanzanian Women's Lawyers' Association (TAWLA) 44–45
tenure systems *see* land rights
Terven, Adriana 76n15, 77n21
TIPNIS (Isobore Secure National Park and Indigenous Territory) *see* Bolivia
Togo, Convention on Consent and minimum Age for Marriage (draft, 1961) 36
torture 10, 117, 119, 162, 170
transnational legal norms and procedures 1, 7, 8, 9, 10
Triqui people *see* Oaxaca, Mexico

UNDP *see* United Nations Development Program (UNDP)
Unidad Revolucionaria Nacional Guatemalteca (URNG) 110, 114
UNIFEM *see* UN Women (formerly UNIFEM)
United Nations: Convention on Consent and minimum Age for Marriage (draft, 1961) 36; Convention on the Rights of the Child (CRC) 36; Historical Clarification Commission (Guatemala) 117–18; International Covenant on Social, Economic and Cultural Rights, 1966 (ICSECR) 36; rights-based approach to land reform 24n15; "Sign up to put an end to violence against women" campaign 114, *115*; Universal Declaration of Human Rights 36; whipping of Marcial Fabricano 205; *see also* CEDAW (United Nations Convention on the Elimination of all forms of Discrimination against Women, 1979); Human Development Index; Office of the United Nations High Commissioner for Human Rights (OHCHR); UN Women (formerly UNIFEM)
United Nations Development Program (UNDP): 2011 Human Development

Report on Sudan 145; Commission on Legal Empowerment of the Poor (2008) 12, 32, 44; poverty statistics (Guatemala) 128n5; self-statement (ascertainment of customary law), support for 13
United Nations Program for Reduced Emissions from Deforestation and Degradation (UNREDD) 12
United States (USA): and CEDAW 133; and Guatemala 112; indigenous women and community justice systems 57
Universal Declaration of Human Rights 36
universalism 6, 16–18, 20, 57, 75, 180; *see also* cultural relativism; liberalism
UNREDD (United Nations Program for Reduced Emissions from Deforestation and Degradation) 12
UN Women (formerly UNIFEM), *Progress of the World's Women* (2011 report) 12
Urañavi, José 205
URNG (Unidad Revolucionaria Nacional Guatemalteca) 110, 114

Velasco, Victor Hugo 205
vernacularization: of gender rights 57–58, 75, 201, 219; of human rights 3, 24n9, 180, 184
vigilante/vigilantism 16, 112, 204, 205
violence against women: Bolivia 215–16; Guatemala 109–10, 111, 114, 117–18, 126–28; Inter-American Convention to Prevent, Sanction and Eradicate Violence against Women (Belem do Pará Convention, 1994) 113–14; and International Council on Human Rights Policy (ICHRP) 23; Mexico 60–62, 64, *65*, 66–67, 69, 72–73; Oaxaca, Mexico 162, 166–71, 172–73; "Sign up to put an end to violence against women" UN campaign 114, *115*; South Africa 129n15; *see also* domestic violence; rape

Weilenmann, M. 89–90, 97
Welch, G. H. 87–88
whipping: Bolivia 205–8, 210, 215, 219, 220; Mozambique 84, 88, 98; *see also* *x'ik'ay* (ritual beatings)
Willemse, Karin 148

Wilson, R. A. 180
witchcraft (*uroi*) 88–89, 92, 95–97, 99
WLSA (Zimbabwean Women and Law in Southern Africa Research Trust) 46, 49–50
Women and Law in Southern Africa-Mozambique (WLSA-M) 90, 97, 101, 102
Women's Legal Aid Center (WLAC, Tanzania) 44–45, 187, 189, 190
women's rights: African Protocol on the Rights of Women (AfPRW) 31, 37, 45; African scholarship on 31–32; impact of globalization on 32–33; International Forum of Indigenous Women (FIMI) 61; UN Women *Progress of the World's Women* (2011 report) 12; *see also* discrimination against women; feminism; gender justice; inheritance rights; land rights; NGOs (non-governmental organizations); property rights; *separate countries/regions*; violence against women
World Bank: Forest Carbon Partnership Facility (FCPF) 12; human rights doctrines and neoliberalism 7; land rights in Africa 24n15, 43; Poverty Reduction Strategy Paper (PRSP) 89; World Development Reports 12, 139
World Conferences on Human Rights (Vienna and Beijing) 37

World Development Reports (World Bank) 12, 139
Wright, Shelly 32

x'ik'ay (ritual beatings) 125, 126; *see also* whipping

Yrigoyen Fajardo, Raquel 76n7

Zambia, impact of colonial legal system 35
ZANU PF (Zimbabwe African National Union – Patriotic Font) 46, 47
Zapatista movement (Mexico) 60, 156–57, 161, 169
Zapatista women (Mexico) 60, 76n2, 77n30
Zimbabwe: colonial legal system, impact of 35; Constitution 46, 47; inheritance rights 46–47, 49–50; legal aid 46, 47; legal pluralism and women's rights 38–39, 45–47, 49–50; *Magaya v Magaya* (1999) 39; *Muris v Murisa* (1991) 46; ZANU PF (Zimbabwe African National Union – Patriotic Font) 46, 47; Zimbabwe Women Lawyers Association (ZWLA) 46, 47; *see also* Rhodesia
Žižek, S. 101
ZWLA (Zimbabwe Women Lawyers Association) 46, 47